Sailed Oct 21st 1933 - Arrived Jan 24th 1934. 94 days

Sailed Feb 22nd 1934 - Arrived June 29th 1934. 126 days

01872 859124

BEFORE THE MAST

In the Grain Races of the 1930s

Original logs written by
Geoffrey Sykes Robertshaw

Edited from the original logs by Elvin Carter

Blue Elvan Books

Published 2008 by Blue Elvan Books
35 Tremayne Close, Devoran, Truro, Cornwall. TR3 6QE

Typeset by Marie Bird of Devoran
4 Carnon Mine, Devoran, Truro, Cornwall. TR3 6NG.

ISBN 978 0 9559950 0 2

Printed and bound in Great Britain by BoothPrint
The Praze, Penryn, Cornwall. TR10 8AA

Sailplan of a four masted barque

Bowsprit Sails	Foremast sails	Mainmast staysails
1. Flying jib 2. Outer jib 3. Inner jib 4. Fore topmast staysail	5. Foresail or course 6. Fore lower topsail 7. Fore upper topsail 8. Fore lower topgallant 9. Fore upper topgallant 10. Fore royal	11. Main topgallant staysail 12. Main topmast staysail 13. Main royal staysail

Mainmast sails	Mizzenmast Staysails	Mizzen mast sails
14. Mainsail or course 15. Main lower topsail 16. Main upper topsail 17. Main lower topgallant 18. Main upper topgallant 19. Main royal	20. Mizzen topgallant staysail 21. Mizzen topmast staysail 22. Mizzen royal staysail	23. Crossjack or crojack 24. Mizzen lower topsail 25. Mizzen upper topsail 26. Mizzen lower topgallant 27. Mizzen upper topgallant 28. Mizzen royal

Jiggermast staysails	Jigger or Gaff sails	
29. Jigger staysail 30. Jigger middle staysail 31. Jigger topmast staysail	32. Jigger driver or spanker 33. Gaff or spanker topsail	

Acknowledgments

My grateful thanks to my brother-in-law, John Robertshaw, for making me the custodian of his uncle's hand written log books, over three hundred negatives of his voyages and many other mementoes. Also for urging me on to publish the logs once he found out I could decipher Geoffrey's writing!

My thanks to all my family for their patience over the years it has taken me to complete.

My most sincere thanks to the multi-talented post mistress of Devoran, Marie Bird for typesetting this book. Her enthusiastic support, tireless attention to details, plus all the hours of work she has done at a time of great stress for her are greatly appreciated. Also to her husband, Ralph, who does not see problems, only solutions, and who, whether it be a boat or a book, simply says "There you are! I don't know what all the fuss was about."

Last words to you again, Marie. Thank you.

E.C. - Devoran
3rd June 2008.

Introduction

Compiled by Elvin Carter from the original logs and photographs of Geoffrey Sykes Robertshaw.

Cover: "Ponape"

Geoffrey Robertshaw was born in Brearley, Luddendon Foot in Yorkshire in 1910. He was the 2nd of the three children of Abraham and Kathleen Robertshaw (née Sykes). He was brought up in a large house with servants, a nanny and even a chauffeur and was educated at a public school in Eastbourne.
The family came frequently to Falmouth on holiday during the 1920's and it is possible that Geoff's life-long fascination with sailing ships began here and also the urge to run away to sea, which he did.
Geoffrey was a "character", outgoing, likeable, obstinate, argumentative, gentle, kind and fearless.
Although slight of build, he would fight his corner and always for the underdog or against injustice.
During the war years, he continued his merchant service on the Atlantic and Russian convoys and to and from South Africa, before being invalided out in 1944.
After the war, Geoff found it hard to settle to life on the land and after a few failed enterprises and his marriage, settled to life as something of a recluse in his family home.
Geoff died on June 13th 1983, aged 73, after a massive stroke, and his remains were buried with his beloved mother (Honey) in the churchyard at Mythelmroyd.

In this book, I have attempted to do justice to the man and the voyages. It has taken me three years to decipher Geoffrey's handwritten logs and they are as near to the exact word as I can get. The photographs have come from some three hundred which were taken at the time but since I only had negatives to work with in the main, there may be an odd one which has been taken on the wrong ship - though how one would know is a mystery to me. In the case of the mix up of the "Lawhill" and "Pommern" taken at sea on his last trip on the "Olivebank" in 1938, I have inserted two photographs one shows a 'bald headed' barque with a deckhouse for'ard of the main mast which I believe to be "Pommern". The other photograph shows a 'bald headed' barque with a Liverpool deckhouse, which I believe to be the "Lawhill", My profound apologies to all the experts if this is not so.

The text is, as it was written. The photographs are, to the best of my knowledge, original, since I have the negatives. Geoffrey was very free with his knowledge, reminiscences and photographs - which he loaned to many people - sailors usually swap all three.

So bearing in mind the 'cabin fever' of young men confined in a small space for sometimes in excess of four months and laying aside all prejudice and criticism, start the journey with a novice sailor where the work was both new and hard and the time to write was brief.

Romantically it is easy to imagine yourself climbing the rigging on a bright, sunny day.

It is less easy to imagine doing this on a wet and windy day with the mast swinging like a metronome and the yards almost touching the sea at the extremity of the motion.

Did you think it as just a straight climb?

How would you fair on reaching the futtocks where the climb is now outwards and you are hanging almost upside down over first the deck and then the raging sea?

This is just one of the hazards of the tall ship sailor and it takes place at twice the height of a normal house.

Expand with the text and quite simply - Enjoy the Trip.

Wishing you fair wind and fine weather.

Elvin Carter. Devoran, June 2008.

Log of the Four Masted Barque

"Olivebank"

From London to Port Lincoln in South Australia.

1932

———

Day 1 Tuesday September 13
Left Gravesend for Australia. Said good-bye to England, very hard work.
Fair to wet.

Day 2 Wednesday September 14
Never shifted from Dungeness all day. Kept on turning the ship.
Fine.

Self in the rigging

Day 3 Thursday September 15
At Dungeness all morning. Fair Wind. Shifted afternoon saw Eastbourne and
Beachy Head.
Fine.

Day 4 Friday September 16
Down in the fore hold chipping rust. No ships all day. Thought of Honey
{mother} and the rest a lot.
Fair.

Day 5 Saturday September 17
Went up to the royal for the first time (mizzen). Cleaned the decks. Chatted with
Bill (English) at look-out.
Fine to fog.

View from the mizzen

Day 6 Sunday September 18
Had a rest. Sat on deck saw St. Austell Bay.
Fair.

Day 7 Monday September 19
Scraped rust down in fore hold. Saw Union Castle Llandovey Castle. Some small birds on deck.
Fair.

Day 8 Tuesday September 20
Reached Bay of Biscay. Down in the hold again chipping rust. She (the cat) catches and kills a bird.
Fair.

4

Deck view with cat

Day 9 Wednesday September 21
Cleaned the life-boats in the morning. Went up the masts to overhaul buntlines. We have a sing-song at night.
Nil.

Day 10 Thursday September 22
Down in the hold again chipping. Left the Bay of Biscay. Sat on my bunk and read during free watch in the afternoon.
Rough-fine to wet.

Day 11 Friday September 23
A very rough night only two hours sleep. Chipped again in the hold during working watch. Saw first ships for five days. Had a sing song.
Fair.

Day 12 Saturday September 24
Washed our cabins out. Saw a cyclone in the distance and we take in most sail in readiness. Washed some of my clothes.
Fair to rain.

Washed some of my clothes.
View from bowsprit looking aft

Day 13 Sunday September 25
Sat on the fo'c'sle head, went out to the end of the bowsprit for the first time and overhauled buntlines up the rigging. Sat on deck and chatted with the passenger.
Fine.

Self on the bowsprit

Day 14 Monday September 26
Went up to the mizzen royal. Nearly lost my life by falling on deck. Chipped rust again in the hold. Sat out on deck again in free watch. A lovely sunset.
Fine warm.

Day 15 Tuesday September 27
Lovely sunrise. Ship wallowing a little today in heavy swell. Had a small fire in the fore hold. Started to bend new sails - tropical.
Nil.

Day 16 Wednesday September 28
Down chipping in the main hold. I have got the "fed up" feeling today. Sat out in the afternoon on deck. Had a row with "Lofty" Horst (German).
Fine.

Self sitting on deck

Day 17 Thursday September 29
Carried on changing the storm sails for the "tropical rags" changed the main and mizzen masts. Went up to the mizzen royal to overhaul gaskets.
Fine. Hot.

Day 18 Friday September 30
Changed all sail on the fore mast. Sat out on the fo'c'sle head in the afternoon. I had my first wheel today and found it rather hard.
Very fine. Very hot.

Man at the wheel. Note it is covered

Day 19 Saturday October 1
Sat out in the morning. Had two hours at the wheel. Read some magazines in the evening.
Very fine. Very hot.

Day 20 Sunday October 2
Sat out on deck most of the day, washed one of my shirts. Read a book in the evening which the passenger lent me.
Very fine. Hot.

Day 21 Monday October 3
Sat out on the fo'c'sle head in the morning. Had a row with the 2nd Mate in the afternoon. Down in the hold chipping again. We got our N.E. Trade Wind. Smooth.
Fine to dull.

Day 22 Tuesday October 4
Chipped rust again in the main hold. Sat out on the fo'c'sle head in the afternoon. Saw my first flying fish.
Fine to dull.

Day 23 Wednesday October 5
Down chipping in the hold again. Sat on the fo'c'sle head in the morning. Chatted with the passenger at the wheel.
Rough. Very fine and hot.

Day 24 Thursday October 6
Sat on the fo'c'sle head in the afternoon. Had a fight with "Niele" Scheibel. Passed Cape Verde and saw the Island. The cat came up to the fo'c'sle head while I am look-out.
Lightning.

Day 25 Friday October 7
Sat on the fo'c'sle head in hot sunshine. A butterfly came on deck today although we are miles away from land. An Italian steamer passes us. Today we reach the Doldrums.
Showers. Smooth.

View up mast sails set to catch every breath of wind

Day 26 Saturday October 8
Cleaned out our fo'c'sle. I'm being dishwasher (backschaft in Finnish) this week. Chatted with the passenger while at the wheel. Sam (English) teaches me a little navigation. Sat out again on the fo'c'sle head.
Fair.

Day 27 Sunday October 9
Washed some of my clothes. Sam again teaches me some sea rules. Tried to revive some swallows which fell exhausted on deck. Sat out on deck. Saw my first whale.
Wet to fine.

Day 28 Monday October 10
Chipped rust again in the morning. We experienced a lot of bracing all night, I slept on deck in the afternoon. Collected rain water at night during tropical showers.
Rough-showers.

Day 29 Tuesday October 11
Slept on my bunk all morning. Chipped rust in the afternoon Got wet through collecting rain water Had a good laugh with Jack the Aussie.
Rough and wet.

Day 30 Wednesday October 12
Chipped rust in the main hold again. Chatted with the passenger out on deck and again while at the wheel. Two large sharks swimming about around the stern.
Nil.

Day 31 Thursday October 13
Slept on my bunk all morning and chipped rust again in the afternoon. Chatted with Sam about sailing ships on the fo'c'sle head in the afternoon.
Moderate sea. Sun.

Day 32 Friday October 14
Chipped rust again in the morning. Chatted with the passenger again while at the wheel. A large cormorant flies round the mast at night.
Smooth. Showers.

Day 33 Saturday October 15
Sat on the fo'c'sle head in the morning. Washed down the deck in the afternoon before coffee time. Played the ukelele at night and had a sing song.
Showers.

Day 34 Sunday October 16
Fished for sharks from the poop by special permission from the Captain in the morning - we caught two. Saw some dolphins and porpoises. Sat out on deck in the afternoon.
Very fine.

We catch a shark
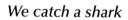

Day 35 Monday October 17
Sat on the fo'c'sle head in the morning. Chipped rust again in the afternoon. Chatted with the passenger at the wheel. Thought of Honey and home.
Smooth. Fair.

Day 36 Tuesday October 18
Chipped rust again in the morning. Worked most of the night turning round the ship. Slept on my bunk in the afternoon.
Smooth. Wet.

Day 37 Wednesday October 19
Slept on my bunk in the morning. Down chipping rust in the hold in the afternoon. Could not sleep for the row in the fo'c'sle and the lights on all night.
Smooth-showers.

Day 38 Thursday October 20
Chipped rust as usual in the morning. Lost my towel overboard. We find a small leakage in the hold and consequently we have to "man the pumps." Had a very busy watch at night bracing.
Rough-rain.

Day 39 Friday October 21
Sat on deck in the morning. Chipped rust as usual in the afternoon watch. Had a fine night and plenty of sleep. We get our S. E. Trade Wind.
Fine.

Day 40 Saturday October 22
Cleaned out the fo'c'sle workshops in the morning. Washed some of my clothes. There was a fight between the sailmaker and Vooristo. Chatted with the passenger on deck.
Fair-wet.

Day 41 Sunday October 23
Sat on deck in the morning and afternoon. Chatted with the passenger on deck. Had a sing song.
Fairly smooth-very fine.

Group with accordion, self 1st on the left

Day 42 Monday October 24
Greased sheet wire in the fore hold. Sat out on deck in the afternoon.
Crossed the line at 6pm. Worked most of the night turning the ship round. A few flying fish about today.
Sea smooth-fine.

Day 43 Tuesday October 25
Sat on deck in brilliant sunshine in the morning reading a book. Saw two very large birds. Greased wire again. Went up fore royal to overhaul buntlines.
Moderate sea-very fine.

Books were read and re-read many times

Day 44 Wednesday October 26
Saw the first steamer for eighteen days at 2am this morning. Chipped rust as usual. 1st Mate chatted with me. Sat out on deck and read my book.
Nil.

Day 45 Thursday October 27
Sat out on deck in the morning. Lovely sunrise. Down scraping rust in the stern of the ship, a hell of a job. Talked politics in the fo'c'sle in the evening.
Very fine.

Day 46 Friday October 28
Getting old and dirty wheat out from the stern of the ship, talk about a smell. Sat on deck in the afternoon with the passenger, Walter Hoffman and Sheibel. Saw some flying fish. I had two hours at the wheel.
Very fine.

Day 47 Saturday October 29

Sat out on deck in the morning and admired the very beautiful seascape. Tried to catch some bonito *[editor's note - any of several tunney-like fish which are striped like mackerel and are common in tropical seas]* from the fo'c'sle head but failed. Again saw shoals of flying fish.
Very fine.

Day 48 Sunday October 30 15.5° South.

Southern Cross seen for the first time. Washed some clothes. Passenger came onto the deck. Chatted with Lofty about the moon and weather influence.
Very fine.

Day 49 Monday October 31

Sat on deck in the morning. Began changing tropical sails for storm sails again. Chatted with the passenger at the wheel again. Had a lot of bracing at night. Thought of home and Honey.
Fine to rain.

Changing sail

Day 50 Tuesday November 1

Cleaned away old wheat from the bilges in the fore hold. Again we carry on changing sails. Chatted with the passenger again.
Dull.

Day 51 Wednesday November 2
Slept on my bunk in the morning free watch. Changed the sails on the fore mast. Scalded my hand carrying hot coffee. Feeling very tired. Thought of all at home. Big seas.
Rain.

Day 52 Thursday November 3
Chipped rust in the fore hold in the morning. Sewed my trousers in the afternoon. We saw a lot of lightning at night. Jack has a bad poisoned eye.
Rain-Rough sea.

Day 53 Friday November 4
Slept on my bunk in the morning. Chipped rust in the hold in the afternoon. Had my free night again.
Rain.

Day 54 Saturday November 5
Cleaned out the fo'c'sle midships. Saw my first albatross flying over the ship. Our black cat is not well. Jacks eye still bad.
Fine.

Day 55 Sunday November 6
In 30 degrees South. Slept on my bunk in the morning. The albatross is still with us. Saw a huge whale at 1pm. The passenger came up to fo'c'sle head and chatted.
Fine.

Men holding albatross

Day 56 Monday November 7
Chipped the galley coal tin in the morning, a dirty job. Sat on deck in the afternoon. Chatted with the passenger and Hoffman on a hatch top. The 1st Mate killed the two black cats which had both been ill.
Fine.

Day 57 Tuesday November 8
Slept on my bunk in the morning. Had two hours at the wheel. The wind became very stormy towards midnight. I had two hours look-out and was very cold.
Fair.

Day 58 Wednesday November 9 34° South 26° West
Made fast all three royals in the morning watch. Gale blowing hard. Made fast all staysails. Gale increases days run 288 miles.
Nil.

Day 59 Thursday November 10
Made fast all three upper and lower to'gallants during the night. I suffered very little sleep. Slept on my bunk during the morning free watch very cold and tired.
Gale and showers.

Day 60 Friday November 11 37° South 20° West
We travel 325 miles in 24 hours the Captain tells me it is a record for the "Olivebank". Chipped rust and greased wires on deck. Chatted with the passenger.
Cold. Fair.

Day 61 Saturday November 12
Slept on my bunk in the morning. Washed the deck down in the afternoon. Had a row with the 2nd Mate and donkeyman. Fed up feeling.
Cold. Dull.

Clean deck

Day 62 Sunday November 13
Had a lot of bracing in the morning watch owing to the variable winds. Sam showed and explained all the different ropes to me, of which there are thousands. Saw some more porpoises.
Dull. Cold.

Knowing the ropes

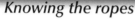

Day 63 Monday November 14
Chatted on the fo'c'sle head with the passenger nearly all free watch in the morning. Chipped rust down the fore hold in the afternoon.
Very fine.

Day 64 Tuesday November 15
Chipped rust in the hold in the morning. Donkeyman is still unfriendly and always rowing. Chatted with the passenger in the afternoon on deck.
Very fine. Cold.

Day 65 Wednesday November 16
Slept on my bunk in the morning. Bill and Sam came up onto the fo'c'sle head while I am look-out and chatted with me. Thought of home and Honey.
Very fine.

Day 66 Thursday November 17
Chipped rust as usual in the hold in the afternoon. Sat out on deck and chatted with Sandholm one of my pals. Had a lot of bracing all night.
Fine.

Day 67 Friday November 18
Chipped rust in the hold again during the working watch. Slept on my bunk during free watch. A beautiful clear night with "Southern Cross" very clear.
Fine.

Day 68 Saturday November 19
Cleaned the fo'c'sle midships in the morning. Read my book in my bunk in the afternoon. Sam explained some knots to me.
Dull. Cold.

Day 69 Sunday November 20
Slept on my bunk in the morning. Chatted on deck with Sam and the passenger. The passenger invited me into his cabin in the afternoon and we chatted about life on sailing ships and the Scandinavians too.
Dull. Warm.

Day 70 Monday November 21
Chipped rust in the fore hold in the morning. A large flock of white Cape pigeons follow us most of the day. Slept on my bunk in the afternoon.
Fair.

Day 71 Tuesday November 22
Slept on my bunk in the free watch. Down in the hold chipping rust in the afternoon. We make fast the mizzen royal in the afternoon owing to the barometer going down. Out bracing most of the night.
Gale. Rain.

Bracing

Day 72 Wednesday November 23
Chipped rust as usual. I wash a few of my clothes. The spanker sail is carried away and the boom breaks in two.
Gale. Fair.

Day 73 Thursday November 24

Slept on my bunk in the morning. The 2nd Mate makes me take five and a half hours look-out, talk about being cold. Chatted with Bill.
Windy. Fair.

Day 74 Friday November 25

Chipped rust as usual. Slept on my bunk in the afternoon. Scheibel and myself make fast the fore royal in the teeth of a gale.
Very cold. Gale.

Day 75 Saturday November 26

"Herzogin Cecilie" passes us at 4am. We take in all royals, upper and lower to'gallents on account of the increasing wind. Scheibel and I wash the deck down in the afternoon.
Wet.

"Herzogin Cecilie"

Day 76 Sunday November 27

We take in the three upper topsails during the night watch. Worked all morning, all though Sunday. Slept on my bunk in the afternoon.
Nil.

Day 77 Monday November 28

Slept on my bunk in the morning. I have three hours look-out as the Mate won't allow me to take the wheel. Took some snaps. Mountainous seas.
Gale.

Mountainous seas

Day 78 Tuesday November 29

Chipped rust as usual. We spent most of the night making sail again. Slept on my bunk in the afternoon free watch.
Fair.

Day 79 Wednesday November 30

Slept on my bunk in the morning. Chipped rust as usual. Had a row with the 2nd Mate and most of the crew. Went up the mizzen royal to overhaul buntlines.
Fine. Warm.

View up the mizzen mast

Day 80 Thursday December 1
Chipped rust in the hold again. Slept on my bunk in the afternoon. Thought of home. 334 miles days run *[Editor's note - this must be a new record for "Olivebank"]. Position 61° East 39° South. Fair.*

Day 81 Friday December 2
Slept on my bunk in the morning. Chipped rust in the afternoon on the fore upper to'gallant yard. Chatted with Bill.
Fair to rain.

Day 82 Saturday December 3
Fed up with the whole routine. Cleaned the midships fo'c'sle in the morning. Sat on my bunk and read in the afternoon. Talked about Australia.
Fair.

Day 83 Sunday December 4
Slept on my bunk in the morning. The port watch made fast all three royals and we make fast the main upper to'gallant.
Showers.

Day 84 Monday December 5
Bailed water out of the tanks, man the pump. Slept on my bunk in the afternoon.
Sun. Cold.

Day 85 Tuesday December 6
Slept on my bunk in the morning. Had a shave. Chipped rust as usual in the afternoon. Went up the main royal to overhaul buntlines.
Fair. Cold.

Day 86 Wednesday December 7
Chipped as usual in the morning. Laughed and joked with Nicky and Walter at lunch. Had another row with donkeyman.
Rain.

Day 87 Thursday December 8 Position 98° East 33° South
Slept on my bunk in the morning. We begin to get ready for Australia.
Fine to rain.

We begin to get ready for Australia

Day 88 Friday December 9
Chipped in the hold in the morning. The port watch commence to man the pumps. Laughed over Esenberg.
Windy. Cold. Wet.

Day 89 Saturday December 10
Slept on my bunk in the morning. Up the main royal overhauling buntlines in the evening, worked continuously during watch on deck at night.
Fair.

Day 90 Sunday December 11
Great gale. Made fast all royals, upper and lower to'gallants and upper topsails. Chatted with Bill.
Showers.

Day 91 Monday December 12 Position 121.28° East 41° South
Got coal for donkeyman with Hoffman. Washed with soda all the white paint on deck. Chatted with the passenger.
Nil.

Day 92 Tuesday December 13
Carried on washing white paint on deck. Had a row with the 1st Mate. Slept on my bunk in the afternoon. Made fast the main royal with Sam.
Rain.

Day 93 Wednesday December 14
Chatted with the passenger while at the wheel. Cleaned the paint on the fo'c'sle head in the afternoon. Sing song on deck in the evening.
Nil.

Day 94 Thursday December 15 Position 36.32° South 134.57° East
"Herzogin Cecilie" again sighted on the horizon 12am. Ship very near at 7pm. Cleaned the white paint again in the morning. Had a sing song.
Nil.

Day 95 Friday December 16
I see the first land in Australia, Neptune Island. Arrived Port Lincoln and dropped anchor at 6am. Made fast all sails. Cleaned brasses and all fo'c'sles.
Arrived Australia.

[Editor's Note - After this first voyage on a sailing vessel Geoffrey jumped ship and made his way back to England on a steamer.

The 'glamour' and the 'reality' of sailing ship life were, evidently, poles apart. The continuous hard work with a virtual skeleton crew to haul such heavy canvas, clearly left its mark. However, just as clearly the pain, hardship, poor food and lack of sleep were soon forgotten - especially in the telling and re-telling of 'salty' stories - and Geoff decided to try again, simply because he loved the sailing ships so much.]

Voyage of the Three Masted Barque

"Winterhude"

From Glasgow to Port Lincoln and back

1934

Day 1 Saturday October 21st

I arrived in Glasgow at 7.32am. Had some breakfast and called in at the office in 58, Bath Street where I met Captain Morn and signed under Finnish law. I left for the boat and found it at 12am. Started work at 1pm. Left the dry dock for Australia at 1.30pm. Passed down the Clyde and had to do a look-out. The tug left us at 1am.

Day 2 Sunday October 22nd

Free watch in the morning I went to sleep on my bunk. Working watch in the afternoon and had a turn at the wheel. Cleaned the deck and swung the yards around a lot. Talked with the passenger (Mr. Brown) at the wheel. Saw the coast of Northern Ireland at 3pm. Left the Scottish coast at 4pm. Turned the ship about again to run down the coast of England.

Self at the wheel

Day 3 Monday October 23rd

Saw the Isle of Man. In the morning watch I was down in the sail locker cleaning and sorting sails, then I pumped water onto the deck and filled up the tank. Passenger came and chatted in the afternoon. Saw the coast of Holyhead at 3.15pm. Had a look-out in the evening.

Day 4 Tuesday October 24th

Cleaning old wheat out of the hold in the early morning. Passed a clan boat at 10am. Chatted with the passenger. Belgier not so well, moustached German ill also. Shifted wheat out of the hold all afternoon. Chatted in the sailmaker's cabin with the sailmaker and the passenger. Had a look-out, got wet through. *Misty.*

Day 5 Wednesday October 25th

Down in the main hold with Belgier cleaning wheat away. Boat rolling heavily but doing 10 knots. Off The Lizard. Went to the wheel 12am to 1pm at the wheel with the passenger. "Olympic" passed and signalled us at 12.30am. Sat in my bunk in the afternoon. Had first look-out in the evening. Fairly heavy sea. *Squally.*

Day 6 Thursday October 26th

Down in the hold in the morning then up on the fore upper to'gallant clearing gaskets, cut my finger. Slept in my bunk in the morning. Chatted with the passenger. After breakfast there was nearly a fight between the starboard watch Germans and the Belgian, Jacques, but it smoothed over. Down in the hold again in the afternoon and the passenger was also down. Had a sing song in the evening.

Dry and fair wind. 196 miles.

Day 7 Friday October 27th

Down in the hold in the morning clearing wood etc. Had a trick at the wheel. Plenty of small birds about. Chatted with the passenger at the wheel. Had a chat with Pongo Thompsen (Dane). Slept on my bunk in the afternoon. Plenty of birds still with us.

Position 48°N 40°W. Squally and wet. 210 miles.

Pongo Thompsen painting

Day 8 Saturday October 28th

Cleaned the pig place out with Belgier. The cat was at look-out with me. Slept on my bunk in the morning. Washed down the deck in the afternoon. Chatted with the passenger at the wheel. Belgier goes up the rigging for the first time. The cat caught a bird. Frachnect was tied up and bound with rope by the rest of the starboard watch, he actually fainted.

Position 41°N 16°W . Calm with a far wind. 167 miles.

26

Day 9 Sunday October 29th

Went to the wheel in the morning. Washed a shirt and towel and darned my trousers. Chatted with the passenger on the fo'c'sle head after lunch. Some of the crew played cards. The sea became very rough in the evening. Strong North East wind.
Position 38°N 16°W. Smooth to rough. 216 miles.

Day 10 Monday October 30th

Washed all the starboard side white paint in drenching rain. Tacked round and eventually got our course South West 1/2 South previously Bi de Vind. Passenger with me at the wheel. Ship strongly lying on starboard side.
Position 35°N 20°W. Sea rough, strong wind and rain. 245 miles.

Day 11 Tuesday October 31st

Finished washing paint all morning on the poop. The cat nearly caught a bird. Slept on my bunk all afternoon. Read "Man from the Carlton". Belgier with me at the wheel in the evening and the 2nd Mate sang sea shanties. Chatted with the passenger at look-out. Course South West 1/2 South then Bi de Vind.
Position 34°N 21°W. Sea smooth, fine and clear.

2nd Mate Andersen

Day 12 Wednesday November 1st

Overhauled buntlines and gaskets and the passenger helped me. Belgier, Franky and Pongo played cards. Down in the hold all the afternoon. Chatted with the passenger at the wheel. Belgier not so well again. Good wind, sailing Bi de Vind. Sea fairly calm.
Position 31°N 22°W. Fog. 192 miles.

Day 13 Thursday November 2nd

Down in the hold again. Some of the boys hunted for bed bugs also some had a gramophone on. Pongo still ill. Most of the crew sat on deck in the evening. Course South South West 1/2 West fair wind, sea calm and a full moon. *Position 28°N 24°W. Fine. 212 miles.*

Day 14 Friday November 3rd

My hand is still sore. Started to change for tropical sails. Started on the main upper to'gallant. In the afternoon we took in the fore lower to'gallant and upper topsail. Very tired. Belgier had three hours at the wheel. Chatted with Heim. Very hot day beautiful sunrise and a very beautiful moon at 6pm. Course South South West 1/2 West sea smooth and little wind, a very fine day. *Position 25°N 24°W. 170 miles.*

Heim young German seaman

Day 15 Saturday November 4th

Changed the fore upper topsail, lower topsail and foresail and one stay sail in the morning watch. I had two hours at the wheel. Heim nearly fell off the lower topsail yard. The passenger cut my hair and I cut his. Frachnect went up to the main upper to'gallant as the crew told him there was a flying fish up there. I had a row with Frachnect. Very hot but clear and fine to dull. Course South South West 3/4 West. Sea calm and little wind. *Position 23°N 25°W. 143 miles.*

Day 16 Sunday November 5th

Overslept. Should have taken the wheel at 6am not 6.15am. Washed clothes after breakfast. Took some snaps also. Chatted with donkeyman and German. Some of the crew played cards. Belgier came for bread into the port fo'c'sle and was eventually kicked out by Bob. Bob and I tried to save a swallow from the cat. It came and sat on the table in the port fo'c'sle, then Bob took it into his bunk. Chatted with the passenger. Beautiful sunrise and sunset a fine, clear, calm day. *Position 20°N 25°W. 149 miles.*

Bob (Yankee) Schmidt (German)

Day 17 Monday November 6th
My backschaft (Fo'c'sle cleaning and mess boy for one week) started. Helped to stow sails in the sail locker, then chipped on the main upper to'gallant first with Frachnect, then with the passenger. Took some snaps from the main upper to'gallant. Washed my brown shirt. Nice sunset again. Slept a little in my bunk. Course South South West 1/2 West. Boat becalmed till late evening. A fine day. *Position 18°N 26°W.*

Looking down on poop and mizzen mast from main upper to'gallant

Day 18 Tuesday November 7th
Chipped the top of the main mast and lower main to'gallant. Row in the starboard fo'c'sle over backschaft. Saw Cape Verde 10am. Chipped on deck. Cut my finger badly in the evening. Cat was with me when I was policeman. The sea is calm and it is fine and clear.
Position 16°N 26°W. 162 miles.

Chipped the top of the main mast

Day 19 Wednesday November 8th
Saw a steamer homeward bound at
8am. Painted the yard of the main
upper to'gallant. Cleaned brushes with
Frachnect. Had a row with Brincks over
waking up the port watch. The passenger
chatted with me in the port fo'c'sle and
he bandaged up my finger. The port
watch got wet through in the afternoon.
We worked continuously during the night
watch from 7pm to 12pm. A big squall at
11pm, thought for a moment that the ship would not last it out. Plenty of brace
pulling. Strong squalls and then we were becalmed. Course South 1/2 East.
Position 13°N 26°W. 180 miles.

Day 20 Thursday November 9th
Cleaned out the pig house in the morning. Cookies food caught on fire. Belgier
in great spirits at breakfast. Feeling very tired as I had only two hours sleep.
Painted the jigger boom then had two hours at the wheel. Ship homeward bound
passed us at 2.30pm. The foresail back wire snapped wrapping the sail, all hands
called. Belgier sent up to paint the jigger mast, very crazy. Bob is called a filthy
name by the 1st Mate. Bob offered to fight him on deck but the Mate was too
timid to come down. Strong wind, boat well on starboard side doing 10 knots. It
is fine and clear.
Position 11°N 26°W. 118 miles.

Day 21 Friday November 10th
Cleaned the Captains bathroom out, then helped to fasten the spare upper
to'gallant to the deck with Heim, Brincks and the 2nd Mate. Got wet through
at the wheel. Slept on my bunk in the afternoon. Saw a flying fish. Reached the
Doldrums. The passenger came forward before tea and chatted. Port watch got
wet through again. Still one green linnet on board. We have squally tropical rain
and it is very hot. Chatted with Brincks at coffee about boats, then with Heim at
look-out.
Position 8°N 25°W. 218 miles.

Day 22 Saturday November 11th

Helped Heim to paint before breakfast, then washed a towel. Looked for bugs in my bunk and took some snaps of the starboard watch on the bowsprit. Cleaned sailmakers and the starboard fo'c'sle out. 2nd Mate

asked our watch questions after coffee. Plenty of work swinging yards around after tea. We are still becalmed and there are some very heavy showers. It is very warm.
Position 7°N 24°W. 81 miles.

Day 23 Sunday November 12th

Had plenty of work all night, then again all Sunday morning. After breakfast some of the crew tried to catch a shark hovering around the stern of the boat. One little green linnet still here and it is now very tame. All of the crew were up forward sitting on deck and listening to Cookies gramophone. Sailmaker, myself, Bob and donkeyman did tricks with ropes etc on deck. Chatted with the passenger and then Cookie at look-out. Cookie pointed out the Southern Star to me. The starboard watch and Keller sang on the fo'c'sle head at night to Stowahse's organ. Becalmed.
Position 6.47°N 23°W. 24 miles.

Day 24 Monday November 13th

Filled up the Captains bath with salt water before breakfast. Had a row with Stowahse over filling the tank, thought he meant finish but really he meant slack on. Helped 2nd Mate with Belgier to secure the spare to'gallant yard. Another row with Stowahse, then at tea between Stowahse and Brincks. Had two hours at the wheel. We are still becalmed and it is fair and hot.
Position 6°N 23°W. 28 miles.

Day 25 Tuesday November 14th

Painted the upper main and lower main to'gallant yard with Heim. Had a very bad night as regards sleep. Port watch got wet through again. Belgier discovered eating bread by the 2nd Mate so was sent up the rigging to overhaul gaskets. I dropped plenty of paint on deck and the Mate got some on his face. Keller as happy as ever, always cheerful whatever is happening. Port watch collected rain water. Tacked round the yards again at 7pm and then worked continuously till 12.15. Then worked again continuously till 8am. I overhauled buntlines. A fairly good wind from the West sprang up at 7am.
Position 5.35°N 24°W. 7 miles.

Day 26 Wednesday November 15th

Belgier told he might as well go back to his bunk and sleep, absolutely useless. Greased wires in the afternoon with Belgier and Frachnect. Had only a look-out otherwise free all night. Wind became very strong about midnight. Passed a fairly large liner homeward bound about 1am. South East Trade Wind arrived about 6pm but the course is still Bi de Vind.
Position 5°N 22°W 38 miles.

Day 27 Thursday November 16th

Greased wires again and painted the white paint over again. Swung the yards around again about 11am. I had a good wash in the afternoon. The passenger started making a model of the "Winterhude". Chatted with donkeyman at coffee about different Captains of windjammers. Saw a very fine rainbow in the morning while at the wheel. The 2nd Mate caught Belgier asleep in watch on deck and made him get out of his bunk. Trade Wind here but not in the right direction.
Position 3.50°N 24°W. Fine and warm. 176 miles.

Day 28 Friday November 17th

Painted the main lower topsail yard. Belgier not allowed to go to the wheel while we are sailing Bi de Vind. Sat in my bunk and read in the afternoon also slept a little. Swung the yards round Westerly again at 7pm. Belgier caught asleep at look-out by the 2nd Mate. The Mate was very angry. I had a wheel and a policeman. Still well off our correct course. Fine and very hot with a good wind.
Position 3°N 21°W. 87 miles.

Day 29 Saturday November 18th

Tarred the main mast and finished it then started on the mizzen mast and Brincks was right at the top. Belgier is sent by the mate right out on the gaff boom. Had two hours at the wheel. Heim cut my hair in the afternoon. Played the mouth organ for a while and donkeyman danced, then he played and I danced. It is fine and warm but a poor wind.
Position 3.6°N 24°W. 87 miles.

Day 30 Sunday November 19th

Had a row with Pongo over coming out at change of watch. Only had two hours sleep. Swung the yards round at 2am our only free watch. Filled the tanks up with fresh water. Washed my towel and handkerchief. Oil tanker passed us bound North East at 6am. Sat on my bunk and read papers in the morning and slept on my bunk in the afternoon. After coffee I listened to the gramophone and thought of Honey (mother). Still Bi de Vind.
Position 2.4°N 24°W. 69 miles.

Day 31 Monday November 20th

Rose early. Passenger said the "Grace Harwar" was in sight at 6.30am and came alongside us within 100 yards at 7.30am. Turned out to be a German school ship the "Scheulschiff Deutchland". Still in sight 2.45pm. Up the main mast painting

lower topsail yard. Had wheel from 11am to 1pm. Chatted with Cookie in the afternoon. Stowahse who was policeman fell asleep and did not hear the Mates whistle, thus all starboard watch must now stand on deck, underneath the poop, during their watch. Sailing Bi de Vind. A fine and clear day.
Position 2.15°N 24°W. 36 miles.

The school ship "Scheulschiff Deutchland" (note cadets manning the rigging)

Day 32 Tuesday November 21st

Our watch got wet through in our watch from 4am to 8am. I was sent up to the main upper to'gallant to overhaul gardings. Turned the ship around again at 7am. I fell on my head and the Captain told me not to go up the rigging. Down in the hold in the afternoon cleaning up with Stowahse, Belgier and Frachnect and also getting oil. Swung the yards round again at 5pm and got wet through. Talked with Heim at look-out. The Mate allowed us to sit in the deck house. Still sailing Bi de Vind and it is very wet.
Position 1.33°N 23°W. 83 miles.

Day 33 Wednesday November 22nd

I slept very well last night. Painted the main mast in the morning. Had a good wash. Chatted with the passenger. Belgier was nearly hit by Bob for stealing sugar. At tea time the port watch and myself pinched some fish left on deck as it was a very poor tea. The 2nd Mate chatted with me at the wheel about the position and when we should pass the Equator. Beautiful moon and night it is very fine and clear. We are sailing Bi de Vind then, at 8.15pm Full and By, course about South West by West.
Position 1°N 25.16°W. 123 miles.

Day 34 Thursday November 23rd

We passed the Equator at 5am. Up the main mast in the early morning painting the left of the main yard. There was a very beautiful sunrise. We have now definitely got our South East Trade Wind. Still painting the main mast and yard, then wet the whole deck with sea water in the evening. Sang songs with the passenger and Pongo after tea. The port watch must now stand on deck as Pongo failed to hear two whistles when policeman, he was sleeping. Course South West by South sailing Full and By. Belgier takes the wheel.
Position 1.14°S 27°W. 182 miles.

Day 35 Friday November 24th

Slept very well. Finished painting the main mast then started on the mizzen mast we then painted the lower gaff, very dangerous as there is nothing to hold onto. Shouted down to Belgier who was at the wheel, he was not looking at the sails, nearly got me thrown off the yard. Read my old diary and tried to sleep in the afternoon. It is mainly fine and clear with a little rain late at night. Sailing Full and By course South South West.
Position 3.35°S 29°W. 215 miles.

Day 36 Saturday November 25th

Chatted with the 2nd Mate while at coffee in the early morning, then carried coal to the galley. Washed my towel after breakfast and chatted with the passenger. Saw an oil tanker bound for South Africa at 8am. Washed the deck

in the afternoon. I hurt my left leg very badly. Plenty of the crew got drunk on rum, especially Schmidt and the 2nd Mate. Plenty of row in the evening singing etc. The 2nd Mate fell asleep for two hours in his watch then came forward and chatted with me. Good wind and it is very fine and clear. Sailing Full and By and course round about South West.
Position 7.50°S 29.46°W. 210 miles.

Day 37 Sunday November 26th
Ceremony of Crossing the Line took place and Keller, Belgier, Stowahse, Pongo, Brincks, Jacques and Frachnect were all baptised. Bob got dead drunk. I did not get the chance of seeing the fun as I had to take two hours at the wheel. Slept on my bunk in the afternoon and chatted. Sailing Bi de Vind and course about South South West but a very fine, hot, clear day.

Belgier being baptised

Day 38 Monday November 27th
Cleaned the deck by brushing it ready for tarring. Frachnect forgot to wake me up therefore Heim woke me up at 5.55pm so I missed coffee. Belgier is told by the 2nd Mate that when he had finished cleaning the pig place, the 'heads' and filled the tanks with water, he could go to sleep. He failed to clean them correctly therefore he had to take the wheel. Tried to sleep on my bunk in the morning but failed as the flies are very bad. We tarred the starboard side of the deck in the afternoon and also the fo'c'sle head. A very fine sunset seen from look-out. It is fine and clear and we are sailing Full and By and then Bi de Vind. The course is about South South West.
Position 14°S 30°W. 192 miles.

Day 39 Tuesday November 28th
Painted the mizzen boom in the morning. A four masted barque seen at 7.30am on the port side. The Captain thought it was "Parma", then as it came nearer at 1pm he though it was either the "Archibald Russell" or "Lawhill", most probably the former. She is gaining slightly on us. At 4pm she is definitely ahead of us and the Captain now thinks it is definitely the "Passat". She looks very pretty.

Chatted with Brincks in the afternoon and then later with the sailmaker. At 8pm the "Passat" is definitely overhauling us. Had plenty of work in the watch as Frachnect has broken his wrist. Sailing Bi de Vind and the course is South South West.
Position 17°S 30°W. 173 miles.

Day 40 Wednesday November 29th
The "Passat" is now definitely directly ahead of us at 6.30am and hull down. Scraped the top of the fore hold this morning and in the afternoon finished scraping the aft hold top. Then I was down in the hold cleaning up etc. I had last wheel and saw a beautiful sunset from the poop. Lights of Trindade seen at 7pm and I saw them at midnight. Saw the very first Cape pigeons today. It is fine and clear and we are sailing Full and By and then later course, South.
Position 20.17°S 29.20°W. 173 miles.

Day 41 Thursday November 30th
Started changing the tropical sails on the main mast. Our watch changed three sails, the upper to'gallant, lower and upper topsail. The 2nd Mate very nearly lost his life by falling from the main upper to'gallant. I went up the main mast taking snaps on the yard. After coffee in the afternoon I sat out on the net on the bowsprit and watched the ship ploughing through the water. Worked a lot in the night watch swinging the yards round as the wind was coming from aft. It is very fine and clear and very warm and the course is still South.
Position 22.33°S 29.20°W. 156miles.

Looking at fore mast from main lower to'gallant

Day 42 Friday December 1st
Went up the fore rigging and overhauled buntlines and gaskets. Washed my towel in the afternoon. Took down the tropical mainsail and then bent and set the stronger canvas. Had two hours at the wheel. Changed two staysails and then I went up the main mast checking gaskets in the evening. Beautiful full moon seen at 7.30pm. I am feeling very hot and tired. Thought of home and wee Honey. The course is now South 1/2 West and it is very fine and warm.
Position 24°S 28°W. 124 miles.

Day 43 Saturday December 2nd

Pulled the braces plenty of times in the morning and got very wet. Battened down all holds then chipped paint on the floor forward. Slept on my bunk in the afternoon. We are now "Running the Eastern Down" very strong wind from the South West lot of sea coming onboard. At 7pm the ship is lying well over on her port side. The course is about South East and we are sailing Bi de Vind and it is very wet to fair.
Position 26.43°S 26.22°W. 172 miles.

Running the Eastern down

Day 44 Sunday December 3rd

The sea is not so rough at 4am. The inner jib on the bowsprit got torn at 4.15am therefore we took it in, also the mizzen staysail is taken in. I sighted a sailing ship on the port side at 4.20am and she was alongside at 8am on the starboard side. Plenty of signalling took place but our Captain could not read it. Eventually the Captain thought it was the "Padua" of Hamburg. I had two hours at the wheel in the afternoon as Belgier sent down yet again, no good. Saw the first albatross this trip at 3pm. The four masted barque now believed to be the "Priwall" still in sight on the horizon at 4pm. Heim showed me how to splice ropes together. The 2nd Mate came up after coffee and showed us tricks with string. At 5pm the sailing ship vessel had worn ship and turned about so we did the same at 7pm. Course now round about East, the sea is fairly rough, there is a strong wind and it is wet to fair.
Position 27.6°S 21.32°W. 240 miles.

Day 45 Monday December 4th

Changed the flying jib and main jib then painted numbers one and two hatch tops. Then at 1pm all hands changed the fore sail. My week as backschaft has commenced. Slept on my bunk in the afternoon and then sat out in the sun on deck. Beautiful moon came up at 9.15pm. The 2nd Mate chatted with me at the wheel. It is fine and warm still and we are sailing Bi de Vind our course was South South West and then South by West.
Position 27°S 23°W. 60 miles.

Day 46 Tuesday December 5th

Had a very good nights sleep. Saw a second albatross at 5.45am. I went up the main mast before breakfast to overhaul buntlines. Thought of Honey in the morning. Managed to get two hours sleep in the morning free watch. Down in the hold in the afternoon clearing old wheat away, then swept the deck and got wet through as the weather is fine to rain. Sailing Full and By then course at 6.15pm with me at the wheel going South South East.
Position 30°S 21°W. 156 miles.

Four jib sails from fore sail yard

Day 47 Wednesday December 6th

The Captain gave us a whole day holiday on account of the Finnish Freedom Day. There are now three albatrosses and some of the boys and the passenger were up on the poop trying to catch one by the ancient method of a wooden triangle and a piece of pork but the Mate lost his line overboard. Slept on my bunk in the afternoon. Chatted with Bob in the evening. It is a fair day with rain at intervals and the sea is smooth. Our course is South by East 3/4 East.
Position 32°S 19°W. 170 miles.

Bob at the Wheel

Day 48 Thursday December 7th

I slept on my bunk in the morning and was down in the hold in the afternoon clearing wheat away and shifting wood. Had a row with all the starboard watch over the course and Belgier. Then at tea time finally a fight with Frachnect in which the whole watch turned against me. Saw a whale at 7pm. Chatted with Bob in the evening. It is very fine and warm and our course is South East by South.
Position 33°S 16°W. 159 miles.

Day 49 Friday December 8th

All the starboard watch are still out with me and nobody speaks to me. I don't care a hang, give me the English. Down in the fore hold again during working watch clearing wheat and shifting wood. Saw a whale on the port side from the poop while at the wheel. Slept on my bunk in the afternoon chatted with the passenger about the row. Thoroughly fed up. Course is South East 3/4 South and the wind is increasing though the weather is fine.
Position 35°S 15°W. 92 miles.

Day 50 Saturday December 9th

Filled the water tanks with fresh water then went down the after hold clearing wheat. Belgier again sent down from the wheel, absolutely useless. Talked with the passenger about the rest of the watches unfairness. A little more friendly with Stowahse and Frachnect. Carried coal to the galley. Row started up again at coffee Bob and Mr Brown stuck up for me but our watch are dead against me. I had two wheels in three hours, dirty work. Saw some Dolphins. Had a very bad nights sleep. The course is now South East 1/4 South and the sea is smooth. There is a fair wind which got very strong by 4pm so we took in the upper and lower

gaff. It took me all my time to hold the wheel and I got wet through.
Position 36°S 11°W. 212 miles.

Day 51 Sunday December 10th
Still unfriendly with the rest of the watch. Chatted with the passenger and Bob in the morning over Leeds and Sheffield. Slept on my bunk before coffee, then again after coffee. Absolutely fed up, my watch are a most unsporting crowd. There is a fair wind and some rain and the course is South East.
Position 37.5°S 6°W. 214 miles.

Day 52 Monday December 11th
Did not sleep at all during the night, so tried to sleep during the morning but failed. Down in the hold again in the afternoon clearing away wheat from the bilges. Now definitely friends again with everybody but Frachnect. One Cape pigeon flying about and plenty of albatrosses. It is very cold and dull with showers. The course is South East 3/4 South.
Position 38°S 2°W. 188 miles.

Day 53 Tuesday December 12th
Again I had only two hours sleep, feeling very tired indeed. It was very cold during the night but turned quite warm during the day. Mr Brown caught an albatross at 12.45pm and released it again at 1pm. Down in the hold again clearing away wheat. Tried to sleep on my bunk in the afternoon but could not at all. Slept two hours during the night. The day was fair and the wind increased at 7pm. Course is South East.
Position 1°E 38°S. 73 miles.

Day 54 Wednesday December 13th
Tried to sleep on my bunk in the morning but again failed to do so. Bob had another argument with the 1st Mate. Two albatrosses still with us. There is a good wind and it is fairly strong. Down in the aft hold in the afternoon clearing water and then chipping in between deck. Had a fight with Belgier, I had offered him the fight at 7pm but he had refused then. It is fine but cold and the course is South East 1/4 East.
Position 2°E 39°S. 145 miles.

Day 55 Thursday December 14th
Down in the middle hold chipping stanchions. The passenger was down with us. None of us did much work, we sang songs and smoked cigarettes. Washed a lot of clothes in the afternoon. Now we are definitely running short of water, only about two days supply left. Chatted with the passenger in the afternoon after coffee. I had two hours sleep. Beautiful sunset at 7pm but it turned very cold. Course South East 1/2 South. Fine day and a fairly good wind.
Position 6°E 40°S. 195 miles.

Day 56 Friday December 15th

Overhauled buntlines and cleaned the pig house out before breakfast and afterwards I had a shave and chatted with the passenger about the countryside of England. Four albatrosses and one small Cape pigeon to be seen. Down in the hold chipping stanchions again in the afternoon. The 2nd Mate came down and chatted with me Belgier and Stowahse about whether we are allowed to go to Mariehamn (Finnland) or not after the voyage. It is a fine day with a good wind but not a fair wind. Course Bi de Vind.
Position 9°E 40°S. 168 miles.

Day 57 Saturday December 16th

Chipped down in the hold again all five hours as I had no wheel. The passenger was down with us and we all sang songs again. Sowed my trousers and a shirt in the afternoon. Plenty of albatrosses about now. After coffee I slept on my bunk for one and a half hours. Wind began to get very strong by 7.45pm and I was at the wheel. One sea came over at 8.15pm near the fo'c'sle head. By 9.30pm the wind was very strong so we took in all mizzen sails and the mizzen top staysail, then took in the flying jib at 10pm. The wind was now very strong and the ship was wallowing and lying well on her port side. Now we took in the two upper to'gallants. Myself, Karlsson and Belgier took in the main. Then all hands of the starboard watch took in the fore upper to'gallant. At 12pm there were three whistles from the Mate and all hands took in the mainsail and eventually turned the ship around, now the course being South West but still Bi de Vind. A fair day and the course changed to North North East and sailing Bi de Vind.
Position 13°E 39°S. 190 miles.

Day 58 Sunday December 17th

I had very little sleep in the night, our watch was very unlucky and had to work almost all night. At 7am we made sail again with mainsail , two upper to'gallants and fore lower to'gallant. Then at 8am in our free watch, the port watch made the other sails. I slept on my bunk from 9am to 12.30pm and then slept again in the afternoon until coffee time. We still have a head wind. Course now West by South and it is a very fine and clear day but a little cold.
Position 14°E 38°S. 58 miles.

Day 59 Monday December 18th

Chipped down in the hold again all morning. Turned the ship around again at 2pm. I had a good nights sleep and slept again on my bunk in the afternoon. Thompsen discovered he had got scabs, so also me. Turned the ship round again at 7pm. Chatted with donkeyman about his trip on "Penang" last year. Fine weather but rather cold and still sailing Bi de Vind.
Position 12°E 40°S. 136 miles.

Day 60 Tuesday December 19th

Chipped in the hold again before breakfast. Turned the ship round again at
5.15am. Slept on my bunk in the morning and then down in the hold again
chipping in the afternoon. Caught two albatrosses after tea through the famous
triangle method. We are now definitely becalmed and in the "Roaring Forties"
too, most unusual. It is fine and clear and we are sailing Bi de Vind.
Position 13°E 40°S. 29 miles.

Day 61 Wednesday December 20th

Down in the hold again chipping. Had a good nights sleep and then a good
wash in the afternoon. Now we are definitely short of water again. Caught
another albatross just before 7pm but let it go again. The starboard watch teased
Belgier again by making him an apple-pie bed. The weather is fine and we are
sailing Bi de Vind.
Position 14°E 41°S. 21 Miles.

Day 62 Thursday December 21st

Down in the hold painting before breakfast. Chatted with the passenger after
breakfast. The passenger came forward and chatted with me about villages in
England. Down in the hold painting and chipping in the afternoon. We have now
definitely got our course back again South East by East 3/4 East and it is fine and
clear.
Position 14°E 42°S.

Day 63 Friday December 22nd

Down in the main hold chipping and had two hours at the wheel. One of the
pigs was killed this afternoon by Alfred shooting it, a very quick death. We have
now got a good fair wind and fine weather and we are sailing South East by East
3/4 East.
Position 16°E 42°S 119 miles.

Homemade Christmas tree

Day 64 Saturday December 23rd

Carried coal to the galley before breakfast.
Slept on my bunk in the morning and washed
the Captains Chart House in the afternoon.
Took in the mizzen topsail. Made Christmas
things for the Christmas tree after coffee. Had
plenty of brace pulling after coffee. Plenty of
stormy petrels about. The 2nd Mate told me,
when I was at the wheel, that at 12.30 am he

saw an iceberg. It is fine and clear and the wind got very strong at night so we took in all mizzen sails.
Position 20.39°E 42.49°S. 182 miles.

Day 65 Sunday December 24th

Had fried pork for breakfast, not bad but very tough. Took in the mizzen boom sail and I helped Heim to tie gaskets around it. The wheel was very hard to hold. Chatted with Bob and the passenger after lunch. We had a very good Christmas meal in the evening, pork, sardines, pineapple, rum and beer. Then both watches came into the port fo'c'sle after tea and chatted and played tunes. The sailmaker got drunk. It has been a dull day and the wind has been strong.
Position 26°E 43°S. 261 miles

Day 66 Monday December 25th
Christmas Day

Carried water in the morning. Took the flying jib sail in before breakfast. I am now once again on friendly terms with everybody. Slept on my bunk in the morning until 12am then chatted with the passenger and Bob. Wrote letters again in the afternoon. Chatted with the 2nd Mate at the wheel regarding dish washer. Had cake and biscuits at afternoon coffee. Took a snap of the passenger on the fo'c'sle head. Went into the starboard fo'c'sle after tea. The Germans sang songs and we had the Christmas tree lighted. Course East 1/2 South and dull with plenty of wind and stormy seas, some coming overboard.
Position 32.1°E 43°S. 263 miles.

Day 67 Tuesday December 26th

Wrote letters again to Jack (brother) and Doods (family nick-name for his sister Audrey) Then read a book and slept on my bunk. Played deck tennis in the afternoon and evening. The 1st Mate caught two albatrosses in the evening. Ate my first orange in the morning. Chatted with Bob and the passenger. Not much wind and the ship is rolling very much. We still have one cat, the little black and white one and it is still very well and strong. Course East 1/2 South it is dull and rather cold.
Position 37°E 43°S. 243 miles.

Doods, Honey and Jack

_____

Day 68 Wednesday December 27th

Down in the main hold shifting wood before breakfast and went up the main mast overhauling. Wind shifted to North West at 7.45am. Down in the hold chipping on the in-between deck in the afternoon. Course East 1/2 South. Fog descended at 7pm and we had the fog horn at night. Rain fell at 11pm and we collected rain water. It has been a fine to dull day.
Position 41°E 43°S. 157 miles.

Day 69 Thursday December 28th

Down in the hold chipping again all morning. Came up no fewer than 8 times to pull on the braces. Rained all morning. A black albatross visited us in the evening. I saw a school of porpoises from the wheel and a beautiful red sunset. It has been dull and rainy and we are sailing Bi de Vind.
Position 45°E 43°S. 223 miles.

Day 70 Friday December 29th

Cleaned the pig place out before breakfast then went down into the hold scraping. The passenger took a snap of the starboard watch with the Christmas tree. Down in the hold again in the afternoon chipping etc. Plenty of albatrosses to be seen. Fog descended again at 6.30pm. Thought of home and Honey. We now have a course again East 1/2 South and it has been fine to fog and rain.
Position 48°E 42°S. 90 miles.

Day 71 Saturday December 30th

Cleaned our fo'c'sle and chips and sailmakers in the morning. We had a look-out all day and fog horn all morning. The mist cleared at 3pm the wind becoming slightly stronger. Slept on my bunk a little in the afternoon. Collected rain water as the day has been a wet one. Course East 1/4 South.
Position 51°E 42°S. 129 miles

Day 72 Sunday December 31st

Rained all day. Finished collecting rain water the tanks are now all full. Slept on my bunk in the morning and read my book in the afternoon. The 2nd Mate played the mouth organ after tea and then I did. The starboard watch played music in the evening and sang. No albatrosses to be seen. We had a look-out all day as it was misty. Course East South East 3/4 East.
Position 56°E 42°S. 216 miles.

Day 73 Monday January 1st 1934 New Year's Day

Washed clothes in the morning and read my book. Slept on my bunk until coffee time in the afternoon. The wind began to increase very much at 4pm and at 5pm boat healing well over on starboard side. Port watch at 5.15pm took in all mizzen sails and at 5.30pm the rope for the main upper to'gallant snapped and

at 5.45pm the port watch took in the fore upper to'gallant. It has been rain to fair today and the course is East South East 3/4 East.
Position 60°E 42°S. 173 miles.

Day 74 Tuesday January 2nd
Tried to sleep on my bunk in the morning but could not. Down in the hold painting the between deck. Plenty of wind now and big waves. The black albatross visited us again in the late evening. Could not sleep again during the free watch so went into the starboard fo'c'sle. Course South East 3/4 East it is wet and there is a strong wind which increased to gale force late at night. Wonderful sea.
Position 65°E 42°S. 252 miles.

Wonderful sea

Day 75 Wednesday January 3rd
Down in the hold painting again. Our watch took in three staysails on the fo'c'sle head. Wind increased again at 12.30pm to gale force. Now doing 14 knots. The main upper to'gallant got a tear in it but the sailmaker stitched it up. The Captain is wonderful, never took a single sail in although at 4.30pm we were doing 16 knots. From 12 noon to 6.30pm we did 100 miles. The sea became very rough at 5pm so that until midnight there were two men at the wheel. It has been fine but cold and the course is South East 3/4 East.
Position 71°E 43°S.

Day 76 Thursday January 4th

Went up and overhauled gardings on the main and fore upper to'gallants very hard with masts leaning over at an angle of 60 degrees.

Then down in the hold before breakfast, painting. Slept on my bunk in the morning. Down in the hold again chipping etc. Had the last wheel again 6pm to 7pm second time in a week. There has been rain at intervals, otherwise it has been fine and clear. Course South East 1/2 East.
Position 77°E 43°S.

Day 77 Friday January 5th

Had a good nights sleep. Down in the hold scraping in the morning. The 2nd Mate came and chatted with me and Frachnect about the "Winterhude". Had a good wash in the afternoon. Had plenty of brace pulling in our watch at night. Course South East by East 1/2 East and it is fine.
Position 81°E 42.12°S.

Day 78 Saturday January 6th

Again we had plenty of brace pulling on our watch on deck. The Captain gave us a whole day holiday for the 13th day after Christmas. Cleaned the pig place out. The wind increased to gale force at 7.30am therefore I joined Heim at the wheel. Slept on my bunk in the morning. Heim and I had two hours at the wheel in the afternoon, there were two men at the wheel all afternoon. On our first wheel we very nearly had the "Winterhude" dismasted. The wind suddenly changed direction all the sails flew back the ship began to roll and pitch in an uncontrollable manner. She now became broached too, the most dangerous thing that can happen to a sailing ship. I was helpless, so too Heim. The Captain came up very worried and helped us, eventually after some 15 minutes hard fighting we got her back into the wind. At 7pm the wind was not so strong and

the wheel much easier therefore only one man at the wheel. Course East South East 1/2 East very wet and misty.
Position 87°E 44°S.

Day 79 Sunday January 7th
Sat on my bunk and read my book till coffee in the afternoon. Chatted with Bob about Australia. Fog descended again at 5.30pm. At 12pm we had only 1972 miles left. Course East 1/2 South. A dull and drizzly day but a fair wind.
Position 93°E 44.25°S.

Day 80 Monday January 8th
Slept on my bunk all morning. Stowahse fell and upset all the Salmon on deck which he was bringing for breakfast. Down in the hold in the afternoon putting burlap down. I had a very good nights sleep. Course East 1/2 North. Showers.
Position 97°E 44°S.

Day 81 Tuesday January 9th
Down in the hold finishing putting down the burlap in the fore hold. Washed a sheet and had my hair cut by Mr Brown. Slept on my bunk after coffee until tea time. Somebody threw our poor little cat overboard a week ago today. A fine to dull day and course is North East by East 1/2 East.
Position 103°E 44°S.

Day 82 Wednesday January 10th
Started washing the white paint before breakfast and afterwards I sewed my shirt and raincoat. We washed white paint again on deck in the afternoon a job I hate. Thought of Honey. Fair weather and course North East 1/2 East.
Position 108°E 44°S.

Day 83 Thursday January 11th
Washed paint again on deck. Fell out with my watch again. They are a rotten crowd. Slept on my bunk in the afternoon and chatted later with Bob and Schmidt. Chatted with the 2nd Mate at the wheel at 7pm regarding Australia. He gave me an oilskin. An albatross flew against the main yard hurting itself and falling on deck. Sailing Bi de Vind.
Position 112.40°E 43°S.

Day 84 Friday January 12th
Started washing white paint again before breakfast. My watch are still unfriendly with me. Chatted with the passenger about them. Again we wash paint in the afternoon. My watch are now friendly again. I chatted with them about football etc. Still sailing Bi de Vind.
Position 116°E 43°S.

Day 85 Saturday January 13th
Finished cleaning the white paint on deck. Then later down in the sail locker aft. Now definitely becalmed. At 11am we get our course again North East 3/4 North. In the afternoon both watches cleaned the paintwork in their fo'c'sles. I am now friends with everybody.
Position 116°E 42°S.

Day 86 Sunday January 14th
Sewed the oilskins the 2nd Mate gave to me in the morning. Made some coffee for Bob and myself. Then in the afternoon I sewed buttons on my coat and washed a towel. All the boys did plenty of washing of clothes. Joked with Bob and Schmidt after dinner. It is fine and warm course North East 1/2 North.
Position 117°E 42°S.

Sailmaker's Sunday washing

Day 87 Monday January 15th
Down in the aft hold in the morning putting down burlap. Sang songs with the sailmaker and Mr Brown and Stowahse in the afternoon, then thought of Honey. Plenty of brace pulling at night. Course North East 3/4 North.
Position 121°E 41°S.

Day 88 Tuesday January 16th

Patched my oilskins and trousers. Had some coffee with Bob, Pongo and the passenger at 11am. Down in the hold in the afternoon putting wood up against the stanchions. In our watch from 7pm to 12midnight I worked all five hours as we are absolutely becalmed so there was plenty of brace pulling. Course North East 1/2 East.
Position 122°E 41°S.

Day 89 Wednesday January 17th

Down in the fore hold scraping the top of the hold, also scraped the tank. Made some toast in the afternoon. We have now definitely got back our Westerly wind. Showed the sailmaker and carpenter card tricks. Course North East by North.
Position 124°E 41°S.

Day 90 Thursday January 18th

Down in the hold before breakfast getting the boat up and scraping the tanks on deck all afternoon, painting the white on the step and cleaning the landing stage. Course North East by North then sailing Bi de Vind.
Position 128°E 39°S.

Day 91 Friday January 19th

On deck painting the white parts in the morning and cleaned the white paint in my bunk in the afternoon. We now killed the second pig. Slept on my bunk in the afternoon. Course North East by North.
Position 131°E 37°S.

Day 92 Saturday January 20th

Worked nearly all night taking in sail. At 4am the fore upper to'gallant ripped open and Brincks and I took it in. Belgier and Karlsson take in the main upper to'gallant. Then all the watch take in the main and fore lower to'gallants and a few staysails. Then I carry coal to the galley before breakfast. The port watch in the morning work on the fo'c'sle head getting the anchor ready. At 10am Keller sights land. Therefore all hands now take in the mainsail and turn the boat, our course now is Bi de Vind around about South West. In the afternoon our watch wash down the deck, then I sleep on my bunk. The wind is now definitely shifting West. Sailing Bi de Vind.
Position 135°E 34°S.

Day 93 Sunday January 21st

Had a very good nights sleep. The wind is now shifting North East. Had pork cutlets for breakfast and lunch, then slept on my bunk in the afternoon. Chatted with Keller, Stowahse and Heim. Turned the boat again at 7pm. Sailing Bi de Vind.
Position 135°E 35°S.

(left) Unbending
_____

*(right) Carrying up
new sail*
_____

(left) Hauling sail aloft
_____

(right) Bending new sail
_____

(all) Changing sail
_____

Day 94 Monday January 22nd

Had a good nights sleep. Had first wheel and witnessed a beautiful red sunrise, a lovely sunset that night too. After morning coffee our watch took down the torn fore upper to'gallant, then Belgier did the same with the main lower to'gallant and I did the fore lower to'gallant. At 7am we turned the boat again and this time we get a course. I started backschaft. Slept on my bunk in the morning. Down in the fore hold in the afternoon cleaning. After afternoon coffee our watch again unbend the torn fore upper to'gallant. I helped Karlsson. Beautiful hot day.
Course North East 1/2 North.

Day 95 Tuesday January 23rd

Down in the hold in the morning. Had plenty of brace pulling as we have very little wind but good course. Putting burlap down again. The 2nd Mate sent me up to the main upper to'gallant to overhaul gardings. Sewed my trousers up in the afternoon.
Course North East 1/2 North. then Bi de Vind.

Day 96 Wednesday January 24th

I had the wheel from 5am to 6am and during that time Hiem, at look-out, sighted Neptune Island. We were alongside at 8am and now we only have 28 miles to Port Lincoln. Cleaned the brass on the poop before breakfast, then sat on the fo'c'sle head and Stowahse played his organ. Arrived Port Lincoln 5pm. I am made night watchman so I sit in the galley all night and read and make coffee and toast. The Mozart is here also having taken the same time, 94 days.

Day 97 Thursday January 25th

Slept on my bunk in the morning. An Aussie friend of Bob came on board in the afternoon, he gave us beer and chatted with me. At 4pm we got ready to sail for Port Germein to load. Left Port Lincoln 5pm and I had 2nd wheel and look-out. A storm arose with terrific lightning. Took in both upper to'gallants.
It is fine and hot.

Day 98 Friday January 26th

Arrived Port Germein at 12am. Had plenty of brace pulling etc. all morning. In the afternoon until coffee we got the anchorage ropes out. After coffee we made fast the sails to the yards. At 4.30pm Thompsen fell from the foresail hitting the side of the ship and falling into the water. He was nearly drowned. Stowahse went in and held him up until a boat came. He had broken his arm and was taken to Port Pirie hospital.
It is very fine and hot.

Day 99 Saturday January 27th

Cleaned all the fo'c'sles out in the morning. Went ashore at 4pm to the pub with Bob and Mr Brown, got very drunk. Had some tea with two Belgians and Jacques

on the "L'avenier", then went back to the village and danced in the dance hall. Spoke to the Australians and came back to the ship at 12.30.
Very fine and hot.

Day 100 Sunday January 28th
Stayed on board all day. Washed my clothes and peeled spuds for Cookie. The Captain and Mates of the "L'avenier" came on board for dinner. In the evening I rowed ashore four times, once to take the 1st Mate and another to bring back Brincks the night watchman. Had plenty of work. Donkeyman gave me some tomatoes.
Very fine and hot.

Day 101 Monday January 29th
Took down all the sails and put them in the sail locker. Then after coffee got ready to sail to the quay but the wind got squally so we were unable to do so until 7pm. Got eventually tied up at 10pm.
Very fine and hot.

Day 102 Tuesday January 30th
Finished taking in sail then helped the gang men from ashore to get the shutes ready for loading. "Mozart" arrived at 4pm. She came ashore on a sandbank, the Captain was drunk, she eventually got off at 9pm and some of our crew and from the "L'avenier" went and helped. Walked ashore in the evening.
Very fine and hot.

"Mozart" aground on sandbank

Day 103 Wednesday January 31st
Shifted the ship further along before breakfast then started chipping over the side. After lunch I helped the sailmaker to shift sails in the sail locker, then chipped again after coffee. Started loading at 3pm. Went ashore in the evening with Brincks, Heim, Bob, Schmidt and Karlsson we went to the cafe.
Very fine and very hot.

Loading

Day 104 Thursday February 1st
I was with Brincks all day painting the starboard side of the boat. Went ashore in the evening with an Englishman off the "L'avenier" and we met some members of "Mozart" crew ashore including an Englishman from Gravesend. There was a dance on the "L'avenier". At night there was a fight on our boat between the 1st Mate and Frachnect. The 1st Mate threatened to lock him up.
Very fine and cooler.

Day 105 Friday February 2nd
Painted the port side of the boat again. In the afternoon my cap blew off so I dived in and rescued it. Went ashore in the evening with an Australian.
Very fine, cooler.

Day 106 Saturday February 3rd
Painted over the port side of the boat again in the morning. Washed the deck in the afternoon. I am night watchman again. Went ashore in the afternoon again and I got very drunk.
Very fine and warm.

Day 107 Sunday February 4th
Tried to sleep in the day but could not as there were to many visitors about etc. Stayed on board all day.
Very fine and warm.

Day 108 Monday February 5th
Slept a little in the morning. Went ashore after coffee in the afternoon. Met an Englishman who wished to join the boat and put him up in the Donkeyroom.
Very fine and very hot.

Day 109 Tuesday February 6th
Still night watchman. Called in at my little cafe near the pier. Cannot sleep at all during the day time.
Very fine and very hot.

Day 110 Wednesday February 7th
Went ashore again after coffee and again called at the cafe. Thompsen came back from hospital.
Very fine and very hot.

Day 111 Thursday February 8th
Went ashore again to my cafe with Thompsen. Met a Yorkshireman from Middlesborough.
Too hot to move about 110 Degrees in the shade.

Day 112 Friday February 9th
Went into the Port again in the afternoon. Called at my little cafe and had some tea. "City of Lyons" passed us outward bound from Port Pirie.
Fair and cooler.

Day 113 Saturday February 10th
Finished night watchman. Washed the deck down. Went ashore at 5pm. Called at the pub, got very drunk and was sick. Had a fight with an Australian.
Dull and wet.

Day 114 Sunday February 11th
Stayed on the boat all day until after tea. Washed my towels, then went ashore in the evening. Called at my cafe and the lady invited me in to tea. Then I went into the dance hall.
Fine to wet.

Day 115 Monday February 12th
Painted the yards up on the main mast, then painted over the side of the boat. Went ashore in the evening and into the dance hall.
Fine and hot.

Day 116 Tuesday February 13th
Painted the port side of the boat with Schmidt. Had terrible pains all day in my stomach. Went ashore in the evening. Wrote letters later.
Very fine and hot.

Day 117 Wednesday February 14th
Painted again over the side of the boat with Schmidt. Went ashore in the evening, then again wrote letters.
Fair and cooler.

Day 118 Thursday February 15th
Painted over the side of the boat again with Schmidt. Washed the deck down after coffee 3.30pm. Had a dance on deck in the evening. The 2nd Mate had a fight with the Captain. Both Mates were drunk.
Fair to wet.

Day 119 Friday February 16th
Carried coal to the Donkey Room before breakfast, then painted with Schmidt. Went ashore with Schmidt in the evening. Wrote letters.
Wet to fair.

Day 120 Saturday February 17th
Painted the name aft with Schmidt then washed the deck down. Went by carrier to Port Pirie and went to the pictures. Slept in a police cell. Met Brincks, Belgier, Jacques and some of the "Mozart" boys.
Fair.

Day 121 Sunday February 18th
Left Port Pirie at 9am for the ship. Met Bob and had breakfast with him. Walked eight of the sixteen miles and then got a lift to Port Germein. Slept on my bunk in the afternoon. Went ashore in the evening and listened to the radio in my favourite cafe.
Very fine and very hot.

Day 122 Monday February 19th
I started backschaft again. Cleaned all the lamps etc. Then in the afternoon I helped Keller to fix one of the staysails. Went ashore in the evening and again listened to the wireless.
Very fine and very hot.

Day 123 Tuesday February 20th
Worked aloft most of the day getting the sails ready. Went ashore in the evening as the Port Germein people gave us a dance in the Palais and a fine supper. The Captain gave a speech. All very enjoyable.

Day 124 Wednesday February 21st
Worked up on the rigging again. Went ashore in the evening. Listened to the wireless in my cafe and then met some very nice Australians.

Day 125 Thursday February 22nd
Bent the foresail and then got the deck ready for sailing. Went ashore in the evening and met Harry. Got dead drunk.

Before the Mast in the Grain Race 1933-34.
The return voyage.

Our stay here in Port Germein lasted five weeks and throughout that period we were hospitably entertained and we were reluctant to leave for the voyage home to Falmouth which commenced on the night of February 23rd 1934.

The Crew - self 1st left back row

Thursday February 22nd 1934
We leave Port Germein on a glorious late Australian Summer night just after 8.30pm, being towed out from the wharfe side by a tug which had to come from Port Pirie, seventeen miles away.

As we leave, the boys from the four masted Finnish Barquentine the "Mozart" give us three hearty cheers and wish us "Good Luck".

At 10.30pm the tug leaves us and we now, definitely, set out on our long 12,000 miles to Falmouth, England. We have the same crew as the voyage out and so we divide up into our same watches.

Starboard watch - self 1st left front row

Day 1 Friday February 23rd

At daybreak we can still plainly see the hills around Port Germein and Port Pirie. During today we anchor no fewer than three times on account of both head winds and no wind at all and it looks as though it will take us all our time to get clear of the Spencer Gulf.

Towards evening a rumour goes round that we have a stowaway on board and about an hour later this is confirmed, for as both watches were up for'd in the fo'c'sles having their tea, a head appears out of the coal hole (opposite the fo'c'sles). He asks us to give him a drink of water and then tells us he is an Australian from Melbourne, that he jumped aboard at 8pm when all was quiet the night we sailed. He begs us not to let on to the Mates or Captain and we promise not to but we warn him that he had better stay down in the fore hold (he had got through here from the adjoining coal hole) until we have left land, which would take about a week at the rate we are going now. We also tell him we will bring him food down every night at tea time (we could not see a human being starve and at the same time none of us liked to sneak about him being here) so he returns to his secret hiding place among the wheat bags.

At midnight the wind again drops to a dead calm and we anchor for the night with all sails set in readiness for a puff of wind to come. We can see some lights which the Captain says is Port Broughton, a small port 30 miles further down the Gulf from Port Germein.

Capstan on the fo'c'sle head

Day 2 Saturday February 24th

As I am dishwasher (in Finnish "Backschaft") this week I must (as is the custom on Saturdays) clean my fo'c'sle (starboard) and also the sailmakers cabin and the carpenters cabin, as well as wash dishes and get from the Steward the weeks ration of sugar and margarine, the allowance being 1lb of each to every man. We never see milk, not even Condensed, except the latter as a special treat while in port.

A slight wind blows up again this morning at 6am but it dies away at 3pm this afternoon and we again anchor. This was excellent and we hoped it would remain calm until Monday morning so that we could have a lazy week-end but just as we had all got comfortably tucked up in our bunks about 11pm tonight, Brinks (Dane) the night watchman comes running up into the fo'c'sles yelling to us to "use up" as there was a favourable wind blowing from aft.

All our hopes for a fine Sunday had now vanished and we come out on deck swearing and cursing everybody and everything under the sun.

Australian Wheat Ketch

We spent a very enjoyable Sunday (I don't think) "tacking" up and down the narrow Gulf and to make matters worse we anchor again at 5pm just off Wallaroo on account of strong head wind. What is the use of it now Sunday is almost over?

The Mates have now found out there is a stowaway on board (we suspect the cook of having informed them) and they proceed down into the fore hold along with three of the boys to search. We thought at any minute they would find him, however,after an hours thorough searching they returned to the deck satisfied it must only be a rumour.

Again tonight the stowaway comes up on deck, looking thoroughly tired and worn out and we give him some food, later asking him where-in-the-devil he was hiding this afternoon when the Mates searched the hold? He tells us he cut a wheat bag in two, emptied the wheat out of it and then got into the bag himself and just kept as still as he could.

The heat down there he says is terrific and he has only about a foot of space between the wheat bags and the deck. After half an hours breather on deck, he again returns to the darkness and terrific heat of the hold.

Day 4 Monday February 26th

A slight wind blows up from aft early this morning at 4am so we again set sail. During the afternoon watch on deck 1pm-7pm, we erect a life line along the starboard side of the deck (the port side having been put up by the port watch in the morning) ready for the gales we shall soon experience.

I take the stowaway his tea down in the hold at 7pm, (or 6 bells). He (who's Christian name is George) tells me he cannot stick any longer than one day more but I tell him just to keep smiling we shall soon leave the land now.

We have got two cats and two dogs onboard this trip, both Australians by birth.

Day 5 Tuesday February 27th

During my working watch from 8am-1pm, (8 bells to 2 bells) I go aloft to grease some of the "buntlines" up the fore rigging. Buntlines is the term applied to the wires and some times ropes employed for confining the "bunt" of the sail to the yard when stowing. In the early afternoon we pass Kangaroo Island at the entrance to the Spencer Gulf .This is probably our last landfall until The Lizard is picked up. We can still discern the flashes from the lighthouse at 7.30pm.

At coffee time (kaffe in Finnish) lasting from 3.30pm (7 bells) to 4pm (8 bells) George the stowaway comes up after having been down in the hold for 5 days. How he stuck it God only knows.

He asks us what he should do and we suggest he should go aft to the Captain who is now up on the poop. He goes up amongst roars of laughter from the crew, as he certainly looked a sight, with his long beard and extremely grubby and worn out appearance.

Returning after half an hour he informs us the Captain was extremely annoyed as he would have to take him to England now but said he would, however, sign him on as an ordinary seaman without, of course, any pay and that he must join the port watch, owing to Bill Thompsen (Dane) being unfit to work just now having fallen from aloft in port thus breaking one of his arms, so they were a man short.

Making fast the starboard anchor, self standing

Day 6 Wednesday February 28th

At 8am this morning we get back our favourable wind which sends us along
at about 9 knots. My Mate (the 2nd Mate), a wonderful friend to me and about
the finest seaman onboard, orders me aloft to overhaul the buntlines up both
the fore and main masts and during our working watch, 1pm to 7pm, Scrayen
(nicknamed Belgier) and myself clean out all the paint brushes. Towards evening
the wind blows up stronger and the sea, once again, becomes rough. It appears
as though we have definitely said "Good Bye" to warm and sunny climates for at
least nine or ten weeks.

At 6.15pm tonight our first wave lops aboard midships and therafter we get many
more. George the stowaway complains of feeling seasick but carries on working.
I see my first albatross so far this voyage, late this evening.
Position 37 South - 136 East.

Day 7 Thursday March 1st

During last night the wind decreased and this morning very little water lops
aboard. During our working watch 8am to 1pm we are down in the 'Lazarette'
aft (where the food stores are kept) once again back at that monotonous job of
scraping rust away, of which there always appears to be plenty.

I might mention at this point that both separate watches (port and starboard) scrape and paint their side of the ship only, likewise with any other job onboard, except of course hauling on ropes when bracing or making fast sails etc.

In the evening, George the stowaway gives us a few tunes on Stowahse's (German) accordion. George seems a decent fellow and gets along well with all the crew. He has no clothes with him except for those he is wearing, so the Captain (and one of the best of Captains too) gives him shirts, underclothing, oilskins and seaboots. *Position 39.44° South - 139° East.*

Day 8 Friday March 2nd

From 4am till 8am this morning we are again scraping rust down in the Lazarette. I might mention here that in this watch from 4am to 8am we don't actually start the real days work until 6am (or 4 bells). Early coffee is drunk from 5.30am until 6am and from 4am until 5.30am if you have taken a wheel, policeman, lookout, or bracing etc. you can have a sleep on your bunk (if the Mate is not about). Usually the Mate finds something for the lucky ones to do and it was always a great joke on the port watch because nearly every morning without fail the Mate would blow his whistle, roughly about 4.20am, just as we (who perhaps had no wheel etc.) had comfortably tucked ourselves in the bunks. A large number of albatross follow the ship today, continually flying round and round, without ever actually appearing to flap their wings.

Early this morning we have to "steer by the wind" (Bi de Vind). This happens when there is a "head wind" and we are unable to sail with the given course and in this case, the helmsman must keep his eye on the main upper to'gallant sail (we have no royals) allowing the lowest corner of the sail (weather side) to flap gently. On no account must the sail be full or

else the Captain will have something to say. *Position 39.53° South - 139.3° East.*

Sails set for By the Wind and steering course

Day 9 Saturday March 3rd
From 8am to 1pm we are again scraping that beastly rust, a job all of us loathe. At 7 bells as is the custom on Finnish sailing ships on a Saturday, we are now free until 6am Monday morning, barring of course, wheels, policeman, look out, bracing and a score of other things. More often than not at the week ends we experience dirty weather and gales, necessitating a considerable amount of work both on deck and up aloft, furling sails etc.

The term "Policeman" which I have mentioned once or twice is applied to the man who must be on deck for an hour during the night watches and he must call his watch should the Mate blow two whistles, or all the hands should he blow three. For one whistle he must go to the Mate himself. Also he must keep an eye on everything and report to the Mate should anything go wrong. The policeman then, follows the hour at the wheel and then he must go up to "look out".

I am the only Englishman aboard our ship which consists of 23 hands all told, including no fewer than 8 different nationalities we have 1 American, 1 Australian (stowaway), 2 Belgians, 2 Swedes. 2 Danes. 6 Germans, 7 Finns. and Mr Brown the Scots. passenger from Glasgow.
Position 41° South 140° East.

Self at the wheel

Day 10 Sunday March 4th

Early this morning I met with an accident. I was taking my trick at the wheel from 5am to 6am and at the time a fairly strong wind was blowing up from the South West which made the wheel sluggish and heavy. Without warning the wind shifted to a head wind, all the sails were thrown back against the masts and the wheel became almost unmanageable for one man, kicking and jumping constantly. I fought like the devil with it, jamming one of my legs hard against the wheel, but I was powerless and in the end it went spinning away out of my grasp, at the same time throwing me completely over it, landing me almost against the charthouse. I was stunned for a few seconds and found I could not move one of my legs which was in considerable pain.

The Mate, who had heard the infernal banging of the sails against the masts, came rushing up on to the poop saw what had happened and immediately blew "two whistles" for the rest of the watch and he himself grabs the spinning wheel.

Heim (German) carries me up for'ard to my bunk and Brincks (Dane) relieves the Mate at the wheel while the rest of the watch work with great haste to bring the yards up into the wind.

Had it not been for the Mate anything might have happened, at any rate some of the sails would shortly have been torn to shreds, as it was we lost none.

The Captain comes up for'ard to see me but is unable to ascertain what is the matter with my leg, which is in great pain and seems to lock and slip just below my kneecap. I am unable to stand up. We have no doctor onboard and except for a bandage and a bottle of Sloans Linement, given to me by the Captain, I have to look after it as well as I can. God help any man who gets an appendicitis as we have neither wireless nor doctor.

I turn out (although against the Captains wishes) to again take my wheel at 5pm this afternoon, how I managed to stand there was sheer will power as I could hardly stand on my legs. I did not wish to lie up if possible as our watch were shorthanded enough already and when a man "lies up" he causes a considerable amount of extra work for the other members of his watch.

There is a big sea running all day and we therefore get a large amount of water on deck. The temperature is certainly getting colder.
Position 44° South 142° East.

Big sea running

Day 11 Monday March 5th

I again turn out with my watch this morning but the Captain orders me back to my bunk and says I must stay there for a few days and then see how it feels.

I lie on my bunk all day and thought it a convenient opportunity to sow and patch up my oilskins, which the 2nd Mate had exchanged for my mouth organ, up to then I had been without oilskins.

My leg is still very painful and when I walk appears to lock near the knee cap. Mr Brown thinks it may possibly be cartilage trouble.

At 4pm this afternoon the wind becomes stronger and we continuously have hail squalls beating down upon us. During the evening it increases considerably so that at 8pm the wind is blowing with gale force and my watch between then and 12 midnight are kept busy furling and making fast the fore and main upper to'gallants, previously having made fast the two mizzen sails, the spanker and lower mizzens (the upper mizzen we shall not use until we reach the Trade Winds). At 12 midnight instead of going below for their free watch until 4am, my watch had to help the port watch to furl the large main sail (the wind now blowing from dead aft).

This was the very devil of a job and extremely heavy work. I was thankful to be in my far from cosy bunk on such a night, so also was Bill (the young Danish boy) who is still laid up with his broken arm, after having fallen from aloft while in port. It certainly is company to have another fellow laid up with you. *Position 45.42° South 145° East.*

Rough weather

Day 12 Tuesday March 6th
I am still confined to my bunk. Brincks (Dane) another member of my watch is laid up now. At 4am my watch make fast the fore lower to'gallant. The wind is now blowing with almost hurricane force, accompanied by heavy hail squalls and she rolls to and fro like someone gone mad. Up here in the fo'c'sle there was a scene of utter confusion, mugs and dishes, sea chests, clothes and in fact anything not fast, were sliding backward and forward. Tremendous waves sweep the length of the ship carrying along with them anything in reach. Bob (Yankee) tells me the deck is standing in water waist deep and that all fresh water in the tanks, situated under the break of the poop aft, has all gone.

At 8am after a hard nights work our watch tired and wet through and hungry are relieved by the other watch. The latter immediately take in and make fast the main lower to'gallant. Stowahse (German) while clearing up ends (ropes) on deck in the afternoon is washed off his feet by a large wave and knocked

Two men caught midships

unconscious against one of the hatches, the rest of the watch at great personal risk to themselves carry him along a dangerous deck to the safety of the fo'c'sle for'ard. Our watch is now reduced to four men.

Later on we almost lose a young German overboard. The boy whose name is Boercher was at the time on his way up to the wheel and had just reached mid-ships, when without warning he was lifted clean off his feet and sent sprawling into the lee scuppers but with luck he managed to grab a belaying pin, hung grimly to it while she dipped her lee rail under water and then while she righted herself rushed along the deck to the safety of the poop, non the worse except for being wet through.

Owing to the extremely heavy state of the wheel, the Captain orders two men to take charge of it and these have to be lashed there to prevent them being washed overboard.
Position 47° South 150° East.

Day 13 Wednesday March 7th
Early in the morning my Mate (second) meets with an accident. He was coming up for'ard at the time and had just reached the deck when he was sent flying into the scuppers and was knocked unconscious. But this Finn, barely 24 years old, was back at his job again within an hour. A man with more pluck, grit and determination I feel sure I shall never meet. There is something about every Finn I meet that makes me admire them. Their seamanship is A1, they always seem to take the bad things with the good without grumbling and they never shirk when it needs a man for some dangerous work. Above all they are great shipmates, always willing to help you when in difficulties.

As the day wore on the wind decreased so that at coffee time 3.30pm, the port watch set the main and fore lower to'gallants and the mainsail but it is still necessary to have two men at the wheel.

Bill, the young Dane who is laid up with me, and I while away the time playing cards, draughts and reading books. Although he is in the port watch while I am in the starboard, I live and sleep in the same fo'c'sle owing to the fact that I was the last to join in Glasgow and consequently my fo'c'sle (which had an extra man) was full up. This was "hell" for me at times and caused me a considerable loss of sleep because when I am "free watch" and trying to sleep, the port watch are the "watch on deck" therefore the boys are constantly talking, whistling and singing, while the lamp is burning all the time and as it is not my fo'c'sle by rights I cannot tell them to shut up. No I must just make the best of things.
Position 48° South 155° East.

Day 14 Thursday March 8th

The wind is still decreasing, so that between 4am and 8am my watch set the fore and main upper to'gallants the five staysails we had taken in and the mizzen spanker. I am still laid up and can just manage to crawl about in the fo'c'sle.

Towards midday the winds again begin to blow up fresh and at 4pm it has again reached gale force. The old ship now sails along at a fine turn of speed, averaging 11 knots, and not a stitch of canvas has been taken in yet.

Our Captain, who is now always up on deck and has been for the past few days (occasionally popping into the charthouse for an hours sleep) refuses to take in one sail until it is really necessary, thus the pressure of the wind on our sails sends the ship heeling well over to starboard, the lee rail at times being almost submerged. To proceed along the deck now is almost impossible and can only be achieved by clinging on to the life line and so dragging oneself along, for at the present the deck is one mass of green water and even in the intervals when there is not so much water on board, it is extremely dangerous owing to the very slippery state of the heeling deck. Bob tells me that at times some of the waves almost reached the height of our fore and main yards.

The heeling deck

At 4.30pm the sailmaker reports a 'cyclone' heading straight for the ship and consequently all hands are called to make fast all sails except the two lower topsails (main and fore). Even George (stowaway) must now go aloft, although he refused and had always refused previously, but there is no leniency shown on a sailing ship and certainly not to a stowaway. He only goes out onto the two lowest yards, the main and fore, flatly refusing to go any higher. In any case, he might just as well be on deck as he was absolutely useless up there and hindered other people, getting in their way.

All hands completely tired, hungry and wet through to the skin work like Trojans almost throughout the whole night. It is absolutely impossible to explain what it is like, to anybody who has never been afloat on a sailing ship deep laiden with cargo, the lee rail at times submerged, a deck standing waist deep in water, hail squalls incessantly beating down into their face almost blinding them, every man (all mere boys) wet through (some without oilskins), hungry and worn out and a 2000 ton sailing ship to be manned by a crew of 26 hands all told. There is all the difference in the world between life on a steamer and a sailing ship.

On board a steamer during a gale people have not to turn out on deck unless absolutely necessary but on a sailing ship, we are always out, either fighting the sails aloft or hauling on the ropes on deck. Then when the time comes for the free watch to go below and get perhaps an hours sleep before another 3 whistles sounds, there is no warm, dry bunk to get into, no warm cup of tea or coffee to be drunk only perhaps a stale piece of bread can be found and if you are lucky you may have some margerine still left. Let those grousers on land make a voyage on a sailing ship around Cape Horn and they will return with perhaps a different outlook on life.

It requires the whole of a man's grit and determination to fight against such elements. It was bad enough laid up in the none to warm fo'c'sle the floor standing in water, which comes pouring in through the door (although shut) and the roof ventilator (which is broken). We stick all manner of old rags up the latter and jam the door up tight but still it comes pouring in. It is impossible to sleep as the ship rolls and pitches at all angles and to attempt to walk on the water covered floor of the fo'c'sle meant probably breaking a bone or two as it was so greasey and slippery with grease dirt etc. it was impossible to stand up. All I could do was to sit patiently on my bunk and remain there.

This was certainly the toughest night I have ever experienced in all my life. Thank God that at any rate I was laid up.
Position 49° South 161° East.

Day 15 Friday March 9th

Still laid up and unable to hardly walk a yard. By 10am the wind had decreased sufficiently so that our watch could set some of the furled sails, the port watch carry on with the work at 1pm so that by 3.15pm we were once again sailing along with all sails set.

Both watches are tired out after having worked throughout the night and there is a considerable amount of grousing among certain members.
Position 49.18° South 163° East.

Day 16 Saturday March 10th

Each watch have a considerable amount of bracing owing to the wind incessantly changing from one quarter to another (bracing is the term applied when pulling or 'hauling' on the ropes to bring the yards and sails up into the wind) however, we sail along at a steady 6 knots.

Owing to the amount of water on the deck the usual custom of washing down the deck on a Saturday afternoon is not necessary.

My Mate comes up for'ard this afternoon to have a chat with me and tells me we have now passed 'Bluff' the bottom-most corner of New Zealand. Although I am only an ordinary member of the crew, the Mate, who has always been a great friend of mine, invariably has little chats with me, in most cases when I am taking my trick at the wheel. I like this fellow immensely. There is none of the old type of bullying about him, which so often occured on ships in the famous Clipper days, in fact he hardly ever shouts at any men. He told me once that he hates to shout at the boys and likes to treat them as human beings. Alfred the Chief Mate is just the opposite but at the same time is also a human kind of fellow and most of his shouting is done when the Captain is up on deck.
Position 49.24° South 167.48° East.

Day 17 Sunday March 11th

Not much of a fine Sunday for the boys today, continual bracing both morning and afternoon. I am still laid up but my knee feels a little better. At coffee time, instead of our usual minute piece of cake (which we only get on a Sunday) the Steward distributes two large biscuits to each man. They looked and tasted more like those large square Spratts Dog Biscuits and what made matters worse was the fact that having been bought last year when the ship was in Australia, they had all gone fusty and soft and in almost every one we discovered large white worms, only Belgier, who eats anything, devoured them with relish.

This evening George and Stowahse give us a musical concert, the former playing a mouth organ while the latter played his accordion. We were a happy crowd

and tried to forget for a few minutes the long miserable road that lay before us to Cape Horn. The weather was overcast all day and towards evening heavy rain began to fall.
Position 49.34° South 172° East.

Day 18 Monday March 12th

The Captain orders me 'aft' to see my leg but as I am unable to walk about without a great deal of pain, he orders me back to my bunk for another two days. During Thursday nights gale our cargo, consisting of 39,000 bags of wheat (equvalent to 3,000 tons) had shifted giving us a heavy list to starboard. So, each watch in turn are sent down into the hold to shift some of the bags back again, extremely heavy and hard work. Having completed this, each watch in turn commence to raise the anchor chains (port and starboard) up onto the deck so that the chain locker (situated at the bottom of the forepeak) can be scraped and painted. This again is hard and very monotonous work for unless you are lucky enough to have an hour at the wheel, you trudge round and round the large capstan on the fo'c'sle head for five solid hours.It was hard and unpleasant work and more often than not there were only two men to heave around the capstan, this was made still more difficult owing to the slippery state of the deck, while the rain beat down without mercy wetting the wretched boys through to the skin.

George is in great spirits today. The Captain has told him he need never go aloft again but must wash the dishes for his port watch every week.
Position 49.42° South 177.35° East

Day 19 Tuesday March 13th

At long last we have reached the Pacific Ocean. Boercher (German) sighted the lonely Antipodes Island while up aloft at 6am. At 4.55pm this afternoon we pass the meridian 180 degrees and for the first time we are supplied with a glass of rum, nine tenths of which was water.

We now definitely head towards the notorious Cape Horn. The weather today has been fine but cold.
Position 50° South 180° East.

Day 19 Tuesday March 13th

Having passed the meridian (the 180 degees mark) we must go back a day in our lives and commence Tuesday again. As is the custom on Finnish Sailing Ships the Captain gives us a whole holiday. But as is always the case the boys have bad luck and spend their holiday hauling on ropes (bracing) owing to the changeable and unsteady wind. Towards the evening the wind strengthens, the sea again becomes rough and we experience heavy hail squalls.
Position Almost the same.

Day 20 Wednesday March 14th

I am still laid up the Captain ordering me to remain another two days. The wind which is blowing up from 'dead aft' increases considerably during the morning, so that at 1pm 'all hands' take in and make fast the mainsail. Prior to this my watch had made fast and furled the fore upper to'gallant.

In the afternoon the sea became very angry, mountainous waves reared themselves up against the ships side and as she dipped her lee rail under water, they deposited themselves on deck with a thunderous roar sweeping along with them anything that was not fast. At 5pm (2 bells) the port watch make fast the main upper to'gallant, of course by now the two mizzen sails and several staysails had been made fast.

During the whole night the wind blew with tremendous force while the ship pitched and rolled to such a degree that it was impossible to sleep.
Position 51° South 169° West.

Day 21 Thursday March 15th

We continue sailing gradually South and shall do so until we have almost reached the Horn, which lies in about 55 degrees South, even then we shall have to go down to about 58 degrees South to clear it safely.

Just before 8am this morning (my watch being on deck) the fore lower to'gallant sheet chain snapped and the sail blows to and fro completely out of control but before any damage is done the sail is clewed up from the deck and three boys are sent aloft to make it fast. Meanwhile the sailmaker (bo'sun, and in our watch) and Karlsson (Swede) also go aloft to repair the damaged chain.

Towards midday the wind has decreased considerably, so that by 3pm all sails had been set again. Peter, one of the dogs, and Napoleon, a cat, come up for'ard for every meal without fail and seem to eat anything and as the food is none to appetising they usually receive plenty to eat.
Position 51.13° South 164° West.

Day 22 Friday March 16th

I turn out for work again this morning the first time for almost a fortnight.

Even now my leg is very painful but I refuse to cause my watch any more inconvenience, at any rate I can do my best. I am sent down, along with Frachnect (German) and Belgier to clean the bilges at the bottom of the forepeak, a hell of a job, especially with my leg in this state. It took me at least ten minutes to get to the bottom and when I got there it was impossible to keep a foothold owing to the heavy rolling. It was icy cold too as we had to stand knee deep in water (foul stinking stuff too) and this had all to be got rid of before we could commence scraping, painting etc. Then again to make matters worse we were continually bracing. This meant continually going up one minute out onto the deck, then down again. No sooner had we safely reached the bottom when again we must come up. There is no sympathy shown to anyone who is suffering from a bad leg. No, you must carry on as best you can.

Later on while going aft to take the wheel, I am swept off my feet by a large wave which sent me flying into the scupper. Owing to the state of my leg I had no time to grab the lifeline but except for getting wet through I was none the worse.
Position 50° South 159° West

Day 23 Saturday March 17th
We are again bracing throughout our afternoon watch but at 5,30pm, while I am at the wheel, we get a head wind and have to steer 'By the Wind' but this only remains for 15 minutes, for at 5.45pm we had our course back again but at 6.15pm there is no wind at all and we lie idly rolling in the longest swell I have ever seen, a sure forecast that dirty weather is approaching. Owing to the heavy rolling we get a large amount of water on deck and towards late evening a heavy hail squall comes up but 10 minutes later we were becalmed again.
Position 50° South 154° West.

Day 24 Sunday March 18th
Another Sunday spent bracing almost without cease. When shall we get a free Sunday? During a brief spell lasting about half an hour I chatted by the warm Galley fire with Cookie and Karlsson (both Swedes) about Captain Eriksons fleet of sailing ships.

Today has been 'fine and warm' most unlike Cape Horn weather.
Position 50° South 150° West.

Day 25 Monday March 19th
I am given the job of 'plaiting' this morning. You take a long piece of tarred rope (about half an inch thickness) double it, bringing the two ends together and then make fast both ends after having stretched it out and made it tight. You then tie round it short six inch lengths of old rope yarn each one by one. This is done by bunging the two ends of the rope yarn over the top in the form of a nail staple, then bring the two ends now over and under and finally pull the rope yarn and the rest (as you carry on) back to the end. This in time forms a frilly appearance and is thus often called a "Baggywrinkle". This is then placed around stays at certain places, where the sails will touch them, thus preventing them from fraying.

The day is fine but cold and we experience a steady wind most of the day, although the deck is continuously awash owing to the heavy sea.
Position 50° South 146° West.

Day 26 Tuesday March 20th

I am again 'plaiting' this morning but having returned from my trick at the wheel, I dicover Stowahse (German) carrying on with my work. After repeatedly asking him to shift and start one of his own and likewise getting no answer, I simply push him away. He resnted this and a fight commenced which certainly was beginning to take on ugly scenes, when luckily in stepped the 2nd Mate, who finished off the whole fiasco by giving us both good hard blows, each on the jaw, which we both thoroughly deserved. He eventually orders Stowahse aft to start on some work there.

It is miserable all day, very cold and heavy hail showers continually beat down upon us. The deck is still water logged which makes it very awkward when bracing and traversing the deck.
Position 50° South 142° West.

Day 27 Wednesday March 21st

Belgier is hurt this morning. At the time our watch were hauling on the lee braces. The wind was blowing strong, while a very heavy sea was running and the deck as well as being extremely slippery was waist deep in water. Every minute we had to make a grab for the life line as wave after wave hurled itself over the side of the ship. During a brief lull, we had begun hauling on the ropes again when without warning she gives a tremendous lurch, causing the lee rail to be completely submerged, while an avalanche of water hurled itself on deck, dragging all of us along with it. We grabbed anything we could, one or two managed to get to the life line. I grabbed hold of a rope, while others caught hold of belaying pins etc. Belgier was not quick enough and was sent headlong into the scupper. He lay motionless and at any moment might be washed overboard but Heim and Stowahse made a grab for his legs and hauled him to safety. Later he was taken up to the fo'c'sle where it was discovered that as well as having been knocked unconcious he had a badly sprained ankle. Except for being wet through the rest of us were none the worse.

During the afternoon we start to raise the starboard anchor chain. Except for half an hour (coffee time) I spent five solid hours trudging round and round the large capstan on the fo'c'sle head, more often than not there were only two of us to perform this heavy work. If we stopped to have a deserved rest we were yelled at from below by the Mate to 'heave away for Satan'.
Position 50° South 136° West.

Day 28 Thursday March 22nd
Belgier, although lame turns out again this morning, he and myself are sent
down into the chain locker to scrape the rust. Another devil of a job. Only one
man can go down here at a time owing to the very small amount of room. In
fact, there is barely enough room even for one person to work in comfort. It is
miserably cold, you stand in water, and being at the very bottom of the forepeak,
the rolling and pitching of the ship makes it almost impossible to stand and
also to work. I go down first while Belgier hauls up onto the deck the water in a
bucket.

I was very nearly washed overboard this afternoon while going aft to the wheel
at the time. I had just reached midships (the most dangerous spot) when without
warning I was literally swept off my feet by a tremendous wave, which sent me
crashing headlong against the lee rail just as she dipped it under the water. For a
moment, owing to the amount of water, I thought I was actually in the sea, when
suddenly I managed to feel something solid which I gripped with all my strength.
It happened to be a stay and it was to this stay that I am alive today. I seemed to
cling there for hours, while it could not have been above a few seconds, when
my Mate who had witnessed the whole thing from the poop, came rushing down
and dragged me at very grave risk to himself back to safety up on to the poop. I
was wet through as I had no oilskins on at the time but on a sailing ship there are
no dry clothes to be changed into, so I took my wheel and stood my hour there
wet through, cold and feeling thoroughly miserable.

At 7pm (6 bells) while the crew (as is the custom on sailing ships every night
at 7pm, 12 midnight and again at 4am) 'muster' aft beneath the break of the
poop, each in their respective watches (this is done so that the Mate can tell
whether any man is sleeping in his bunk when he should be on deck) Theo
Keller (German) is knocked against one of the capstans by a wave. He gets up
screaming and yelling unable to straighten his back or walk, so he is carried up
for'ard where we discover he has hurt his spine. It is a sheer wonder to me that
no one has been killed or washed overboard so far, every day every minute you
have to take your life in your hands.

Jacques (Belgian) is laid up with boils all over his arms and legs due to the bad
food etc. The Captain cut one of them this morning to get rid of some of the
poison and the method he used was unbelievable. He cut the boil with a pocket
knife, squeezed the poison out, then scraped round the large hole formed with
the blade point and to finish up he almost emptied a bottle of iodine into the
cavity making the wretched boy scream 'murder'. All the same, it cured it.
Position 51 South 130 West.

Day 29 Friday March 23rd

During a.m. watch on deck in the afternoon we are again scraping rust down in the chain locker. As the day wears on the wind increases and large waves come crashing without cease on deck.

Just before 7pm the wind veers round to 'dead aft', so at 7pm (6 bells) instead of going off duty until midnight, and also getting our tea which was ready waiting for us, 'all hands' are called out to 'take in' the mainsail. Before going aloft we must break all the buntlines (i.e. snap all the yarn which keeps them in place), let go the sheet, clew up and countless other things, commencing always first on the weather side. Having completed this, we all go aloft to make fast and stow the sail onto the yard.

The work on deck is always 'hell' as more often than not we are standing waist deep in water, hail and rain beats down into your face and eyes without cease, at times almost blinding you. As the main mast is situated midships (the worst spot) we have to continually jump for the life line to prevent ourselves being carried overboard by tremendous waves. We get wet through (no oilskins can prevent the water getting through), we are cold and tired out, but we must carry on.

On this particular night, I had no oilskins. Mr Brown (passenger), who had joined the port watch the other day, and I, used to share oilskins. Owing to him being in a different watch and not being prepared for a 'all hands' call, at 6.45 (15 minutes before our watch went below) I handed them over to Mr Brown until midnight when I should come on deck again. All I wore was a mackintosh over my work suit, which was useless as I got wet through the very first minute and in time I became so hunched with cold that when up aloft helping to make fast the angry, wet, heavy sail I could feel nothing. We fought like the devil out there on the yard for a solid hour, trying our utmost to heave up the heavy sail onto the yard. But owing to our shorthanded watch it was useless and in the end the port watch, who had successfully made fast the port side, came over to give us a hand. Even then it took us all our time to haul it up onto the yard, while the continual yelling at us from the Mates on deck only made matters worse and roused our tempers up.

It was no joke out on this yard which continually kicked and heaved about as the ship rolled. Sometimes the yard was hanging at a terrifying angle which almost chucked us off but we fought like madmen and at last after an hour and a half's strenuous work we safely hauled the heavy wet sail onto the yard and made it fast.

Hungry, wet through, cold and tired we came down to go off duty, only to find our tea was now stone cold and the galley fire almost out. What a life. Between

8pm and midnight the port watch took in and made fast the fore upper to'gallant and two staysails. Having only had two and a half hours sleep (if that) our watch come out again at midnight for our watch on deck.

So is the sailors life.
Position 51° South 126° West.

Day 30 Saturday March 24th

During the morning the wind decreased considerably and we were busy setting sail again, but by 3pm it had again strengthened and it looked as though we might again be in for a rough night. Typical low Cape Horn clouds were flying past, some almost touching the top of the mast, while the sea had turned its old angry grey colour once more. To make matters worse Mr Brown told us the barometer was falling rapidly.

Just before 5pm another fight takes place. This time between Bob (a Yankee and my best friend on board) and the Steward (Finn). At the time Bob was in the galley making some toast (a thing not allowed although very often done, as the galley is out of bounds to all except for the Cook and Steward). Along comes the Steward, who immediately strikes Bob. On hearing the row, along comes the Cook and the 2nd Mate who also set into Bob thus making three men attacking one. Bob put up a plucky, but vain fight and retired to the fo'c'sle raving mad, with a cut lip, bleeding nose and a nasty black eye but says he will pay them back, even if it means being dismissed the ship in England for attacking his superiors.

Just what we all expected, at 7pm 'all hands' again take in the mainsail (tonight the port watch will suffer as they are free from 7pm till midnight). The conditions were as bad as last night but this time I did have the protection of my oilskins, even then I was as good as wet through.

I am informed today, it is Summer Time down here, then God keep us if it was Winter Time.
Position 52° South 120° West.

Day 31 Sunday March 25th

Between 4am and 8am our watch are continuously bracing, this is none to pleasant on a deck waist deep in water. Since we furled the mainsail last night at 7pm the wind has gradually increased so that by 8am this morning the port watch took in and made fast the fore upper and lower to'gallants.

The deck is again waist deep in water and huge waves repeatedly come crashing down on deck making it extremely dangerous to be out anywhere on deck.

Brincks (Dane) is now laid up with a badly poisoned hand. Throughout today two white and one black albatross follow us, continuously flying round and round the ship never once appearing to flap their wings.

During the afternoon I chat with Cookie and the sailmaker (Finn) and they show me different knots and how to splice wires.

I get wet through while at look-out tonight. For a solid hour I stood up here on the exposed fo'c'sle head while large waves continually crashed on the deck wetting me through.

Look-out, a lonely job

I could find no shelter and I attempted to stand on the lee side of the large capstan but this was almost useless and every minute I had to grab hold of the capstan as a stay, as the ship rolled, to prevent myself being either chucked headlong against the rail or possibly overboard. It was terrifying at times to stand here and gaze at those mountainous waves and deep valleys and for a minute it made me wonder as she dipped her bowsprit under the waves whether she would ever right herself again.

Those who have never been at sea in these regions will not be able to realize what terrifying forms the sea can take. It is impossible to describe in writing. *Position 52° South 114° West.*

Look-out, a dangerous job, too

Day 32 Monday March 26th
Frachnect (German) and myself are sent down into the chain locker to scrape rust. At no time is this a pleasant job, but this morning it was ten times worse, for between 8am and 1pm we experienced no fewer than six 'two whistles' for bracing. This meant constantly going up onto the deck to 'brace' then down again into the locker. No sooner had we reached the bottom again and commenced scraping, when there was another two blasts from that damned whistle, (nicknamed the Mates best friend). We got so fed up with this confounded business, that in the end we pretended we had never heard the whistle and remained down in the locker, but we soon learnt our lesson, as the Mate ordered us both up on deck and gave us a good 'sound leathering', which no doubt we deserved. As the wind had again decreased we also set the mainsail, the two staysails and the two mizzen sails, (the spanker and the under mizzen). The third one, the 'over' mizzen, is down in the sail locker and will remain there until we reach the kindly Trade Winds.

Mr Brown gave each member of his port watch some rum tonight and as I was awake I got a share also although I'm in the starboard watch.
Position 52° South 111° West.

Day 33 Tuesday March 27th

At 6am this morning, I go aloft to overhaul and clean all buntlines and gaskets, the latter are small ropes attached to the yard for making fast the sail to the yard when 'stowing'. While to 'clean' them, simply means tie up those that have come undone in the special way, so that they can be readily and quickly undone again when required.

Having completed this I am sent down into the forepeak to clean away water from the bilges, how it gets there I don't know. The stink from the water down here is enough to give you fever, and this is another detestable job.

Bob's great chance has come at last. During his working watch 8am to 1pm, he is ordered to paint down in the Lazarette, underneath the poop, where the food supplies are kept. Every morning roughly about 9am the Steward goes down there to fetch the days supply up. Bob realized this and waited patiently. Just after 9am down goes the Steward and half a minute later an infernal scream arose which could be heard all over the ship, Bob had sent him reeling headfirst onto the floor. The Captain and Chief Mate, who happened to be in the chart house at the time, go rushing down to see what was the matter. The Captain sees the Steward on the floor and without asking for a question aims a blow at Bob, but the latter foresaw this, and got his in first, giving the Captain a large black eye. The Chief Mate now has a go, but he is no match for Bob and so suffers like the rest. A few minutes later the Cook goes down too but his effort also was all in vain.

I like Bob, he's afraid of nobody, barely 23 years old and yet he's a man. A man in the true sense. He's been seasick, had boils all over his arms and legs, had a poisoned ear, which caused him hellish agony, yet he has never laid-up and never missed a watch. He has no oilskins, no sou'wester, no seaboots, in fact he has very little clothing at all, he gets wet through repeatedly and like others he is overworked, often tired out and always hungry. He never grouses, always cheery and ready to help anybody in difficulties and lastly, without doubt, he is the finest seaman aboard bar none. A man in the true sense and the best pal I have ever had.

During my watch on deck 1pm to 7pm I meet with another accident but not serious enough to prevent me from working. I was down in the forepeak clearing water away from the bilges at the time. Belgier had just hauled the bucket up on to the deck to chuck the water overboard and was letting down the empty one, when for some unknown reason it became loose from the rope and came hurtling down onto my head knocking me clean out for a few minutes. I certainly was stunned but carried on again after a few minutes rest.
Position 53° South 106° West.

Day 34 Wednesday March 28th
I spent four hours with Stowahse and Heim (Germans) heaving round and round the capstan on the fo'c'sle head, letting down the starboard anchor chain into the freshly painted locker.

We see plenty of sea birds of all descriptions today. The albatross of course, several Cape pigeons, stormy petrels, three sea swallows and several other species. It beats me what these birds live on down here in these wastes miles away from any land.

We set the 'flying jib' (outer staysail on the bowsprit) so once again, except for the 'over mizzen', we have every canvas set.
Position 53° South 103° West.

Day 35 Thursday March 29th
I am again sent down into the forepeak to clear the water away from the bilges. It always appears to fall on me to perform this detestable work.

During my free watch, I have a row with Frachnect for using my tin (which I use for washing myself with) to clean a filthy and oily hurricane lamp, while later on another row crops up. Belgier, who always keeps his case locked, discovers the lock broken and tries to find out who has done it. As a matter of fact the whole of our watch including myself had a hand in this. If there is anything we hate it is for another man to keep his case locked up. These boys never steal from another boy. I have been on two sailing ships and I never had a thing pinched, therefore, to teach him the ways of the sailing ships, we taught him a lesson.

The weather is again dull and extremely cold, yet it is supposed to be Summer down here. I cannot remember when I saw the sun last.
Position 53° South 99° West.

Day 36 Friday March 30th
Today is Good Friday but we get no holiday. It is my turn to clean the pig house out this morning. We took three aboard in Port Germein and up to now they are still alive.

Just before 1pm the wind blows up strong and veers round to 'dead aft' so to enable our large foresail to get more wind, at 1pm 'all hands' furl the mainsail.

As the afternoon wore on, so the wind increased, the port watch make fast the fore upper to'gallants and two staysails; while previously they had made fast the two mizzen sails.

84

Just after coffee I have a fight with Jacques (Belgian) outside the galley over the usual thing 'food'. We rammed in at each other right and left, and eventually while clinched together (to the great amusement of the other boys) we both fell down into the water filled scuppers, still fighting desperately. At last after a ten minute hard battle we both gave up each admitting it was a 'dead heat'.

Half an hour later there is another fight, this time up in the starboard fo'c'sle between Bill Thompsen (Dane) and Frachnect (German). This was certainly the hardest and longest fight I have witnessed. An hours incessant 'battering' at each other and although their faces were covered in blood and bruised almost out of recognition neither would give in or admit defeat, so in the end they had to be separated. They kicked each other and punched each other black and blue, while pots, cases, in fact anything within their reach went flying in all directions.

Bravo Bill Thompsen, although you were recovering from a broken arm, you stuck up to him well and I admired you for refusing to give in.

Later on I have a row with Mr Brown (passenger) about 'nothing'. These rows and fights are always cropping up but are to be expected when young fellows see only themselves day after day, sometimes for as long as five months, perhaps even longer.

We have a splendid wind at present, ploughing through the water at about 8 knots but owing to the heavy rolling, we get a large amount of sea on deck. *Position 53° South 93° West.*

Day 37 Saturday March 31st
As the wind has been blowing steady throughout the night without increasing further, between 4am and 8am, we set the mainsail, fore upper to'gallant and the two staysails which we had taken in last evening. This was completed by 7am and as is always the custom on a Saturday, coal must be brought up from the coal hole (situated up for'ard under the fo'c'sle head) and carried to the galley midships. The Mate orders me down into the hole along with Stowashe. This is another job loathed by all members.

It is pitch black down here. I will admit you are given a lamp of some description but every now and again the lamp along with yourself are sent flying against the ships side as she continually rolls. The lamp is out and you feel for it, but you cannot find it in this blackness, while up on deck the Mate is yelling murder waiting to know why coal is not being sent up. Again I get a bucket on my head, this time through the carelessness of the man on deck, who should, before chucking the bucket down, yell out 'look out' but the fool failed to do so. The consequence being I suffered from a badly cut head.

I have a little arguement with Bob at tea time tonight over some jam (if you can call it jam) which the Cook had given me for helping him to peel some spuds during my free watch. I gave him a little and he said I was 'stingy' and had not given him barely a spoonful. It blows over and as usual Bob and I are the best of pals.

It is very cold all day and we have heavy hail squalls.
Position 53° South 87° West.

Day 38 Sunday April 1st
How we all long for the Trade Winds and a dry ship. For two weeks now we have had a deck standing in water, a fo'c'sle (where we live) always wet, wet clothes, wet bunk, in fact everything is wet.

Mr Brown (passenger) tells me this morning that, although the door leading into the Captains, his own and the Mates quarters was cemented up just before leaving Australia (they now have to get in through the chart house) to prevent the water from getting in, actually the whole place was literally awash.

The 1st Mates cabin was completely flooded out and he now has to sleep in Mr Brown's cabin. Every morning for about two and a half hours the Steward was kept busy baling out the water, even then it was scarcely any better.

Up for'ard in the two fo'c'sles life is just as miserable. We sleep on wet bunks, all our clothes are wet, there is no stove to dry them (we have only one fire on board, the galley, and here only the privileged Officers are allowed to dry their clothes).

The fo'c'sle floors are standing in water and even when we are free watch we get straight into our bunks, sometimes even with our oilskins and seaboots on, as it is useless to attempt to change when all spare clothes are wet too. This makes life very miserable as we never get our blood warm and we just remain, day after day, frozen stiff.

Belgier makes me an 'April Fool' telling me the Captain wishes to see me but I have him back a few minutes later.

During the afternoon the wind shifts round from 'dead aft' to blow fairly strong from the South West and we sail along at about 8 knots. But about 6pm it returns to 'dead aft' so at 7pm all hands take in the mainsail.

Mr Brown is thrown from the wheel tonight and sprains his wrist. She is extremely heavy to handle, as I found out later. It took me all my arm and leg strength to prevent it again throwing me.
Position 54° South 82° West.

Day 39 Monday April 2nd

Before breakfast I overhaul all 'buntlines' up the fore and main masts. The wind strengthens during the morning and by 2pm it had increased almost to gale force. The sea was now a mass of mountainous white capped waves, which thundered against our sides, eventually hurling themselves without mercy on our reeling deck, the flying spume at times almost reaching our lower topsail.

She ships heavy seas continuously but she's a game old ship and gallantly rises up again after each one passes. As the wind is coming from 'dead aft' she rolls very badly causing first the weather side to be submerged and then the lee rail. It is very dangerous to be on deck now.

At 3.35pm while Frachnect (German) was at the wheel and the rest of us drinking coffee, we are almost 'pooped', the very worst thing that can happen to a sailing ship and more often than not results in the ship being dismasted, (take the Hougomont for example), this was only just averted by our splendid and always alert Captain who rushes to the wheel and helps the terrified helmsman to bring the ship back to safety, while the Chief Mate (nicknamed Alfred) rushes up for'ard for another boy to come to the wheel. I was free watch at the time and in my bunk reading.

Just prior to this happening, there was a fairly strong wind blowing, and we were shipping rather heavy seas without warning, there was utter confusion. The ship pitched and rolled like something incredible, large waves were depositing themselves on deck with a thunderous roar, while all the sails which were now back were banging against the mast, causing an infernal din and the deck was literally one mass of green swirling sea.

Up here in the fo'c'sle we were flooded out, the lamp was smashed, plates, mugs, boys cases and sea chests were floating about in all directions while the lower bunks were flooded out. The poop, where the wheel is situated, also had its share although it is raised above the deck, while the Captains quarters below the poop were standing in water.
The Galley midships was also awash, the fire out, and Cookies dishes and pans, tins of beans and Bully Beef were floating about, some on deck.

All hands were called out to man the braces and we certainly had a gruelling time dodging the waves and hauling on the braces on a waterlogged deck.

It was caused through the wind which had been blowing up fairly stormy from 'dead aft' suddenly shifting to a very strong head wind. After two hours strenuous work on deck (during which we all got wet through) we had brought her back to normal once again.

A water logged deck

All this happened within 160 miles of the dreaded 'Horn' where so many fine sailing ships have met their doom, never to be heard of again. We carry no wireless, so if the worst had happened, we should have gone down without a soul knowing. Another Cape Horn victim. Bravo "Winterhude" you stuck it gamely. Bob (American) who was in the Hougomont when she got dismasted two years ago actually thought for a few minutes our end had come.

The weather is bitterly cold but fine.
Position 55° South 76° West.

Day 40 Tuesday April 3rd
Cookie laid up this morning, therefore Belgier, who is a great eater and always in the galley, takes on the role of Cook.

In our morning watch on deck I am again down in the forepeak scraping rust and then red leading it prior to painting. The wind is steady all day and we average roughly 5 knots.

At 8pm tonight we pass Cape Horn in glorious weather and with every canvas set. A really splendid trip, having taken us only 34 days from our last landfall Cape Berda. I was at the wheel from 8pm to 9pm and as we actually passed the horn at 9.10pm, I feel that at any rate, I have actually steered an old sailing ship round the Horn.

Glorious weather off Cape Horn

I might mention here, that our wheel, which is situated in a very exposed position aft on the poop, has no wheelhouse for shelter as on my last ship the four master "Olivebank" and we stand here for one solid hour, sometimes even two hours in the worst weather imaginable. More often than not one gets wet through and the cold icy winds bite your face, hands and ears. No gloves will keep you warm and no oilskins will keep out the heavy rain and damp experienced down here in these latitudes. Then having finished your hour at the wheel, there is no warm fire to go to, no warm cup of coffee or tea to drink, you must first carry on, brave the elements and be cheerful like the rest.

A great surprise awaits us tonight. We each get a glass of rum given us in recognition of having passed Cape Horn. Spirits have now bucked up tremendously, every day will bring us nearer to the Trade Winds and Falmouth.

We all sing songs up in the fo'c'sle this evening. The weather is very wet and cold. *Position 57° South 69° West.*

Day 41 Wednesday April 4th
We are now definitly steering in a Northerly direction.

This morning I have my first row with my friend the 2nd Mate. I was sent aloft to overhaul the buntlines on the fore upper to'gallant. While I am up there the Mate yells an order to me, which I fail to hear on account of the wind pressure. I try to discover what it is he wishes me to do, I go out on the yard on the deck side of the mast, but fail to see anything wrong. Finally the Mate, who is now furious and yelling murder at me, orders Stowahse up aloft to carry out the order, while at the same time yells for me to come down on deck.

When I reached the deck, the Mate played the very devil. I tried to explain to him that it was impossible to hear up there but it was useless and I certainly felt a damn fool having been ordered down on deck. But, as usual, it blew over after a few minutes and again we are loyal friends.

In the evening Mr Brown caught two albatross by the ancient method of dangling a triangle overboard attached to a long piece of thin rope. Attached to this triangle is a large piece of pork. The bird sees the pork dives down to get it and gets its hooked beak caught in the triangle. We haul them aboard but as usual they are both sick (water sick) and they cannot walk or rise while on the deck. After about half an hours time, we liberate them again, we dare not kill them as it is an old sailors superstition. To kill them means 'bad luck'.
Position 54° South 64° West.

Day 42 Thursday April 5th
During our working watch we are again scraping rust down in the forepeak. We see scores of birds today from the large and stately albatross down to the small sea sparrow.

Towards evening we again have a head wind necessitating us going 'by the wind' and as the wind was blowing fairly strong and taking us to far out of our course, we take in and make fast the mainsail and fore upper to'gallant, while towards midnight it had increased to about gale force.

We are still feeling very tired and worn out. We seem to be always working and never sleeping. We work 14 hours one day and 10 the next as well as sometimes being called out during free watch.
Position 54° South 57° West.

Day 43 Friday April 6th

The wind is still a strong head wind. My watch between 4am and 8am take in the fore lower to'gallant and the main upper and lower to'gallants. Brincks (Dane) and myself make fast both the upper to'gallants, which was extemely difficult and dangerous work lying out on a reeling yard high above the deck and which every so often gave a kick which nearly sent us hurtling down on to the deck.

You can readily imagine the velocity of the wind up there when I tell you I had my shirt ripped clean off my body, I didn't even see it go.

At 7am (6 bells) 'all hands' are called out to take in and make fast the fore upper topsail. There only remained on deck the Captain, two Mates Cookie, Steward and helmsman. To have sent every hand aloft with so few on deck was a very dangerous decision; as, I soon discovered when I got aloft, that the collar which attached the yard to the mast had broken and consequently the yard was banging and swinging about in a very dangerous manner. Any minute it could easily have fallen down on deck taking all of us down with it and in all probability killing every hand. Before I knew what was the matter and as I was actually stepping from the rigging on to the collar, Brincks pulled me away and only just in time. Had I stepped onto the collar, I should have had my foot crushed to a pulp by the yard which was repeatedly swinging inwards against the mast.

Out on the yard it was absolute hell and none of us felt safe while Bob called the Chief Mate every name under the sun for having sent us all aloft. It was the devils job attempting to make fast the sail to the yard as every minute the yard jumped and kicked in a very vicious mood, I almost thought any minute we should all be down on deck. After three quarters of an hours hard battle we eventually made the sail fast, at least in a fashion, and we were all very thankful when we reached the safety of the deck again.
Position 53° South 56° West.

Day 44 Saturday April 7th

Just before 8am the wind shifts from the starboard to the port side and consequently we must 'about' or 'turn' the ship and the operation is as follows. First the helmsman takes the wheel hard over to the port (he must hold it there until the foresail yard is squared, which is almost at the end of the operation).

The Mate now slackens the Lee Main Braces while the crew haul tight the weather braces (the ship is now going over to port) and having done so haul on the slack from the Lee Braces. Then for'ard to the fore braces and when these have been hauled tight the fore and main 'sheets' are made fast to the respective capstans and then hauled tight.

All staysail sheets must be taken over to the opposite side and made fast too. The three mizzen sails, the spanker, upper mizzen and lower mizzen (which had

previously been taken in before the operation began, to ease off the pressure on the stern) are set also, but on the opposite side. The four small sails out on the bowsprit (the flying jib, outer jib, inner jib and the fore topmast staysail) are also taken over to the opposite side by their sheets and made fast.

The four jib Sails

Finally, all ropes and wires must be cleared up either on deck or on the pins, according to the Mates instruction. This operation takes our short handed watches roughly twentyfive minutes to complete in fair weather and about forty minutes in rough weather. 'Wearing Ship' is the term applied to this operation and in very rough weather it can at times be excedingly dangerous.
Position 52° South 55° West.

Day 45 Sunday April 8th

The donkeyman who had worked all day yesterday making a new collar for our fore upper topsail yard, continues again this morning although a Sunday. By 1pm it is ready to be fixed aloft, consequently it is hauled up and fixed in position.

At 3pm the fixing work is finished and as it is my watches hours on deck we have the bad luck as usual to set the sail again and as the wind is only moderate we set the fore upper and lower to'gallants too, which meant us having plenty of work.

Fo'c'sle head from fore upper topsail yard

Two albatross and two Cape pigeons follow us all day.
Cold and hail showers.
Position 51° South 54° West.

Day 46 Monday April 9th

We commence washing the white paint up on the poop, this being done by first cleaning it with warmed up rain water mixed with soda, and then washing it off with ordinary salt water. As most of the crew were suffering from cuts and sores on the hands, the soda caused considerable pain. Having completed this, we now commence scrubbing the poop deck, in my opinion one of the worst jobs I did throughout the whole trip. The operation, which is most ancient in its form, is as follows. Each man is given a small tin containing sand, a larger tin filled with a mixture of hot rain water and soda, and lastly a large block of sandstone, known as a 'Holystone'. We now get down on our knees and commence scrubbing the starboard side with these stones.

As I had no 'wheel' between 8am and 1pm, I scrubbed without hardly a stop for five solid hours. A back, neck, arm and knee aching job. I was extremely glad when 2 bells were struck at 1pm.

When the deck has been scrubbed all over, we swill it off three or four times over with salt water until the Mate considers it clean enough.

By 8pm at night, the wind had increased considerably so that my watch had to make fast the fore and main upper to'gallants and during this I stand for two solid hours at the open wheel in bitterly cold and wet weather and although cold and wet through I go straight from there up to the fo'c'sle head to spend an hour as 'look out'.
Position 49° South 51° West.

Day 47 Tuesday April 10th

Cookie caught George (stowaway) pinching food in the galley this morning. This pinching of food has been going on all the trip so far, not only by George but also by myself and other members of the crew. We pinched onions, cocoa, tinned meat, in fact anything edible that we could lay hands on and during our cold watches at night, we would fry the onions, cook the tinned meat and make ourselves a nice hot drink of cocoa or coffee. All this cooking was done over the small kerosene lamp up in the fo'c'sle. We could not refuse this temptation of pinching, as we never seemed to get enough to eat and as we were always cold, wet through and hungry during our night watches it was certainly a God Send.

Poor old George is reported to the Captain.

By 8am the wind had decreased in force, so my watch again set the main upper to'gallant, while at 9am, the port watch set the fore upper to'gallant. We are again sailing with every canvas set.

Jacques (Belgian) and Brincks (Dane) are laid up with boils on the legs and arms. During our watch 1pm to 7pm we carry on that foul job scraping the poop with the 'Holystones'.

The weather today has been fair and slightly warmer.
Position 46° South 48° West.

Day 48 Wednesday April 11th

We finish scraping the poop this morning and commence cleaning and washing the white paint down on deck, but again, only the starboard side. I chat with Bob (my best friend) and Brownie in the evening.

I always considered Wednesdays food the worst. To give you some idea as to what we have for our breakfast, dinner and tea every Wednesday, I will explain. For breakfast we have terribly salted bacon, (which hardly anybody eats). For dinner Pea Soup (if you can call it that) and pancakes (which are as tough as leather). For tea a kind of cake which is a mixture of rice, raisins, currants and meat. After eating the latter in an hours time you are hungry again.
Position 44° South 46° West.

Day 49 Thursday April 12th

We again wash the white paint on the deck this afternoon. I have a row with young Frachnect. He would persist in washing paint very close to where I was working, although there was heaps of other places which wanted cleaning. I told him to have a little sense and start somewhere else but he is very stubborn and refuses to move, at the same time tells me to 'go to the devil'. I suggest we fight it out on deck but he refuses this also. But later on when I come down from look-out at 7pm, he meets me and says he believes I wanted him 'on deck'. I told him it was bright coming now but that I was still prepared to fight him. We got to grips, and for the first five minutes it was level pegging, then as we are both clinched together, we stumble over something and both fell on the deck. My back is out for he falls on top of me and, gripping me between his strong legs, lunges in at my face with all his strength and eventually knocked me clean out, as I was powerless to move. When I come round, I discover I have a very sore, swollen, black eye and my upper lip is all puffed. We soon make friends again. I like all the foreigners on this ship, we have our little fight but that is nothing.

Just after the midnight muster another row crops up. Keller (German) accuses George of stealing his cigarettes and immediately others say they have lost things too and accuse him also. George punches Keller in the face, giving him a very large black eye. Keller (always a baby) rushes aft and reports to the 2nd Mate that he has been struck by a stowaway. The Mate comes up fo'ard and plays the very devil with George and tells the whole of my watch (starboard) to give George a

good hiding, but I refuse flatly to do such a thing and tell the Mate he has done no harm to me. Bob (who, owing to his strength, everybody fears) now steps in and tells the Mate to go to the devil and what a bad trick he was ordering, seven men to fight one. Then he warns the starboard watch (who were just about to set into George), that if they dare touch him, he (Bob) would fight the lot of them single handed. That warning certainly made them 'think twice'.We are becalmed today although down here in the 'Roaring Forties' of all places.
Position 44° South 44° West.

Day 50 Friday April 13th
We finish washing white paint on deck this morning. This afternoon we kill one of the pigs consequently, as one died two weeks ago, we have only one left after this. Alfred (1st Mate) who is the only person on board who has a pistol performing the deed. He's certainly a good shot. At any rate we shall get fresh food for a time, only the best parts will go 'aft' to the Captain and the Mates.

Everybody friends again. Only, after the row last night, the Captain orders George to join our starboard watch and Frachnect (Kellers best friend) forms the port watch.

Fine and warmer. Becalmed.
Position 43° South 41° West.

Day 51 Saturday April 14th
Still 'becalmed' early this morning. We get a slight wind about midday but this later becomes a head wind and we must sail 'by the wind'. In the afternoon we commence scraping teak wood up on the poop, such as the wheel, doors to the chart house, sail locker hatch cover etc. During free watch in the afternoon Heim (German) explains a few knots to me.

Fine but cooler.
Position 42° South 39° West.

Day 52 Sunday April 15th
We still have a head wind and sail 'By the Wind'. Heim (who everybody nicknames the ships barber) cuts my hair and also other members of the crew. This boy cuts hair ten times better than some of these 'so called' qualified barbers on shore. All the boys who have grown 'Cape Horn Beards' shave them off this morning, hoping that we shall get a 'Fair Wind'. Also, as the weather is so much warmer, one or two of us pinch some fresh water from the galley and have our first real wash for well over a month.

Fine and warm.
Position 40° South 39° West

Day 53 Monday April 16th

Before 8am our watch set the fore upper to'gallant. Just before 3pm and during our free watch, the wind suddenly springs up to gale force and we take in both the mizzen sails. While Jacques and I are making fast the 'under mizzen', Jacques lost his foothold but just saves himself crashing down on to the winch on deck by grabbing hold of a gasket (rope for making fast sail to the yard etc.), luckily the gasket did not break. Certainly a very close shave. Having made this fast we rush for'ard and help take in and make fast the flying jib and jigger staysail. The main upper to'gallant staysail now blows out into shreds.

At 4pm we take in the fore upper to'gallant, Belgier, Jacques and myself are sent aloft to make it fast. Owing to the tremendous force of the wind the ship was heeling well over to starboard and occasionally the yard would kick and jump which made our work up aloft extremely hard and dangerous. Neither of us felt too safe up aloft, especially when the yard kicked, as the starboard side was broken and corroded away out at the end of the yard. In fact it was so bad that you could almost get your whole arm inside.

The wind continues to increase and at midnight it is blowing a regular hurricane. We take in the main upper to'gallant and Stowahse, myself and Belgier are sent aloft to make it fast.

At one time the force of the waves which were crashing on deck were so strong that one sent the whole watch, 7 men and the Mate, sprawling in all directions. Luckily none of us went overboard and although we were all wet through to the skin and feeling frozen stiff and tired out with the continuous work, every man kept on smiling and taking it as a great joke.

What wonderful fellows these foreign windjammer sailor boys are. They seem to laugh at everything, take everything as a joke, they are always willing to come out in a free watch to help on deck. You hardly ever hear one grousing, except of course about the food, but who wouldn't. They are all fine fellows to me, the only Englishman aboard, they are all the best of pals.

Frachnect (German) fell on deck this evening while carrying a pot of boiling water up for'ard and scalds his arm and leg rather seriously.

Waves all day sweep the deck from end to end. Owing to the force of the wind we only have a few staysails set, these only being left to help to make the steering easier.
Position 38° South 42° West.

Day 54 Tuesday April 17th

We are again scraping teak wood on the poop during our working watch this morning. I find the wheel exceptionally hard to hold this morning on account of the very heavy swell, this causes it to kick considerably. I was unable to prevent it swinging three points each side of the given course but I find out later I am not the only one to be in such a quandary as most of the other boys experienced the same thing. At 12am and for fifteen minutes we have to sail 'By the Wind'.

We have blood pancakes for our dinner today and also for tea later on. They did not look very appitising and certainly would not have done on shore but I certainly devoured them with relish as there was nothing else. When the pig is killed all its blood is collected in buckets and later made into these pancakes. What cannibals we are on this ship. But we must eat something.

A new moon appears tonight and the Mate tells me we shall now get good winds and better weather. A heavy sea is running all day and we get plenty of water on deck.

The weather is fine and warmer.
Position 37° South 37° West.

Day 55 Wednesday April 18th

The wind decreased considerably during the night, so that by 9am our watch again set the fore and main upper to'gallants. There is a very rough sea although no wind, this again causes the wheel to be very heavy and hard to steer.

The carpenter (nicknamed Chips by me and called 'Timmerman' by the Finns) is almost washed overboard this afternoon. He was going along the deck at the time and had just reached midships when without warning the ship gave a sudden lurch, while at the same time a large wave came crashing down on deck taking Chips along with it, in its stride, eventually chucking him hard against the lee scuppers and just as she dipped her lee rail well under the green sea. As she rights herself again, Chips makes a rush for the ladder going up to the poop and except for a thorough soaking he is none the worse.

Before breakfast, that is at 4 bells (6am) after having drunk early morning coffee, it is my turn to carry the daily ration of fresh water to the two fo'c'sles, galley, donkeymans, Timmermans and sailmakers cabins and lastly to the pantry aft and while the Mate is not looking I pinch a bucketful for myself for washing, (as we are short of water). This has to be done regularly every morning at 6am, when also all buntlines and gastets must be overhauled too, so also must the pig house be cleaned out. The Galley is allowed six buckets, the carpenter, donkeyman and sailmaker have to share one bucket, while the two fo'c'sles for'ard are allowed two, one for each fo'c'sle. There are fourteen men up here, so this is not very much supply for each man and we are always thirsty.

At 6pm the wind blows up strongly and this time from dead aft.
Position 35° South 34° West.

Day 56 Thursday April 19th
Again scraping teak wood up on the poop (very lazy and most enjoyable work) but we are often called away from work for hauling on the braces, owing to the wind repeatedly shifting from one direction to the other.

Today sees the passing away of one of our dogs, Peter, who was given to the Chief Mate in Australia. Alfred (Chief Mate) killed the dog himself, owing to the fact that for the past week it had been far from well and could only manage to crawl about.

According to Brownie (passenger) it was one of the cruellest deaths (although not meant) that he had ever witnessed. The Mate hit it on the head with a large hammer no fewer than ten times and then, although still alive and blood gushing forth from its head, he chucked it overboard. The water around instantly became a mess of red caused by the blood. The poor animal is torn to pieces and devoured by scores of albatross which were following the ship.
Position 34° South 32° West.

Day 57 Friday April 20th
At 6am this morning I am sent aloft to overhaul buntlines up both the fore and main masts. It is a glorious morning and when I reach the top of the mast and get out on to the fore upper to'gallant yards, I spend a few minutes admiring the scene. How really beautiful the "Winterhude" looked from up here, her sails were full and she was cutting through the water in a very graceful manner, only occasionally giving a very slight roll.

During my free watch from 8am to 1pm I spend my time washing dirty clothes in fresh water, which I have again pinched from the Galley tank. This is the first time I have had the opportunity of washing clothes since leaving Australia. By jove, and weren't they filthy.

During our working watch from 1pm to 7pm we scrape rust off the white paint up on the poop, prior to painting. The scraping of the teak wood is now complete and the port watch varnished it over this morning.

The 1st Mate who is now the sole owner of any cigarettes (the Captain forgot to buy a fresh supply in Australia consequently we have been without since the

98

first week after leaving port) is offering tins (he has only 5 left) of 50 Abdullas for fifteen shillings a tin, or 3d a cigarette, but except for Belgier who bought one tin, and a few boys who bought one or two at 3d each (including myself), Alfred does not find trade too brisk. Most of us pinch coffee beans from the Galley, roast them, cut them up into small pieces and use them for tobacco. There is also a shortage of matches, nearly every box the Captain has left are all damp and no use, having suffered like everything else from the sea water which flooded the Captains and our quarters, in fact, the whole ship on the road to 'Cape Horn'. *Position 33° South 31° West.*

Day 58 Saturday April 21st
We finish scraping the rust off the white paint on the poop and commence red leading it.

There is only a very slight wind blowing all day, which sends us along at only about two knots. There is no sign of the South East Trade Wind yet, although we should get it at any time now.

The weather is very fine and warm and during our free watch in the day we sit in the sunshine up on the fo'c'sle head. It is a beautiful evening and Alfred thinks it a good time to bring out his violin and he plays a few tunes while he sits on the poop. He certainly is an artist with the fiddle and the music was really worth listening to on such a beautiful night.

How that music made me think of home and England. I thought of Englands countryside in all her spring beauty.

Music makes peoples minds wander.
Position 31° South 28° West.

Day 59 Sunday April 22nd
We experience the best Sunday (as regards work) so far this trip. The wind blows steadily from one direction and consequently we have no braceing.

During our watch on deck in the afternoon I only have one hours work, which was spent at the wheel, and that was so easy it cannot be actually called work. The rest of the time I spend sitting on the hatch midships both reading and basking in the warm and brilliant sunshine.

George tries his hand at fishing but is not successful, although he had told us previously he was excellent at the job.
Position 28° South 26° West.

Day 60 Monday April 23rd

We commence changing our strong heavy Cape Horn sails for our lighter 'Tropical Rags' and we commence with our largest sail of all, the 'foresail' which on account of its enormous weight requires 'all hands'.

This job of changing sails takes place twice every voyage. Firstly when we get our South East Trade Wind and then we change back again to our heavy sails when we get to about 30 degrees North when by rights the North East Trade Wind leaves us and we experience strong North Atlantic winds. It is extremely heavy work, running up and down the mast all day long and usually in tropical heat and every man is dog tired at the end of the day.

We have now definitely sailed completely round the world, having once again found our outward route to Australia. On the outward trip we sail around the Cape of Good Hope and homeward we sail round Cape Horn. So, both on the outward trip from the Cape of Good Hope to Australia and likewise on the homeward from Australia to Cape Horn we 'Run an Eastern Down'.

The weather is again fine and very hot, so different to what we experienced on the road to Cape Horn.
Position 27° South 25° West.

Day 61 Tuesday April 24th

This morning I am ordered to carry the huge block used for hauling new sails aloft and lowering the Cape Horn sails down to the deck, up the fore mast to the 'Truck', (the very top of the mast) and I must then make it fast there. The block is a terrible weight and takes all my time to reach the top, how I managed to get over the 'futtocks' and 'cross trees' God only knows.

Having completed this my watch commence to change the fore upper to'gallant and we just manage to get the tropical rag fixed in its place as 8 bells are struck, meaning we are free watch until 1pm.

Changing sail

During our afternoon watch we change the fore upper topsail, fore lower topsail and the fore lower to'gallant. By 7pm when we were again free watch I was completely done, the heat had been terrific all afternoon and what with running up and down the mast, hauling on ropes and trudging round and round the capstan it had completly finished all of us.

Hauling on ropes completely finished all of us

I am afraid my weariness caused me to disobey an order from my Mate. He told me, although it was 6.30pm and nearly time to finish, to go up the fore rigging and overhaul all gaskets and buntlines. As all the sails on the fore mast had been changed during the day, naturally all buntlines and gaskets required overhauling. But, for one man to overhaul the lot, it would have taken close on an hour to finish, so I refuse to go aloft but after ten minutes heated argument I think it wiser to obey the order, especially as my Mate had always treated me throughout with great fairness.

Owing to the terrific heat during the day the crew had been very thirsty, consequently all the days ration of fresh water had been consumed by 8pm at night. I am at the wheel from 11pm to 12 midnight and during that period I suffer greatly from a bad thirst. I knew there was none up for'ard and as I was almost crying out for a drink, when I am relieved, I go quietly down to the pantry in the Captains quarters and had just swallowed one mugful down and about to swallow another, when who should step in but the 1st and 2nd Mates, The Chief Mate knocks the mug out of my hands, tells me to go up for'ard and at the same time gave me a hell of a kick which sent me sprawling headfirst along the deck. I deserved it, I suppose, if only I had asked the Mate to allow me a drink I should have got it, but now, without doubt, I will be in for a rough time from both of them.

There has been no wind all day, the ship has lain 'idly becalmed'. *Position 25° South 25° West.*

We finish changing sail

Day 62 Wednesday April 25th
We finish changing the sails during our morning watch, and what a relief. We commence scraping rust off the white paint on deck. I used to detest this job but except for the fact that your eyes get choked up with pieces of rust, give it to me any time to changing those sails.

At 3.15 pm our very long looked for South East Trade Wind arrives. What a difference it makes to our spirits. Whereas for the past few days we have all been grousing and looking thoroughly fed up with things in general, now every man looks happy, smiling and thoroughly content. *Position 23° South 26° West.*

Day 63 Thursday April 26th
Just before 8am this morning Jacques while up aloft sights another sailing ship far down on our lee side horizon. There is great excitment and all the boys, Captain and Mates rush up the mast to make sure whether the statement is correct. She's there safe enough but very faint. The Captain, however, brings his telescope out and discovers she is a three masted barque carrying 'royals' (which we dont carry). He says it must be the 'Penang' which left Australia a week before us. At 11am she is much clearer and if anything she appears to be slowly gaining on us. We can now pick her out to be a three masted barque without the aid of a telescope. By 1pm owing to the weather being hazy we have lost sight of her.

My watch is reduced to four men, namely Stowahse, Belgier, George and myself. Heim and Karlsson have become 'daymen', that is, they work all day from 6am to 4pm and have no watch to keep during the night. Their work consists chiefly of either sowing and patching sails (which have been torn coming round the Horn) working aloft in the rigging and splicing ropes and wires plus numerous other jobs which require immediate attention, also they are not required when bracing.

This taking out of some of the boys from the watches to become daymen is the usual custom aboard Finnish sailing ships when we reach the Trade Winds as there is never so much bracing and what there is, is not heavy work. By rights we should have 5 men left in the watch but Brincks (Dane) is again 'laid up'.

This reduction in the watches of course means double the work for the rest of us. It means double strength from each man when hauling on the ropes and instead of perhaps only having one wheel during one's watch at night (like the 7pm to 12 midnight watch) the boy who has the first wheel from 7pm to 8pm now has four solid hours of work and only one hour free consisting of two wheels, one hour 'look out' and one hour policeman. Remember, this is after having worked during the day too.

George who up to now has never taken the wheel, must now learn it so as to keep us out of the difficulty, at any rate a little. But when we are sailing 'By the Wind' which unluckily it nearly always is now, the 2nd Mate wont allow him at the wheel, as he cannot steer when it is so.
Position 21° South 26° West.

Day 64 Friday April 27th

Carried on scraping rust off the white paint on deck during our morning watch. We experience today our first real good rainfall since leaving Australia that we have been able to catch and store in the tanks. Although it rained often on the way to Cape Horn, owing to the heavy weather and dangerous water logged state of the deck, we were unable to catch any. So, every conceivable thing possible from barrels, buckets, tins down to the pots and even mugs are brought out on deck to keep on catching as much as we could. This was the afternoons work as long as it kept on raining, as we are in dire need of fresh water. Three hours later we had collected enough, all tanks were full, barrels and every conceivable bucket. So, although it was still raining hard we required no more and the rest was left to waste.

We notice two peculiar birds following us in the evening, their body was a whitish colour, they had fairly large sized wings and a very long neck but were not very strong fliers like albatross and stormy petrels but nobody is able to distinguish what they are.

We are becalmed all day.
Position 20° South 25° West.

Day 65 Saturday April 28th

From 6am to 8am we again scrape rust from the white paint on the deck prior to red leading and painting. It is my watch's turn this Saturday to wash down the deck, a job I always like.

During our watch on deck tonight from 7pm to 12 midnight we short handed company of only four men experienced two and a half hours continuous work 'wearing ship' and 'Going about'. The wind flatly refused to blow steadily from one direction and no sooner had we completed the task of 'Going about' from port to starboard and were coiling up ropes on their pins, when back went the wind to the other side again. This went on time after time, sometimes with perhaps a ten to fifteen minutes interval of steady blowing between, but we must carry on with this however annoying it may be because it is only by catching these unsteady puffs that we get through these regions at all. By right our South East Trade Wind should be blowing us steadily along but it somehow refuses to come. This terrific heat and our very short handed watch make matters considerably worse.

During the afternoon (although sharks were seen only yesterday) Mr Brown goes overboard for a swim having previously let a rope hang overboard, by which to climb up again, luckily for him there were no sharks about today.

Tonight on account of the terrific heat and large numbers of bunk bugs at present being experienced by all members up for'ard (these bugs thrive in warm weather and delight in sucking human blood) we are forced to sleep out on deck, where things are at any rate a little more comfortable.

Just before 'turning in' and during my free watch tonight, I watch the most wonderful sunset I have ever seen before in all my life. As the sun sank slowly down beyond the horizon the sky turned to all colours of the rainbow, while just as the very last tip of the sun was sinking below, a beautiful, olive full moon came up in the east, the 'Southern Cross' twinkled down upon us, while the sky had now changed to one solid mass of a glorious purple shade. A most heavenly sight and as Bob remarked to me, no artist could possibly paint such a picture. I am sure a very true remark.

We are becalmed for the second day in succession. The atmosphere on a sailing ship becalmed, especially at night, is one of peace and loveliness, something that will live in my memory for always.

Tonight when I am at the wheel from 12 midnight to 1pm I see and feel the loveliness of our ship becalmed in this wide expanse of water. I simply stand there, with my wheel hard over to port, all the sails are back and lying listless, the Mate is sitting on the starboard lee rail staring out to sea. Occasionally I catch a glimpse of the dark form of the man at look-out up for'ard on the fo'c'sle head leaning over the rail. The sea is as calm as a duck pond and you cannot even hear a ripple, while up above the moon and stars shine down upon us from a wonderfully clear night sky.

We have no engine to disturb this unbounded peace, and we remain a happy little crowd of 23 men living entirely alone in this peaceful, imaginable world of our own.
Position 21° South 26° West.

Day 66 Sunday April 29th
About 9am this morning a puff of wind blows up but while we are in the middle of 'wearing ship' it leaves us. During our free watch in the afternoon George and I discover a large shark swimming about directly under the bowsprit, so we hurriedly fetch a large chain and hook (used for this purpose) from underneath the fo'c'sle head, get a large piece of salt pork from Cookie, attach it to the end of the hook, lower it over the side into the water and wait patiently for the result.

Half an hour later he made a grab (after smelling it repeatedly) and we hauled him up onto the deck. What a weight he was and didn't he half fight. It took 10 men all their time to haul him onboard. They're tough fellows these sharks. It took us close on an hour to kill him, although he had been hit on the head with a capstan bar at least ten times. Even when the boys were cutting him up to get souveniers of his fins and back-bone, he was still living and occasionally gave a kick.

We are 'becalmed' for the third successive day. Another very fine sunset this evening but not a patch on that seen last night.
Position 20° South 27° West.

Day 67 Monday April 30th
During my free watch from 8am to 1pm I commence making a pair of sandals out of sail, having previously made a pair of work trousers out of sail too. One or two of the boys including Brownie (passenger) are making models of the "Winterhude".

During our afternoon watch on deck, we carry on scraping rust off the white paint on deck. In the evening just before dark, as is the rule after a very hot day, we swill down the whole deck with salt water.

At tea time today the Steward brings each fo'c'sle a large glass jar of Lime Juice. We always receive this when we are in tropical weather. In fact we receive it when we get our South East Trade Wind and leave it off again when our North East Trade Wind leaves us in about roughly 30 degrees North of the Equator. In the olden days the English sailing ships were then nicknamed the 'lime juicers' on account of this lime juice which we receive in the hot climates.

Becalmed for the 4th successive day.
Position 19° South 27° West.

Day 68 Tuesday May 1st

Just after 4am this morning we again get back our South East Trade Wind and this time it actually is blowing a shade stronger. Let's hope to God it remains now.

During my free watch I carry on making my sandals, while during our working watch we again scrape rust on deck.

I have a row with Cookie this morning. During the outward trip and also during the homeward trip up to now, I have always kept a mug full of coffee left over from the afternoon coffee and which I always put on the Galley top to warm it up at tea time, as I did not like tea without milk. I warmed it up again as usual this evening, only when I began drinking it, it tasted to me full of pepper. I go straight back to the Galley and ask the cook whether he has applied any pepper to my mug of coffee, to which he says, 'Yes.' I ask him the reason for this low down trick and he replies that my mug takes up too much room and in future I must not do it. I refuse to obey this stupid rule of his, much to his annoyance, and for the rest of the trip I shall warm it up and stand in the Galley until it is hot enough to take away again.
Position 16° South 27° West.

Day 69 Wednesday May 2nd

During the night the wind has increased and this morning we are cutting through the water at a steady 6 knots. At 7am (6 bells) a squall suddenly springs up tearing to shreds our main lower topsail. My watch 'unbend' what is left of it while the port watch who relieve us at 8am 'bend' a new and stronger sail in its place. Just as this was completed the 'outer jib' (out on the bowsprit) blows out too. These tropical rags or sails are only light and in most cases old and very worn. They are not meant for squalls and strong winds. These squalls are very rare up in these Trade Wind regions but when they do 'pop up', they are usually very severe.

We carry on scraping rust off the white paint on deck.
Position 14° South 27.14° West.

Day 70 Thursday May 3rd

During our working watch this morning we carry on scraping rust off the white paint on deck and by 1pm (free watch) we have reached the fo'c'sle head, having finished the length of the deck. We are well ahead of the port watch who up to now have only reached midships. There is always great competition between the two watches in any work, as to which watch works the hardest and makes the best job of it too.

During free watch in the afternoon, I sit up on the fo'c'sle head with donkeyman (a Finn and one of the finest fellows aboard) and talk about Finland and her fine fleet of sailing ships.

George today takes his first wheel entirely alone and as the Mate put it to me, 'That boy he steers plenty good.'
Position 11° South 27.9° West.

Day 71 Friday May 4th

We experience heavy rain all morning and owing to the large amount of clothes washed since our last downfall, it is once again urgently needed, so both watches are kept busy collecting it.

At 11am the mizzen staysail blows in two and we have to take it down and 'bend' a fresh one. The sailmaker is far from satisfied with these three sails which have lately been torn, as he has already enough work on hand repairing those damaged round Cape Horn.

We experience heavy tropical rain all day and both watches get wet through collecting it, but up here in these warm regions nobody cares about it.

The Southern Cross is still clearly seen at night but each day brings it further down onto the Southern horizon.
Position 8° South 27° West.

Day 72 Saturday May 5th

We commence scraping rust off the white paint up on the fo'c'sle head. Thank goodness this scraping job will soon be finished and we shall then start painting.

Jacques (Belgian) is caught sleeping by the first Mate, while supposed to be look-out and receives a good hiding.

These so called 'bunk bugs' are annoying everybody, consequently most of us overhaul the bunks. I paraffin mine all over even the matress but it appears to do no good whatever and they still thrive.

This evening our S.E. Trade Wind leaves us again having to go 'by the wind' owing to a head wind, while later on this dies away completely so once again we are becalmed.

There is a considerable amount of lightning tonight but no thunder.
Position 6° South 27° West.

Day 73 Sunday May 6th
From 4.35am till 8am my watch work without almost a stop both bracing and 'wearing ship', the wind refuses to blow from one quarter.

I have yet another fight, this time with Belgier, a watch mate. I was taking my 'trick' at the wheel when it cropped up. It is the custom on Finnish sailing ships that if the Mate orders a man to perform a job, he must completely finish this before (as was the case here) he comes to take the wheel. Belgier always relieved me at the wheel, and five minutes before he was to come and relieve me, the Mate ordered him to overhaul a buntline on the main upper to'gallant. He had got half way up the mast, when I sounded 6 bells (3pm) and immediately he begins descending the mast again, not even having attempted to overhaul the buntline.

When he comes up on to the poop to relieve me, I tell him to go and finish the job before he thinks of coming here, as I refuse to do it for him. Belgier always disliked going up the mast and naturally refuses and grabs the wheel, but I refuse to budge an inch. He then starts pushing me away and being thoroughly roused and annoyed, I leave go of the wheel (a terrible thing to do on my part) and hit him right and left. The 2nd Mate had evidently heard the row and comes flying up onto the poop and without asking us men a question, hits both of us as hard as he possibly could (and we deserved it too) but I am afraid Mr Belgier gets the worst of it, for evidently the Mate had noticed that the buntline had not been overhauled and orders him up aloft again, telling me to take hold of the wheel and as he departs yells at both of us that we shall hear more about this later.

George and I later on in the afternoon, try to catch some 'bonito' fish which had been swimming all day underneath the bowsprit, but they are much too cunning and refuse to take the bait.

George, Bob, Brownie and myself sing Scotish songs up on the fo'c'sle head in the evening.

We are still becalmed.
Position 5.18° South 27.29° West.

Day 74 Monday May 7th

I am 'dishwasher' again this week, the third time this voyage. One's turn lasts a week starting Monday morning and finishing Sunday night. I have never seen such a way of washing dishes before in all my life. Both on my last ship, the "Olivebank", and my present one, the "Winterhude", we used hot salt water for washing the dishes and knives, this caused the knife blades to rust, while the spoons and forks went a peculiar yellow colour. Then, for washing and drying we used any old shirt or rag sometimes even a piece of burlap or sacking. I think they could do with us in the Savoy Hotel London.

Jacques is again caught sleeping while supposed to be keeping 'look-out', this time the 1st Mate does not let him off so lightly and he looks a picture of unhappiness what with a large black eye and a face swollen almost out of recognition.

George, who has had to sleep on a borrowed hammock all the trip under the fo'c'sle head and who experienced 'hell' round Cape Horn, through always being wet through and so unable to sleep, now makes one of his own.

Tonight I sleep on a borrowed hammock from Brincks (Dane) up on the fo'c'sle head and slept like a log.
Position 4.33° South 27.39° West.

Day 75 Tuesday May 8th

Brownie, George and myself have a great discussion about Communism and its many evils and here I should like to point out that we have not a single Communist member amongst our crew of 23 boys.

We finish scraping the white paint up on the fo'c'sle head and thank goodness. We now commence painting up on the poop. My Mate told me this morning that before we reach Falmouth the whole ship must be painted except for the masts and yards, which we painted on the trip out to Australia, and even portions of these must be painted again.

Tonight I discover a fresh place for sleeping, I refuse to go back to my bunk on account of those detestable bugs which thrive there and suck you almost dry. I take my matress into the small carpenters shop midships, place it on the floor and sleep solidly for five hours it was a little hard lying there and occasionally, owing to the narrow space between each wall, I struck my head against the wall as she gave a lurch, but I was content with this new 'boudoir'.

We are becalmed for the 4th day running.
Position 3.55° South 27.41° West.

Day 76 Wednesday May 9th

During my working watch I scrape and paint the staircase rail leading up to the poop and having completed this I commence painting the white painted section up on the poop.

George is the next to lie up with boils. I somehow, thank God, don't suffer from these agonising things. This reduces our watch to only three men, Stowahse, myself and Belgier but Brincks (Dane) expects to be fit again tomorrow.

About 10am this morning a slight wind blows up from the South West and this blows us along at about 3 knots, it is not very fast but at any rate we are moving. Our South East Trade seems to have left us definitely now, as we are too near the Equator to get it back.

During my free watch in the afternoon, I again wash some of my clothes. This afternoon I see my first shoal of 'flying fish' so far this trip while tonight five porpoises follow us.

The weather all day was very hot with occasional showers.
Position 2.20° South 27.44° West.

Day 77 Thursday May 10th

This morning we finish giving the poop its first coating of white paint and commence painting on deck. During the afternoon we experince a great amount of bracing and during this we get wet through in Tropical rain which beats down without ceasing throughout the whole afternoon.

Bob, Brownie, Schmidt, Keller and myself play cards up in the fo'c'sle at night, but I am afraid not for money as there is none to be had, simply for matches which are very scarce indeed.
Position 1.43° South 27° West.

My three best pals Bill, Bob and Schmidt

110

Day 78 Friday May 11th

We are again painting on deck. George and myself make another attempt to catch some 'bonito' which are swimming round the ship but as before we are again, unsuccessful.

In the evening we all have a great sing song up in the port fo'c'sle and George who has now recovered from his boils plays Stowahse's Accordian.

We are again becalmed. Give me any day the stormy Cape Horn winds and gales even with all its misery, to these days of stagnant calms. Everybody becomes bad tempered. The only possible means of ever getting out of these dreadful calm belts or regions is by squaring the yards and sails to every puff of wind that blows however faint it is. This means a considerable amount of bracing but it is worth it in the end.
Position 1.30° South 27° West.

Day 79 Saturday May 12th

Just before 8am this morning we sight our first steamer since leaving Australia (our 79th day) but she is too far away out on our starboard horizon to ask her to report us to Lloyds. Until today it has just seemed as though we have been living in a little world just of our own, we have seen no papers, no ships, no land and no people except ourselves, yet we are a happy carefree crowd. We have had fights etc. but those are bound to crop up when men get hemmed in on a sailing ship for 79 days without seeing anything of civilisation except for the ship and the other members of the crew.

At 2pm this afternoon, while our watch are busy washing the deck, the 2nd Mate sights another steamer directly ahead of us but heading westwards. Evidently she has seen us for at 2.15pm she had altered course and was now making straight for us. By 3pm (6 bells) she had come very close and we discover she is a large two funnelled liner. When she approaches a little nearer, we notice she has her national flag flying and immediately the 2nd Mate and Karlson (Swede) rush off aft onto the poop to send the Finnish flag (Blue cross on a White background) up the mizzen mast.

She is the Spanish liner "Gabbo-Santo-Tame" bound for Montevideo from Spain and she comes so close that you could chuck a bucket over onto her deck. Her decks were thronged with excited passengers and heaps of pretty girls which we all took special notice of. When she is alongside our port side, she slows down to a 'dead slow' pace and sends aloft some code flags, asking us where we have come from and where we are bound for. We reply in the same manner and she then sends aloft another section wishing us 'Bon Voyage' and carries on her way and as she leaves dips her countries flag three times out of respect, to which we reply.

We are all at a loss why our Captain did not ask her to report us to Lloyds as in three or four days time she would be in Montevideo. We can still pick her out at 5pm far away on the horizon.

A violent squall accompanied by hail springs up unawares at 5.15pm and blows to shreds our outer and inner jibs. We were the watch on deck at the time and since one man was at the wheel there remained only three of us to haul them both in and make them fast. Owing to the very strong wind we experienced extreme difficulty in hauling them in. The torn portions of the sails were flapping about in all diretions while to make matters worse the hanks of the inner jib flatly refused to slide down the stay and we almost hauled our guts out trying to get them to slide down the stay and thus bring the sail down with them. In the end Stowahse and myself went out onto the bowsprit, climbed the stay (at great personal risk as the torn portions of the sail were flapping about doing their utmost to knock us over into the surging sea) and while Belgier and the 2nd Mate, who had now come to assist us, hauled on the downhaul, Stowahse and I tugged at the hanks and in the end after three quarters of an hour's hard fight we got the sail down far enough so that we were able to make it fast.

White wings

This evening I once again have a row with my Mate. At the time I was up for'ard in the starboard fo'c'sle washing up the dishes etc. Evidently he had blown 'two whistles' which summond our watch on to the deck for bracing. I failed to hear this and a few minutes later he appears in the fo'c'sle hauls me out on deck and wants to know what in the devil I think I am doing not being on deck when he has blown 'two whistles'. I try to explain the reason why; but it was utterly useless, as he refuses to listen and simply pushes me along the deck, telling me to help the rest of my watch with the braces. I am afraid I have let myself in for all this through pinching that water from the pantry the other night. I can see clearly he thoroughly dislikes me at present, all the same I still like him immensely and even now I think he is too lenient with all of my watch.

While I am look-out tonight from 9pm till 10pm George, who is now 'Policeman' and supposed to remain on deck, comes up to me on the fo'c'sle head and begs me (as he says he feels so tired) to listen out for any 'two whistles' from the Mate and also to wake him up when I hear the helmsman ring 4 bells (10pm). I tell him it is alright to me, so he dosses down beside me up on the fo'c'sle head, while I sit on the port side pin rail. About 15 minutes later, the Mate suddenly appears, orders me to stand up and not sit down and go to sleep when 'look-out'. He asks me where George is and I reply that I have no idea. Just as he is returning to the deck again, he stumbles over George's leg. George waking up suddenly from his sleep, yells out "What is up Geoff." and before he knows what is the matter, the Mate grabs him by the shoulder, punches him three or four times in the chest and says "I see you go sleep when 'Policeman', alright I see about you later, go down on deck and remain there". Like a fool I start arguing with him and ask him whether he has never slept in the Tropics during watches? But it only makes matters considerably worse, for he now orders me to 'dishwash' for my starboard watch until we reach Falmouth. I tell him point blank, that I will refuse to do this.

I discover later the reason for the Mate coming up so quietly to the fo'c'sle head while I was look-out and George was sleeping. Brincks (Dane) and in our watch, who was a great pal of the Mate, had evidently heard George asking me to listen out for him while he slept and when the Danish boy went to the wheel he informed the Mate.

I let Brincks know what I thought of him later on and offered him a fight, but he being considerably stronger than I was, I am afraid I came off the worst. Just as I am getting a thorough good 'socking' from him, Bob, who had been woken up on account of the noise (during his free watch), steps into the fo'c'sle and lands Brincks a heavy blow on the jaw, which sent him reeling against the table. He certainly deserved it, as he was far too keen on sneaking to the Mate about the rest of us and he certainly received his punishment from the best person, as everybody is afraid of Bob and I don't think there is a man on board dare fight him.

But once again things blow over and Brincks and I are the best of pals again. One cannot help these rows and it does one good to have fights occasionally. Although I have had scores of fights with different members of the crew there is not one man out of the twentythree I dislike. They are all fine fellows and the best of shipmates.

We 'Pass the Line' at 8.15pm tonight 79 days out from Australia and we celebrate by having a glass of rum each, sent for'ard by the Captain.
Position (at 12 Midday) Half a degree North 27° West.

Day 80 Sunday May 13th
There is another fight early this morning, this time between two Germans in the port watch, Schmidt and Boercher.

During our watch on deck from 8am till 1pm, although a Sunday, we work continuously. Not only do I have the breakfast dishwashing to do, which usually takes me about an hour, but I have two wheels (one hour each) while the rest of the watch is spent bracing and bracing and bracing. We square the yards for every cats paw of wind. We are now in that belt of calms and uncertain winds known as the Doldrums. I never mind a stagnant calm when the ship simply lies idle and there is no bracing required, but these regions called the Doldrums where, for one minute you lie becalmed the next minute there is a puff blowing up from dead aft and we square the yards, but no sooner have we done this when the wind blows up perhaps a little stronger from another quarter, again a few minutes later, back to another quarter then calm for perhaps ten minutes or so. This means continual bracing and in this Tropical heat too, while the persperation simply runs off your body.

Frachnect caught a small shark single-handed before breakfast, he seems very proud, and asks me to snap him standing beside his prisoner. We see one or two Dolphins today and of course scores of our old friends the 'flying fish'.

George, who like all Australians I have come across is exceptionally keen on puzzles, gives Chips and myself one or two to work out, but I am afraid they were too hard for either of us.

It is a glorious day and very hot. This afternoon we all sit out on deck listening to Cookies gramophone which he had very kindly lent us for the afternoon. The deck resembled a laundry, it was one mess of clothes which we had washed this morning , while also we bring bunk matresses, shore suits etc. out on the life-line to air, certainly a good opportunity in this warm sun.

At 3pm Bill Thompson (Dane) sights a steamer aft but she passes us too far away to make out what kind of a steamer she is. Another beautiful sunset.
Position Half a degree North 27° West.

Day 81 Monday May 14th
Early this morning our watch 'wear ship', as the wind was now blowing from the starboard quarter. We sight another steamer at 6am this morning. There is always

intense excitment on board when a steamer is sighted, but this is only natural after being cut off from civilisation for 81 days on end. We seem to be 'dead on' the shipping routes at present, for at 12am another steamer passes fairly close bound South.

During our afternoon watch we carry on painting on deck. While I am at the wheel from 3pm to 4pm, the Captain sights a large steamer heading straight for us from dead aft. As she draws nearer there is great excitment up on the poop and the code pennants and the Finnish flag are hurredly brought out on deck in readiness. At 3.45pm she is alongside, and she passes so close to our stern that for a minute there was great consternation aboard our ship as to whether she would cut our log in two. She passes us on our lee side and we discover she is the Dutch liner "Zeelandia" bound for Amsterdam. Similar to the Spanish liner that passed us on Saturday, her decks were a mass of cheering people. She is so close that our Captain instead of sending the pennants aloft, asks the liners Captain, through a megaphone, the correct position, as he fears our Chronometer is a little out. He got a reply and as he thought we are a little out, which means us altering course a shade. As she leaves us she dips the Dutch flag in respect and we dip ours too.

I forgot to mention that when I turned out after breakfast this morning, I started dishwashing according to my Mate's orders, as a punishment for the other night's affair. As I had not refused to obey his order, he thought he would let me off, for I had hardly begun, when he came up to me and said, 'Alright Geoff, you dishwash no more, I tink you plenty good, so I give you another chance.' I thank him most humbly and apologise for the other night. We both shake hands and it is over. A great fellow this Mate, in fact too kind. A finer Captain and Mates no one could wish to work under on a sailing ship. They make life worth while here. *Position 1° North 29.32° West.*

Day 82 Tuesday May 15th
We steer now slightly to the North West, so that we shall pick up the North West Trade Wind later on. Should we sail too near the African coast, we shall meet "Celius".

During our working watch we are again painting on deck but I am ordered up the main mast to paint the portions of the yard where the paint has rusted away. I am told to start on the top yard (the upper to'gallant). It is no easy task carrying a large tin of paint up aloft as you have only one arm by which to hold on to the ratlines as you proceed up. The hardest parts of all are when you reach the 'futtocks' and later on the 'cross trees', in negotiating the former you climb outwards instead of upwards and so hang out over the deck.

Sharks are seen swimming below our stern, so one of two of the boys including myself go up onto the poop armed with the famous chain, hook and a piece of salt pork. Owing to the noise we made the Captain found it impossible to sleep in his cabin below and orders us to go down on deck. Strictly speaking the poop is out of bounds for everybody except the Captain, Mates, Cook, Steward, helmsman and of course ourselves when we are working up there.
Position 1.5° North 29.39° West.

View of the poop

Day 83 Wednesday May 16th
Stowahse and George caught a large shark before breakfast this morning. We have often pulled George's leg over the fact that he never caught anything, although he professed he was excellent at the job. Anyhow now he has one back on us all, because it certainly was a tremendous size, about fifteen feet long. He is very proud and asks us to snap him beside it.

My bunk is still infested with 'bunk bugs' nothing seems to prevent them from thriving and I suppose we shall not be able to definitely get rid of them until we paint the bunks and fo'c'sles later on before we reach Falmouth. They have even got into my case and made their nests and laid fresh eggs in my shore clothes.

This afternoon I paint the whole of the starboard pin rail with brown paint.
Position 1.20° North 29.41° West.

Day 84 Thursday May 17th

I commence giving the white paint its second coating up on the poop. For the past three days we have only had a very slight wind and consequently we have just been crawling along at almost snails pace, but I suppose we cannot grumble, we are moving if only very slowly and lucky to be doing even this, for here we are in the famous Doldrums.

This evening Heim, Schmidt, Brownie and myself perform some gymnastic tricks on the life-line. Some of the stunts the two Germans did really were marvelous. I tried them time after time but failed. The strength these Germans have in their arms, really is wonderful. These gymnastic stunts on the life-line have been a great pastime throughout the trip, there is no doubt about it this keeps you fit and brings your arm muscles up considerably.

The Southern Cross can still be picked up but is getting very low down on the Southern horizon. A large number of swallows follow us all day evidently making for the warm summer climates up North. We throw scraps of bread over to them and they seemed to enjoy them and in time became quite friendly. *Position 1.49° North 29.44° West.*

Day 85 Friday May 18th

We are becalmed again all today and our sails lie back against the masts, completely lifeless, and give me the impression they are tired out with the voyage and looking for winds to spread them out and make them full of life. Brownie (passenger) who has worked in the port watch from Australia until the last week and who is now having a well earned rest, comes up for'ard and sits with us during our free watch this morning.

Just after 10am Brincks sights a steamer on our port side and making straight for us. At 11am she passes our stern and we read quite plainly this time the "S.S. Peterton" of London. She is only a small cargo boat of about five or six thousand tons. But what a thrill it gave me to see the British flag and a British ship after so long. Our Captain again asks, by means of pennants, for the correct position and the Britisher replies. As she leaves us she dips her ensign three times and wishes us 'Bon Voyage'.

Frachnect caught a young shark this afternoon and it took close on an hour to kill it. Two more steamers lights are seen at midnight. *Position 2° North 29.50° West.*

Day 86 Saturday May 19th

It rains hard all morning and so we commence that detestable job again of scraping rust down in the sail locker. A steamer is sighted at 9.30am and the 2nd

Mate tells me we should see 'plenty' more now as we are in the tracks of about four different shipping routes.

Although it is raining, we are much more cheerful today as we have quite a strong breeze blowing which sends us along at about 5 knots.

Bob very nearly has a fight with Alfred (1st Mate) this morning. Bob was free watch at the time and was attempting to catch a shark just for'ard of midships. Up comes Alfred and without saying a word snatches the chain and hook from Bob's hands and chucks it overboard. Bob asks him the reason for this very unfair act and Alfred replies that all the freshly painted deck is getting dirty and spoilt with this 'Damn shark fishing' as he put it, and it must now cease. Bob plays the very devil with him and asks him who he thinks he is but Alfred is afraid and quickly retreats to the safety of his cabin.

Tonight during my free watch I read again one of Edgar Wallace's thrillers the 'Man from the Carlton' given to the "Winterhude" boys by the "Missions to Seamen" *[Editor's Note - now the 'Missions to Seafarers']* when she was in Awkland New Zealand last year.

The weather is hot all day but raining.
Position 2.25° North 29.36° West.

Day 87 Sunday May 20th
At 4am we get our North East Trade wind and the Captain says it has arrived much earlier than he thought it would. We all pray it will blow us steadily along and not leave us like the South East Trade did below the 'line'. It blows us along at a steady 5 knots and what a joy it is to see those sails full of life again.

George, Brownie, Bob and myself sit up on the fo'c'sle head all morning experimenting on different knots. How we all like a Trade wind as Sundays can always be called Sundays then. There is no need for any bracing and we only have one hours work and that cannot really be called work. By this I mean one trick at the wheel but it is so easy to steer that all you need do is to stand there and perhaps just occasionally take a glance down at the Compass, to see you are on the right course, which nine times out of ten you are.

George sees his very first 'flying fish' this afternoon.

After tea the two fo'c'sles looked exactly like a second hand clothes dealers shop. Most of the boys were busy swapping or exchanging hats, ties, shoes, suits, shirts, socks in fact anything, for either money or some other article of clothing that another member may wish to exchange. Belgier was a great hand at this.

118

He was about the richest member on hand and consequently he had heaps of good brand new shore clothes, which he was showing, but he would only take money or photo snaps taken on the "Winterhude" in exchange. I managed to get a brand new linen shirt from him for only six small Number 2 Brownie photo snaps. I considered that a very good bargain. He tried every conceivable way to make me exchange my camera for a suit but I flatly refused to do so.
Position 3.1° North 31° West.

Day 88 Monday May 21st
I wash my shore shirts, collars and ties this morning. A 'flying fish' comes aboard and I give it to Napolean (the cat) but it was a long time before he realized it was a fish.

Tired Tim (2nd cat) and my little pal, dies today. He had been ill for the past three days and so Bill and I had taken it in turns looking after him and tucking him up in our bunks when we went to sleep etc. He was a pitiful sight and could not walk an inch. I suggested putting him away but Bill would not hear of it, so in the end I am afraid he died rather an agonising death.

I still pick out the 'Souhtern Cross' at nights, although I had heard it could not be seen North of the Equator and yet here we are in 3 degrees North.

View from the bowsprit

This evening I go and sit out on the 'sharks fin' right out at the end of the bowsprit. This is my favourite spot on all the ship. Here I feel entirely alone and everything is so peaceful. As I sit there I look back at the ship, how really beautiful she looks in the moonlight. Her freshly painted deck shows up so clean and her sails gleaming bright spread themselves out, taking in the fair wind. Then I watch her bow cutting through the clear water. Everything seems so peaceful, no noise of an engine, just the faint sound of the water as she cuts her way through. She just seems human to me. I

love her immensely and feel proud to think I am one of her 'workers'. It is truly remarkable how a fair wind alters peoples tempers. Up till yesterday people were glum, short tempered and always grousing. Today everybody seems happy. For instance while I am at the wheel tonight the Mate strolls up and down the weather side of the poop singing sea shanties, occasionally stopping to ask me if I know the shanty he is singing, and as I leave the wheel he says 'Soon Geoff we reach Falmouth.' but I wonder.
Position 4.31° North 32° West.

Day 89 Tuesday May 22nd
The Mate caught Stowahse asleep on his bunk this morning, when he should have been the 'Policeman' on deck. He plays hell with the young German and for a punishment we all suffered, for in future all the watch must remain aft on deck underneath the break of the poop during our night watch on deck. Stowahse is thoroughly disliked by the rest of his watch, but the poor fellow, we all do it including myself only he just happens to be the unlucky one.

I go to the Galley at tea time to enquire of the Cook why such a small portion of grub tonight and tell him that three men out of our watch of seven have had nothing. He says we are very short of food on the ship and we can have no more. I tell him we cannot damned well starve and that we must have some more or else our watch will all go aft to the Captain. This brings him to his senses and he goes aft to fetch some more but while he is away, I made myself six large pieces of toast, which I distributed later to the rest of my watch. It was lucky I did this as the amount he brought us up was not sufficient to fill a babies mouth. I flatly refuse to starve for anybody however short of food we are. If I had not received some more I should have gone aft to the pantry and pinched it myself.

During the day we are again busy painting on deck.
Position 5.33° North 34° West.

Day 90 Wednesday May 23rd
We commence painting up on the fo'c'sle head today having given the white paint on deck its first coating. George is laid up again this time with a deep abcess on his chest.

Food is getting short and things are not looking too cheerful. We are completely out of potatoes, having to eat tinned Finnish potatoes which taste like nothing on earth but which are eaten. However, we seem to eat anything on board while at sea but we cannot starve and must eat to be able to work.

120

During my free watch I sit out on my favourite place the sharks fin and read my book. There is still one small swallow following us, the rest left us over a week ago but this little fellow looks booked for England.

From midday yesterday to midday today we have covered 134 miles which is not bad.
Position 7.40° North 35.35° West.

Day 91 Thursday May 24th
We are again painting down in the sail locker, a job we all like as we are all out of the Mate's sight and can now and again have a few minutes rest sitting down on the sails.

We average roughly 7 knots throughout the day. Belgier falls on deck and twists his ankle, which necessitates him going to his bunk for the rest of the day. This continual laying up of men is causing our already too short handed watch a considerable amount of extra work, which we few who remain thoroughly resent.

Position 9.45° North 36.50° West.

Day 92 Friday May 25th
My watch (starboard) is now reduced to three men but our Mate helps us along with all heavy work, such as bracing etc.

I go up to the main to'gallant yard to scrape and paint a few rusty spots and on coming down on deck for free watch, I receive a good 'talking' from the Chief Mate for the large amount of paint I have let drop down onto the deck.
Position 11.30° North 38° West.

Day 93 Saturday May 26th
Belgier turns out for work again this morning but is caught by the Mate during the working watch eating bread up in the starboard fo'c'sle, whereupon he is ordered up both the fore and main masts to overhaul all buntlines. This Belgian lad is the worst helmsman we have on board and in fact he cannot steer as well as George who has only just been allowed this privilege. Even in the Trade Winds, where all one has to do is to stand there and hold the wheel, he is unable to hold the given course. He had not been above ten minutes at the wheel this morning before the Mate was shouting out for another man to take his place, on account of his bad steering, as he leaves the wheel the Mate tells him that he might just as well go to his bunk and sleep.

Brownie today cuts my hair and except for a few hairs he pulled out in his efforts, he made an excellent job of it.

George, Stowahse and myself spend two hours this morning carrying coal to the Galley, a job we all hate.

Just before 8 bells (4pm) this afternoon the fore lower to'gallant splits just below the yard on the starboard side, consequently the sailmaker and Karlson spend the rest of their free Saturday afternoon repairing it, the sail having of course been clewed up previously to allow them to reach the tear. As usual these Scandinavians carry on, although by rights free, without a murmer or even a sign of a dull face.
Position 14° North 39° West.

Day 94 Sunday May 27

I have a row with one of my friends Bill Thompsen (Dane) at 2am this morning. During my watch on deck from 7pm until midnight, we had been 'wearing ship' and bracing almost incessantly and this naturally made us very tired, and we were all very thankful when free watch came at midnight. Two hours later we were roused up from our free watch by Thompsen (who was then Policeman in the port watch), in order to help his watch 'wear ship'. Being very tired and feeling thoroughly annoyed at being roused up during free watch, I flatly refuse to budge out of my bunk, whereupon Thompsen hauled me out and punched me a hard blow on my face. This 'wearing ship' took us a good half hour so that by the time we got into our bunks and had fallen asleep again it was 3am and at 3.45am (one bell), struck to raise the watch, we were roused up again for our next 'watch on deck'.

Owing to the shortage of hands in my watch I take two wheels this morning and as is the case on Sundays, we experience a considerable amount of bracing etc. and this is supposed to be the day of rest.
Position 16.14° North 40° West.

Day 95 Monday May 28th

Owing to the fact that we are sailing along and steering 'Full and By' (Full and By is usually the case in the N.E. Trade Winds homeward bound) we are consequently veering much too far West and this 'Westing' is bound to make the passage to Falmouth a lot longer.

During our watch on deck we again paint. If any of us at any time cannot get a job at sea, at any rate we should be able to obtain a job as a painter after all the experience we have had.

Brincks (Dane) and one of the finest seamen in our watch, is again confined to his bunk, this time with a badly poisoned finger.

We observe large shoals of 'flying fish' today but soon we shall be saying Good-Bye to these little Tropical fish.

Tonight during our free watch the sailmaker and myself chat for about an hour on deck and we can both still pick out a portion of the 'Southern Cross' and yet we are sailing 17 degrees North of the Equator.
Position 17° North.

Day 96 Tuesday May 29th

Painting again during working watch this morning. This time we commence applying the second and last coating to all the white paint. Owing to our very short handed watch I again take two 'tricks' at the wheel, whereas in normal times and with a full watch, I should have only one - if that - but this hour at the wheel I always look forward to, it comes as a great respite especially when we are at that terrible job of chipping rust. Belgier is again sent down from the wheel, what a useless lad he is.

Brincks appears again when we turn out tonight but is not able to take his turn at the wheel, so instead he takes three look-outs while one of us takes his wheel.

Where on earth has our N.E. Trade Wind disappeared to now? Throughout the day we only have a catspaw blowing.
Position 18.27° North 41° West.

Day 97 Wednesday May 30th

This morning George receives a sound 'ticking off' from the whole of my watch. Since he commenced his week of dishwashing on Monday morning, his washing and cleaning of the mugs, dishes, spoons, forks etc has been far from satisfactory. He complains he does not receive enough time in which to wash them but that is an old complaint. Sailing ship life may be rough and ready and we may be looked upon by landlubbers as a gang of tough guys but at any rate we do like clean things, clean fo'c'sles, clean bunks, clean ship etc.

This afternoon I commence painting the fresh water tanks which are situated under the break of the poop. Everything must be painted by the time we reach Falmouth and as Alfred (Chief Mate) put it plainly to us the other day, she must sail into Falmouth in yacht like appearance.

We still pick out the 'Southern Cross' but the two pointers (which are supposed to point directly to the South Pole) have fallen beyond the Southern horizon. *Position 19.43° North 42° West.*

Day 98 Thursday May 31st

As most of the white painting is now completed, we commence painting all odd things such as anchors etc. and I am detailed to paint the spare anchor which is lying up for'ard not far from the fo'c'sle head.

This afternoon I have three hours at the wheel without a break, it may have been a little leg aching standing there all that time, but all the same I enjoyed myself immensely, as all I had to do was stand there and lean against the wheel, just occasionally giving her a turn or two, while the rest of the time I spent looking out to sea, watching the sailmakers sewing their sails and now and again admiring the beauty of our sails as they filled out with the occasional puffs of wind and lastly, I had to keep a watchful eye on both the Mate and the Compass. We sight another steamer apparently making for the West Indies.

The donkeyman who is totally blind in one eye through getting a piece of rust in the ball of his eye while serving on the three master "Penang" has, for the past few days, been gradually losing the sight of his good eye, probably through excessive strain and he fears he may go blind. He is unable to work and is only just able to find his way along the deck.

Bob, who is 'Policeman' from 11pm to 12pm tonight and who should have roused up my watch (free watch) ready to come out on deck at midnight for mustering aft, fails to do so, as he has fallen asleep on one of the hatch tops. At 12 midnight as is always the custom the helmsman sounded 8 bells and Bob should have replied by striking eight bells up for'ard on the fo'c'sle head; but he is sound asleep, so also all my watch and the rest of the port watch and consequently nobody appears for the muster aft.

Alfred (Chief Mate) comes tearing up for'ard like a mad bull to discover what is the reason for all this and catches Bob sound asleep. Bob is woken up by a good clout on the jaw but Alfred, for the time, says nothing. But when we are all mustered aft, Alfred commences to yell at Bob and calls him a filthy name which Bob thoroughly resents and, being the type of fellow who most others listen to, asks the Chief Mate what he means by calling him such a fithy name and also demands from him whether he has never slept during watch on deck. Alfred again calls him this fithy name and Bob roused up to a pitch of great excitement yells out to Alfred to come down on deck and have it out, to the great amusement of the rest of the crew. But Alfred refuses and turns away to the safe retreat of his cabin, because he realizes only too well what he will get should he fight Bob. I don't think there is one member of the crew, even the Captain, would actually offer to fight Bob, as they know only too well what the result would be. *Position 21.14° North 43.19° West.*

Day 99 Friday June 1st

I notice that we still have two swallows following us, evidently having made up their minds to accompany us to England. We (both watches) commence painting all stays and I am ordered up aloft to paint the stay belonging to the main upper to'gallant staysail. This stay runs almost from the 'truck' (the very top of the main mast) to just below the 'futtocks' of the fore mast. I am given a bo'suns chair, two peices of 'burlap' and a tin full of paint. I now attach the chair to the stay by means of a shackle and then the Mate fastens the chair to the main upper to'gallant staysail haliard rope. He now orders me to sit on the chair and he and the Cook haul away at the haliard until I reach the top. The staysail, of course, had previously been taken in. I feel none to safe swinging about in mid air far above the deck but soon get over this. I now commence painting and when I have reached as far enough below me as I can possibly manage, I call down to the Mate, (who stands ready by the haliard down on deck) to lower me a little and carry on doing so until I reach the bottom.

I again quarrel with Cookie over the small amount of food dished out to us nowadays. But of course he is not responsible for the shortage of food but as is nearly always the way, he gets blamed for anything dealing with the food question.

We are again running short of fresh water, in fact all the food stores are running short. Up to now we are totally without the following, potatoes and coffee and I hear from reliable sources that the supply of Kerosene (paraffin) for our lamps is dwindling very fast. The Captain has given orders for all food, oil and fresh water to be rationed in future.

Tonight again the sailmaker and myself pick up the 'Southern Cross' but of course not the two pointers. *Position 22.28° North 43° West.*

Day 100 Saturday June 2nd

During my working watch this morning, I paint the stay belonging to the mizzen staysail and having finished that commence painting the stays (mizzen) which run down to the deck on each side of the mast.

Judging from the amount of Sargasso weed observed floating past the ship all day, we cannot be far from the famous Sargasso Sea, which lies in approximately 29 degrees North of the Equator.

This region and further North is known as the 'Horse Latitudes'. Here one can experience winds from a dead calm, to a light wind and quite often strong squalls. This is the belt situated between the N.E. Trade Winds and the stronger winds experienced in the North Atlantic.

George and I sit out on the 'Sharks Fin' my favourite spot situated far out at the end of the bowsprit and sing songs while some of the boys chuck buckets overboard attached to ropes in order to catch some of this Sargasso Weed. One or two of them did manage to get some on board and it really was amazing to notice some of the forms of life which lived on this weed. One could easily term them, after having studied their ways for a short period, spieces of the lowest form of life. *Position 23.45° North 45° West.*

Day 101 Sunday June 3rd
At 5am this morning we got back our N.E. Trade Wind. How relieved everybody is when the Trade Wind is blowing, for usually the wind stays for day after day, blowing with the same steady force unlike the Doldrums where one has to haul round the yards for every catspaw. The watch on deck now, only tighten the braces and haliards just before 7pm (6 bells) every night. Also, unless one had wheel or look-out in the night watches, one is able to snatch a few hours sleep without any fear of 'two whistles'.

This morning I clean out the pig house, we still have one pig left, he is very tame and friendly. I try my hand at playing Stowahse's concertina and find it easier than I expected.

Brownie, George, sailmaker and myself chat and crack jokes on deck this evening. *Position 24° North 45.32° West.*

Day 102 Monday June 4th
We are again becalmed. We have had no luck with our Trade Winds this voyage. I go up the main mast, this time to tar the upper to'gallant and upper topsail haliards. Everything possible is being put shipshape for Falmouth.
This afternoon we see a large Sword Fish swimming beneath the bowsprit, but we fail to catch her. We still see the Southern Cross but only now at sunset, she is definitely very low down on the horizon.

As I am painting one of the main mast stays, the hook which holds me to the stay, suddenly became detached and I was sent swinging to and fro on my bo'suns chair at least 100 feet above the deck, the paint flying all over the place. Eventually the Mate came along and lowered me to the deck.

The food is getting very short indeed now, consequently we do not get enough to eat. The crew are dissatisfied and grumble continuously. Everybody agrees that sailing ship life is a 'dogs life', poor food, poor pay, all work and very little sleep, but a good life.

Again a wonderful sunset.
Position 24.51° North 46° West.

Day 103 Tuesday June 5th
I overhaul buntlines up both the fore and main masts before breakfast this morning. Again we have continuous bracing, to catch every catspaw of wind, which is very slight.

The 2nd Mate has very bad toothache today, but stout fellow as he always is, he carries on with his work. The Captain says he doubts we shall now pick up our N.E. Trade Wind again, as we are too near the Horse Latitudes.

I again paint the main mast stays.
Position 26° North 46° West.

Day 104 Wednesday June 6th
This morning we scrape the anchor winch up for'ard underneath the fo'c'sle head, while in the afternoon 1pm - 7pm, we tar the deck. This is another job everybody dislikes. It is always done on a boiling hot day with the sun beating down from directly overhead, making things almost unbearable. Each man is given a large pot of tar and two or three pieces of burlap and we commence aft (starboard side only) and work for'ards. For five solid hours (if you have no wheel) you must kneel down on a deck which is so hot it nearly burns through your trousers and rub the tar onto the deck with the burlap. Your arms and hands are covered with tar by the finish and it takes weeks to clean it all off again.

Chips and myself still see the three top stars belonging to the Southern Cross and yet here we are in 26 degrees North.

Last night I slept once again on my bunk but not again before it is painted. I have never ceased scratching my body all day through those devils the bunk bugs. Nothing seems to kill them, and in this terrific heat of course they thrive all the more.

We have not moved one inch since midday yesterday to midday today. The sea resembles a duck pond. It really looks as if we are doomed to stay here for always.

Becalmed.
Position 26° North 46° West.

Day 105 Thursday June 7th

Still becalmed again, not a breath of wind. I again paint the main mast stays. George tells most of the boys that Belgier and myself had been talking filthy stuff and acting in a filthy way. This is absolutely untrue and I make him apologise, tell him he is nothing but a mischief maker and a lowdown liar.
I sleep the whole night from 8pm till 7.30am except for the two musters aft at 12 midnight and 4am. During our watch on deck 12pm - 4am I have no wheel, no look-out and there is no bracing, in fact we are definitely standing still, so I make the most of it and sleep soundly on deck up on the fo'c'sle head, Stowahse is also a lucky one and sleeps alongside me.

Again for the second day running we have not moved an inch. We are in the same position at 12 midday today as we were two days ago. This calm beats everybody and everything. Tempers are again getting ruffled and the Mate yells at you for nothing at all. Give me the gales round Cape Horn any day to these distressing calms.

Again a wonderful sunset.
Position 26° North 46° West.

Day 106 Friday June 8th

Gave the water tanks aft their second coating of paint, then went aloft on the main mast and oiled all buntlines and every wire. These have constantly to be oiled, they very soon rust, in fact anything does at sea.

Bill Thompsen (Dane) has a heated arguement with the Chief Mate Alfred but it blows over, before there is a fight. The top three stars of the Southern Cross seen again tonight.

For the third successive day we have not moved an inch and at midday today we were again in the same position as at 12 midday three days ago and the side of our ship is now covered with barnacles and moss.

My left hand is poisoned today. It was caused three days ago when overhauling a buntline on the fore lower to'gallant. The buntlines wire must have been years old, it was one succession of pricks sticking up and very rusty. Consequently I gripped it not thinking and cut the palm of my hand rather badly. I applied Iodine immediately but it seems to have had no effect. This buntline was later pulled down and a new one put in its place, about time too.

Becalmed 3rd day running.
Position 26° North 46° West.

128

Day 107 Saturday June 9th

This morning when I go to clean the pig house out, I discover our lovely fat gentleman dead, evidently having died peacefully in his sleep. We were short enough with our food without losing him and we had all been looking forward to some fresh meat, as he was going to be killed next Friday.

The Mate says we will now get wind, an old sea superstition that if a pig dies at sea, wind comes, but his tip is not altogether correct, as we only get a very light breeze which lasts about one hour.

Two Dolphins swim round our boat all day.

Another fight this evening between Cookie and Jacques in the galley. Jacques comes off considerably the worse, getting a badly cut lip. It is caused through the same old food shortage.

A small swallow follows us all day. We are becalmed again, the 4th day running.
Position 26.30° North 46° West.

Day 108 Sunday June 10th

I attempt to patch up what is left of my only pair of work trousers, making the patch out of an old piece of sail. I again clean my bunk out and oil it to kill the bugs.

This morning at 11am (6 bells) for three quarters of an hour we get our course again (a slight breeze) the course now being N,N.E 1/4 E. Our other cat is now ill.

Today is again glorious and most of the boys spent their free watches either sleeping on the hammocks on the fo'c'sle head or fishing for sharks.

Becalmed for the 5th day.
Position 26.47° North 46° West.

Day 109 Monday June 11th

My little friend the cat became so hopelessly ill today, that the Steward out of kindness killed it by hitting it on the head with a large hammer.

We again change all sails, that is we unbend the Tropical Rags and bend in their place our stronger Cape Horn sails as sometimes up here in the North Atlantic the weather can be very rough even in the summer time. Before breakfast we unbend the main upper to'gallant and bend the stronger one in its place. Then in the afternoon all hands change the large mainsail and our watch complete the lot by changing the fore lower to'gallant, upper topsail and lower topsail. We don't change the foresail as it is a fairly new sail and in all probability will withstand the stronger winds until we reach Falmouth. We also don't change two of the staysails.

A few flying fish seen today. At 4pm the wind blows up fairly strong, the sea comes back to life and once again we get water on deck.

I again sleep on the floor in the carpenters shop, I sleep like a log here and being midships there is never any row from people talking, singing etc. in the port watch.

A steamer sighted tonight at 10pm on the starboard side.
Position 28.29° North 44.25° West.

Bending a new lower to'gallant

Day 110 Tuesday June 12th
A small French cargo boat passed very near to us at 5am this morning. They sent up their ensign and we replied with ours. Our Captain then asked for the position by means of pennants and although very near to us, (she could easily read our message) she fails to relpy and leaves us dipping her ensign, but instead of acknowledging it by dipping the Finnish flag, the Captain, who is now in a furious temper over not getting a reply, orders our flag to be hauled down.

This boat was a complete mystery to all of us, not only had she no wireless but she was also miles off any recognised shipping route and simply making for nowhere.
I grease and oil all the sheet wires again and then paint under the fo'c'sle head, first in the paint locker and then the bo'suns locker where all spare ropes, blocks, chains and wires are stored.

I today patch up again my delapidated pair of work trousers. Fine and warm.
Position 30.18° North 43.30° West.

Day 111 Wednesday June 13th

This morning our watch commence to scrape and wash down the paint up in the starboard fo'c'sle for'ard, ready for painting and we are ordered to take all our matresses, bunk clothes, cases etc. down into the fore hold, where we must all now sleep until the fo'c'sles are finished.

This afternoon we get a head wind and consequently steer 'By the Wind'.

The Southern Cross has now definitely left us and we shall not see it again this voyage.
Position 32.7° North 41° West.

Day 112 Thursday June 14th

We are now definitely heading towards Falmouth sailing in a North Easterly direction. I slept very soundly my first night on the wheat bags down in the fore hold. It was very cosy and one or two boys brought their lamps down (against orders) and read a little before going to sleep, thus making the atmosphere look more homelike.

Another steamer sighted at 11.30am this morning far out on the starboard side. We again scrape the rust off the paint in our fo'c'sle (starboard) ready for painting.

Brownie gives me a new work shirt today (I have only one) and Bob gives me an old pair of trousers. I should now last comfortably until Falmouth. In the afternoon we commence to paint up in the fo'c'sle.

It is getting much cooler now as we come further up North.
Position 33.40° North 40.23° West.

Day 113 Friday June 15th

Another steamer sighted far off at 11am. We again lose our wind and get becalmed. We are again painting up for'ard in our fo'c'sle. We have to paint also in our free watch as the 1st Mate says we must have it finished before we reach Falmouth.

It is remarkable what a keen interest is taken in the work during our free watch. Each man paints his own bunk and everybody tries to make his bunk appear the smartest. There is keen competition.

Another swallow is following us, evidently making for the summer weather up North.
Position 34.30° North 39.30° West.

131

Day 114 Saturday June 16th

This morning I scrape the rust off the paint on our landing stage. The ship is now definitely looking like a yacht as regards smartness. Everywhere looks very clean and freshly painted, in fact you cannot touch anything without getting covered with paint.

I sleep in the hold during free watch in the afternoon. A few patches of Sargasso weed float by today.

At 11pm tonight a dense fog descends upon us and we have our fog horn out. *Position 35.2° North 39° West.*

Day 115 Sunday June 17th

A slight breeze blows up early this morning but we all ask the same question, will it stay? Brincks who has just painted his bunk boards, now places them on the pin rail, a very stupid place, because there is always the possibility of people having to stand up there to hang up the foresail sheets on to the hangers, should the wind shift. As it happens it does shift and I am ordered to hang up the wire which is dangling over the side. It is impossible not to tread on them, consequently I dirty them. Brincks sees me and starts arguing but I tell him to go to the devil and next time place his boards in a more sensible place.
Although it is Sunday both watches carry on painting their respective fo'c'sles. I sit on the fo'c'sle head in the evening and chat with the Donkyman, carpenter and sailmaker, they all speak good English.

We are again without any fresh water except of course drinking water. I have a fight this evening with George. This had been brewing up for a long time, both having lately held heated arguments. At the time, we were both in the sailmakers cabin along with donkeyman and Chips. We were all trying different knots, when George for no reason at all, suddenly stands up and says I have followed him in to tease him. I tell him he is a big baby and start laughing. But before I know exactly what was happening, I found myself sprawling about in the scupper on deck. George, who is extremely strong, simply picked me up and chucked me bodily out of the cabin. But I was not going to stand this and immediately get up and land him a good punch. This started the fire burning properly and I was only saved just in time from being severly mauled, by Bob dragging George away and telling him, if he gave me one more blow, he would knock George overboard.

Bob always stuck up for me, chiefly because I was considerably lighter in weight than most. On at least three occasions, if it had not been for the timely intervention of Bob, I should have had, in each case, a thorough good licking. *Position 36.18° North 38.27° West.*

Day 116 Monday June 18th

Brincks and myself clear away the water which has again collected down in the bilges in the forepeak. I go down below and fill the buckets while Brincks hauls them up on deck. How the water gets down here I am unable to tell. George and I have another row, he refuses to come down below and relieve me, when Brincks goes to the wheel. He is content in staying up on deck hauling the buckets up, he never will try to do a kind act for anybody and it is useless to argue with him.

We discover a large amount of bird feathers on deck this afternoon and try to find out where they are coming from. It does not take us long to find out the reason for them being here, for sitting on the main yard directly above us is a large hawk, which at this very moment is eating alive one of the small swallows. It has no sooner devoured this when it swoops down on another, goes back to the yard and devours the whole of this one also. The Cook says he will borrow the 1st Mates pistol and shoot it, but Alfred (1st Mate) refuses to lend it. *Position 37.48° North 37.24° West.*

Day 117 Tuesday June 19th

I overhaul all buntlines and gaskets on both the main and fore masts before breakfast. I then haul up the water from the forepeak. George is actually down below this morning but only on account of the Mates orders. In the afternoon we commence to give the sail locker its second coat of paint.

Heim (German) and I are great pals now. I always have liked this fellow but up till now, although always on the best of terms, we have never been actually pals. Today we have been averaging roughly 5 knots having at present a good wind blowing from dead aft. Bill Thompsen (Dane) and Bob give an exhibition fight this evening. A perfect scream, they are both real humourists and the life and soul of this ship, without them it would be 'hell'.

Much cooler.
Position 39.48° North 34° West.

Day 118 Wednesday June 20th

At 1am this morning a large liner passes our stern and judging by the length she must have been easily 15000 tons. Again at 8.30am a Swedish oil tanker overtakes us steering the same course. Then again at 11.30am a large American liner the 'Ex Gemiou' (bound for New York from Marsellies) alters her course comes alongside and goes completely round us, actually stopping her engines for a few minutes to give her passengers a chance of having a good look at our old ship the "Winterhude". Our Captain asks her to report us to Lloyds and to tell them 'All's well'. She replied that she would, gives us three large blasts on her sirens dips her flag three times (we acknowledge this by doing the same) and then she swings completely round and makes for her correct course again. Evidently the Captain was an old sail trained man, to have taken such great interest in our ship.

Our Captain says he never remembers, during his many years on sailing ships, a steamer come so far off her course and then come so close and actually stop the engine. This was a sight I shall always remember. After nearly 5 long months at sea without hardly seeing a soul except our own crew and then to actually be within a stone's throw of a large American liner crowded out with human beings, made it appear as though we had been dead all this time and suddenly come back to life. That is exactly how I felt.

We are again painting in the sail locker, while during our free watch in the afternoon, we commence to give our starboard fo'c'sle its second white coating. We still sleep down in the fore hold. Except for one or two wheat bugs and an occasional rat, everything down there is very cosy and comfortable, in fact too warm.
Position 41.30° North 33.32° West.

Day 119 Thursday June 21st
We pass a small schooner early this morning, what on earth she was doing here I cannot say, unless she was making for the West Indies from some port in Spain. I fell asleep in the hold during free watch in the morning and when I wake I find I have been locked in but after ten minutes hard shouting, George hears me and lets me out.

We have a great deal of bracing in the afternoon, the wind refuses to blow from one quarter only. Belgier and myself are ordered to finish painting the sail locker. There is very little to paint so we take our time, occasionally when the Mate is not about, we have a puff or two from a cigarette made from dried coffee beans. I cannot actually recommend this to anybody.

A Portuguese Man-of-War (large jelly fish) swims past us this afternoon. It can swim underwater or float on the surface when it feels tired.

There are a large number of shore birds about all day, a good sign that we are not so far from land.
Tonight in our watch on deck from 7pm to 12 midnight, we have no fewer than 14 'two whistles' for bracing, This wind flatly refuses to blow from one quarter for longer than five or ten minutes and therefore causes us a considerable amount of extra work. But now at any rate we have our full watch of seven men, the daymen having resumed work in their watches at the latter end of last week.
Position 43.30° North 30.30° West.

134

Day 120 Friday June 22nd

We again have a large amount of bracing during our working watch 8am to 1pm and at 11am it rains hard, so once again we bring out all manner of things, from barrels down to coffee pots, to catch all we can before it again stops. This rain water is as precious as gold to us just now. I just wish it would rain food and cigarettes, we should then be complete. It clears up again at 12 midday and I now paint the name S.V. "Winterhude" Marieham on the lifebuoys, a ticklish job, I am ordered to make a good job of it, I make myself a small wire brush.
The deck this afternoon is crowded out with shore clothes being aired, washing hanging up etc. evidently we all take it we shall get no more calms or head winds. But we must see.

We have now finished painting the fo'c'sles and they certainly do look and smell clean and fresh. In fact, as Bob said to me, 'fit enough for King George to sleep in and eat his meals'. So, Alfred (1st Mate) gives orders that everything must now be brought up from the fore hold and we must go back to the fo'c'sles. I think I shall not suffer any more from those pests the 'Bunk Bugs' at any rate not this trip.

It is much colder today.
Position 45° North 26.45° West.

Day 121 Saturday June 23rd

A large Hamburg America liner the 'Portland' overtakes us this morning at 11am bound for Hamburg from Vancouver. She is a very smart looking boat and she leaves us dipping her German ensign, making the same course as ourselves.

At 7.15pm this morning a gale springs up without warning, the sea all in a minute turns angry and with great force tremendous waves throw themselves on deck midships. To make matters worse the wind changes to a head wind and we have to go 'By the Wind'. The main upper to'gallant Saysail blows in two and we have to haul it in before it is torn to shreds. The wheel is kicking like the 'very devil' when I take my trick from 9pm to 10pm and I have to hold it with all my strength to prevent it from throwing me again, like it did off New Zealand. In fact twice tonight it as good as does the trick again, only I wedge my right leg against the spokes and thus help to grip it the better with my hands. Owing to sailing 'By the Wind' our compass is pointing almost due East and thus we are instead of steering our course N.E 1/2 East, now heading straight for the Spanish coast, but luckily at one bell, 11.45pm (this bell is given to 'rise up' the free watch for coming on deck at 12 midnight to releive our watch) we get back our course again, the wind dies away.

Fair but cold.
Position 45.29° North 24° West.

135

Day 122 Sunday June 24th
The New Zealand Shipping Companies steamer the S.S. Rotorua bound from Auckland to London comes alongside and very near at 11am this morning steering the same course. She is still in sight at 1pm.

Today at dinner each man gets a glass of rum and one cigarette, given by the Captain. I heard later from the Steward that he had suddenly found a tin of 50 Abdulla cigarettes.

Some of the boys who did not smoke were offering their cigarette for sixpence and George gave his to a German for a piece of cake, (we always get a peice of cake on a Sunday afternoon at coffee time).

Heim, who has not missed a day through illness since leaving Glasgow last October, has now to lie up through a very sore abscess in his ear, which causes him considerable pain.

At 7pm the wind shifts to dead aft. I again wash some of my clothes.
Position 46° North 21.20° West.

Day 123 Monday June 25th
Everybody is again in the best of tempers, we have a good wind again. While I am at the wheel this morning, my Mate comes and chats to me and tells me that if we can average 4 knots until Saturday, we shall reach Falmouth that afternoon. While at look-out from 11pm - 12 midnight, I see a steamers lights heading straight for us, (evidently his look-out was asleep) anyhow she alters her course when almost on top of us. She passes us very close to and when she is alongside, she stops her engines and commences to morse but I am afraid she had to morse in vain, firstly because we had no morsing apparatus and secondly even if we had, no one could work it on our ship.

During my working watch this afternoon, I helped Stowahse and Brincks to scrub the teak floor of the Captain's saloon aft by means of the famouse Holystone, mentioned and described previously.

We are today averaging roughly 7 knots and we have now only 600 miles to Falmouth.
Position 46.30° North 17.30° West.

Day 124 Tuesday June 26th
I sight a large oil tanker on the starboard horizon evidently making for England. Fifteen minutes later she has definitely altered her course and she is now making straight for us, a most unusual thing for an oil tanker to alter her course, but

136

evidently her Captain is an old sail trained man. Half an hour later she comes alongside and very near indeed. The whole of her crew are on deck and seem to take a great interest in our ship. Our boys wave but get no reply. As she leaves she gives us three blasts on her sirens. I might mention here that this steamer failed to show her ensign. It is the custom at sea that a steamer must send her ensign up before a sailing ship, out of respect, but as she failed to do this our Captain refused to send ours aloft. The foreigners, especially the Germans on my ship were very annoyed over this affair and they all agreed it was typical English. Although I get on very well indeed with all these foreigners on my ship, I can plainly see that the English people on the whole are disliked by the Germans. At 2pm a dense fog descends down upon us with heavy rain, this certainly seems more like the English weather. As usual when we get a fog the wind, which has blown continuously for the last three days, dies away completely.

The port watch this afternoon get the anchors ready up on the fo'c'sle head. This is a sure sign that Falmouth is not very far off now. Everybody now in a great state of excitement, no wonder, after 124 days at sea without having seen land of any description.

There are scores of land birds following us today but up to now I have not seen the friendly seagull.
Position 47.49° North 15.44° West.

Day 125 Wednesday June 27th

As we go aft to muster this morning at 4am, we find a large up to date Swedish oil tanker alongside and going in the same direction. She also morses us but again we cannot reply. Another steamer passes us on the port side at 7.30am.

Our watch wash the poop this morning and after it has dried up we oil it. An oil tanker outward bound passes us at 1.30pm and another again at 4.30pm. We are now almost at the entrance to the English channel and in the centre of all the shipping routes.

The Mate thinks the main upper to'gallant yard on the starboard side has not been painted well enough, so sends me aloft to give it another coat. A strong wind blows up from dead aft at 7pm this evening. Heim is still laid up with his poisoned ear.

I have another fight with George (Australian stowaway) we have been on very unfriendly terms during the past six weeks, he is an extremely moody person, I cannot weigh him up.
Position unknown but somewhere round about the entrance to the English Channel.

Day 126 Thursday June 28th

Several French fishing trawlers pass us early this morning, one of them getting very annoyed with us for sailing over one of its flags (left to indicate the spot where the nets are). We are evidently going to arrive in style for this morning we average 9 knots. This morning we clean all brass, portholes, door handles etc. Today my old friends the seagulls have at last turned up to greet us.

At 12 midday the Captain says we have now definitely only 42 more miles to the Scilly Islands and 120 miles to the Lizard, so if the wind remains, we shall arrive tomorrow morning.

At 3.30pm a large Royal Mail liner passed us outward bound. Two Dublin trawlers pass us at 4,30pm. The Captain says we should pick up Bishop's Rock lighthouse roughly about 6pm this evening, so at 5.30 all the boys, in great excitement each congregate up on the fo'c'sle head and every man tries to pick it up first. But George who has meanwhile gone up aloft (an unusual thing for him) is the first to see it, picking the lighthouse and the island ahead at about 6.15pm. We tell him he is fooling us but soon we discover he is correct. This is the first land we have sighted since we passed Kangaroo Island Australia, after 126 days at sea. At 6.30 St. Agnes Lighthouse (Scilly Island) is picked up, again by George.

I feed the seagulls with stale bread while up here on the fo'c'sle head, I should think roughly we have 30 seagulls following us now.

At 8 pm the Wolf Rock Lighthouse (off the coast of Cornwall) is sighted, while 15 minutes later the flashes from the Longships Lighthouse at Lands End are seen.

At long last, exactly at 9.30 pm, Brincks picks up the sweeping flashes from the famous Lizard light, this light can be seen 15 miles away, so evidently we must yet go another 15 miles before we are opposite the Lizard point. We have steamer lights all around us now, definitely back once again in the congested English Channel.

Day 127 Friday June 29th

When our watch come on deck at 4am this morning, we are dead opposite the Lizard Point. We signal Lloyds station and give our name. We sail along close in to the coast, what a rare sight for anybody who is lucky enough to be out on the cliffs just now.

I plainly pick out the villages of Cadgwith and Coverack and the dangerous Manacle Rocks. At 5.15am, we get our first glimpse of Falmouth, nestling in this fine bay and at the same time we pick out two more sailing ships at anchor well up in the bay. All the crew are now laying bets on which ones they will be. Some say the "Olivebank", others the "L'Avenier" while some say the "Beatrice" (this latter is an impossibility as she sails the seas no longer). Whichever they may be they are two four masted Barques.

Owing to a slight head wind we are unable to sail staight in, so we make for 'Black Rocks', (opposite St. Austell Bay), then we 'go about' and finally drop our anchor at 7.30am, one mile from the shore.

"Winterhude" at anchor in Falmouth 1934

We now find out the two sailing ships at anchor are the "Archibald Russel" and the "Ponape" (both Finns). They left different ports in Australia on the same day, came round the Cape of Good Hope and sailed into Falmouth within an hour of each other after 128 days at sea. We had beaten them both. We had beaten the winner of last years race the "Parma". We had beaten that fine four master the "L'Avenier", which was in Port Germain with us. This latter was a great delight to all of us, as the "L'Avinier's" crew had repeatedly laughed and sneered at our old ship the "Winterhude" while in Port Germain and yet we had beaten her by 13 days. The "Olivebank" (my last ship) however, had made a better passage, having made the trip in 108 days, while the winner so far is the large German four master "Padua" with 106 days. She may yet be beaten for there are still those two fine sailors the "Pamir" and "Herzogin Cecilie" to arrive. (However both these two arrive later with longer passages.)

139

The crew at Falmouth

All the ships this year made really bad passages and except for the "Favell" 144 days the next worse was last years winner the "Parma". Luck plays its part, without a doubt.

"Favell"

We remain anchored here for 8 days, eventually getting ordered up to Lyme Dock South Shields, sailing the short distance in 11 days. We were out of luck having a head wind and fog all up the English Channel as far as Dungeness, first having to make for the French coast, then back to the English coast no fewer than 5 times before we picked up a fair wind off Dungeness which took us through the narrow straits of Dover. Had we met a head wind here, we should have had to anchor owing to the narrowness of the strait.

After passing Dover fog descended again and we were almost rammed by the Newcastle steamer 'Thistlegarth' but luckily she saw us in time and immediately altered her course (it is a rule that all steamers must give way to sailing ships). The fog remains all up the East coast and we eventually dock safely in Lyme Dock at 6am on Wednesday July 18th.

I eventually sign off and go home on Saturday July 21st, just in time to see the last match at Leeds.

It may have been hell at times, we have been short of food, fresh water and cigarettes, we have had fights, we have been wet through hungry and thoroughly worn out with continuous work, but it has been worth it. I am fit, strong and healthy.

I love the sea and what is more I love the old sailing ships and without a doubt Cape Horn will call me back again......
and I shall not refuse.

[Editor's Note:

And call him back again it did for in 1935 Geoffrey signed on once more in the four masted barque "Ponape".]

Log of the Finnish Four Masted Barque "Ponape" to Australia and back to England

"Ponape"

Outward Journey

1935 - 1936

Day 1 Saturday September 21st
Polished all the brass with Clapperton (Aussie) in the morning. Tug came alongside at 2pm left Gravesend. Washed down the deck until 4.30pm. then muster aft for watch picking. I am in the starboard watch. I take my first wheel 6.30pm to 7pm. Free watch 7pm to 12 midnight.
Fine.

Starboard watch, self 3rd from right

Day 2 Sunday September 22nd
Our watch set 3 staysails during watch 12 midnight to 4am. Wind shifts round at 2am to due West - headwind. So we anchor at 4am. Tug leaves us at 4.30am. We anchor opposite Deal, the coast is visible. Captain, being drunk, falls from the deckhouse roof onto the deck. I am dishwasher this week, hateful job. Chat with Clapperton and the passenger on deck in the morning. Slept on my bunk in the afternoon. Mrs Duff came aboard on a fishing boat at night and left about 10pm.
Sun. Cold.

Day 3 Monday September 23rd
Carried water to the fo'c'sles etc, then down in the hold getting ballast ready. Had a sing song in the fo'c'sle in the morning. Motor boat from Deal came around with people in the morning. Down in the hold with two Finns heaving the ballast up secure. Another motor boat crowd came out just before coffee time. Had a sing song in the evening. Still a head wind.
Fine . Warmer.

Day 4 Tuesday September 24th

Painting over the side with the Danish boy Christensen, we get wet through, heavy sea. Clapperton a great joke with all the boys as he is useless. Gale with heavy rain at night.
Stormy.

Crew of the "Ponape", self 1st left

Day 5 Wednesday September 25th

From 4am to 8am we steam up the donkey boiler, as we now have a fair wind. I carry water to the Galley and the fo'c'sles. A four masted Schooner seen at 7.30am. Think of home and everybody during free watch 8am to 1pm. Had gramophone on and chatted. Down in the hold in the afternoon scraping rust. Clapperton's kitten is getting a lot braver and plays a lot with the dog. Had a sing song near forward hatch after 6pm. I had a whole nights sleep.
Fair. Cold.

Day 6 Thursday September 26th

I have a bad poisoned right hand and can hardly work with it also I have a boil above my left eye. Down in the hold scraping rust again at first during watch 8am to 1pm then painting the side of the ship fo'ard with Christensen (Danish friend). I go to the Chief Mate after lunch and have my sceptic hand seen to. The two fishermen come out again this morning and a small steam yacht comes

146

round the ship. We have another sing song in the afternoon. Some of the boys start making models of the "Ponape". Wind gets up again towards midnight with rain.
Fine.

Christensen

***

Day 7 Friday September 27th
I never slept one minute last night, my hand is very painful. Carry water to the Galley before breakfast. After breakfast I go up to the Chief Mate and have my hand cut and dressed. Very heavy sea and wind running. Still anchored here. Down in the hold chipping rust in the afternoon. Rain and fog set in at night.
Fair

Day 8 Saturday September 28th
I clean out the fo'c'sle and midships and chat with Laurie Clapperton about the ship and people. I have my hand dressed again. Some more people come out in a motor boat. It is a lovely day and I wish and long to be on shore and I think about Honey, Ada and all. Sat out on deck in the afternoon. Plenty of people come out and large liners pass us including the new liner "Alloa" and the "Highland Monarch". We have a sing song. I chat with Clapperton and the Bosun at night. We all get our share of tobacco at night.
Fine.

Day 9 Sunday September 29th

We are free all day. In the morning those same people come out again in the motor boat, and Laurie Clappertons girl, they bring us papers, and took back the boys letters. They came out in a very rough sea and thought it best not to come aboard. Slept on bunk in afternoon and read all my letters, and wrote to Ada. In the evening we had a wonderful sing song, six people in all.
Very rough. Wet.

Day 10 Monday September 30th

Terrible wind blowing and hail. I have first look-out from 8am to 9am and get wet through. Then, as usual on sailing ships in wet weather, we are put on to cleaning the white paint on the poop and get wet through. Several ships pass with lists through the gale and one small steamer passes with one of her masts broken. Then we are down chipping rust in the hold. We start making our drum (for our Jazz Band) during free watch in the afternoon and it is finished by 6pm, so we commence playing in earnest, then again after tea out on deck. Laurie comes up forward.
Wet to Fair.

The Jazz Band, self seated with ukelele

Day 11 Tuesday October 1st

Still anchored here. During watch 6am to 8am we haul up water for the donkey boiler and then we go down into the hold and chip rust. I long for home and everybody. Sleep on my bunk during free watch in the morning. Down in the hold chipping in the afternoon. Then at 5pm Christensen and myself go down into the port side chain locker and guide the anchor chain into its locker. Then we both carry water to the donkey boiler. We again have a sing song after tea.
Fair. Cold.

Day 12 Wednesday October 2nd

Down in the hold chipping again. We are all fed up with it, five long hours. We are still anchored, when shall we get a wind. Our Jazz Band practises again in the afternoon, we are getting quite good now. Wind gets up to gale force with heavy seas at 9pm. Captain is dead drunk tonight and wakes up the Chief Mate and Timmerman and plays up with the 2nd Mate.
Rain.

Day 13 Thursday October 3rd

We are again down chipping before breakfast. Things are going along much better now and I feel happier. We again practise our jazz band after breakfast. Passenger is well again now. Finnish boy gets rust in his eyes and has to go ashore with the Captain. Down in the hold scraping in the afternoon and heave up anchor.
Rain.

Day 14 Friday October 4th

I am down in the coal hole all morning and Johansen carries it to the Donkey Boiler. The "Aseama" and the "Hekusen Mary" pass us. I get fed up and filthy down in the coal hole, I always seem to get this job. We now hear we shall sail on Sunday but none of us believe it. Mrs Duff comes aboard in the afternoon. Our Jazz Band practises again. A small Finnish steamer belonging to Erikson passes close and dips her ensign. I have a good laugh this afternoon over things in general. Some of the boys are real characters. Christensen who is dishwasher finds mouldy bread, bad fish and heaps of old milk tins in a cupboard (laugh). The gramophone records are all getting broken and they repeat in places. Stranberg in our watch is a great fellow never heated and always willing to show me anything, he gets teased a lot but always takes things well. We are a very happy crew. Still anchored, looks like us being here over Christmas.
Very cold.

Day 15 Saturday October 5th

Down in the hold chipping rust before breakfast. I make a little sail bag during free watch in the morning. "Pacific Grove" passes us bound for London.

Clapperton this morning , though supposed to be look-out goes aft instead of for'ard what a joke. He is a great sailor, I don't think. We heave up the anchor again for about the 20th time. This is a great joke amongst the crew as it is unnecessary. We now hear we are sailing tomorrow but we don't believe it as we always keep on hearing we are sailing. Captain and the Chief Mate are very drunk this afternoon. In the morning after tea the starboard watch hold a great sing song and we get two bottles of Rum from the Captain and we all get drunk.

All the Mates come up for'ard and join in the fun, I dance with the Chief Mate.
Showers.

Day 16 Sunday October 6th
I am dishwasher again. Mrs Duff comes aboard this morning and has tons of luggage. Our other passenger leaves us as he is sick. We are supposed to sail at 1pm but at just one minute to one we hear we don't sail. Clappertons girl comes aboard in the afternoon. A fight between Lund and Eriksen this afternoon, the first this trip. It is a great joke on board about this sailing business. Played the Gramophone in the afternoon.
Fair.

Day 17 Monday October 7th
While I am 'policeman' from 2am to 3am we get a fair wind and so we stoke up the Donkey Engine. At 4am (free watch) all hands are called out to make sail but at 5.30am, with most of the sails let loose, we again have a headwind and anchor, but at 8am all hands are called out again (during our free watch again) to make sail again. I overhaul all the buntlines on the main mast. The motor boat comes out again this morning to bring us fish and papers. Our watch, although free, work until 11am then we are free and I and Christensen (Dane) sit out on deck in brilliant sunshine. The wind keeps shifting all morning and we about ship plenty times. We pass close to the South Goodwin Lightship. It is slightly foggy.

I take my first wheel onboard the "Ponape" this afternoon, she is a devil to steer.

We make fast both the anchors in the afternoon. For our tea we have fresh fish which the boatmen from Deal gave us. At 4pm we leave the English Channel and reach the North Sea. We have a pigeon and three chaffinches on board.
Very fine and warm.

150

Day 18 Tuesday October 8th

During our watch 12am to 4am early this morning the wind freshens and we do about 12 knots and consequently have two at the wheel. I am with my Danish

friend Christensen. We are surrounded by trawlers in the Dogger Bank and nearly run down two of them. We have plenty of bracing to do. Down in the hold between 8am and 1pm and we have look-out all day. We still have two at the wheel and again I am with Christensen. At 1pm the wind freshens to gale force and the port watch make fast all three royals. Clapperton goes up the main mast and everyone in our watch turns out on deck to watch the scene. He goes up aloft in his glasses. Pots etc. fly all over the place in the fo'c'sle. We have the grammy on during our free watch and I sleep a little. We are sailing "Bi de Vind" so only one at the wheel. *Position 54.33°N - 3.36°E. Fine at first then rain showers.*

Man at the wheel taken from mizzen rigging. Note lack of cover

---

Day 19 Wednesday October 9th

During the port watches watch 12am to 4am they take in the three upper to'gallants as the wind is no good. Then at 4am all hands take in the mizzen sail. Clapperton tells me he had a row with Karlsson over going up the fore mast. I fill the water tanks up on the poop before breakfast. Danish boy Pedersen falls down into the hold and has bad concussion and cuts on his head he has to lay up in his bunk. I sleep on my bunk all morning. Down in the hold chipping rust in the afternoon. The wheel is very easy and we have "course". I am free all night. Timmerman is very drunk tonight and wakes everybody (laugh).
Position 58.30°N - 0.43°E

Day 20 Thursday October 10th

We wash with soda the white paint on the deck. It is very cold with hail showers and we are 'Bi de Vind' and the wind keeps shifting making it very hard to steer. A four masted barque sighted this morning , everybody thinks it is the "Passat".

We gain steadily on her, and we set the three upper to'gallants and the three royals and the fore upper to'gallant at 12.30am. We adieu the ship as we must now go South. I chat with Mrs Duff about the birds. Everybody is wet through. I have a row with the cook, I seem to have these every day. He is a devil and nobody likes him. Four small birds still with us. We pass between the Shetland Islands and the Orkneys and clearly see Foula Island. Have a sing song in the afternoon. The wind increases and at 5.30pm the port watch take in all three royals, at 7pm the wind is at gale force and all hands take in and make fast the main sail and mizzen sail. Then at 8.15pm our watch take in all three upper to'gallants. I and Johansen make fast the fore upper to'gallant. The sail was kicking about like a madman and we both nearly got knocked down on deck. It took us all our time to make it fast. While at the wheel between 11pm and 12pm we sight a lighthouse also a steamer which morses us and wants to know our name. Her name is the "Litenek" (Norwegian) she passes close by. A terrific hail storm at 12.30pm while I am at the wheel and I get wet through and terribly cold. The Mate chats with me.
Position 60.16°N 3.12°W Very cold.

Day 21 Friday October 11th

A lovely sunrise but very wild looking. This morning at 6am we can still see Foula Island. I carry water to the Galley the rest of the boys wash the white paint on deck. We turn the ship again at 8am. The Danish boy Pedersen turns out for work again this morning. I hear Clapperton the other day while at the wheel steered two points off. He's a great seaman. In the afternoon watch on deck I have one and a half hours look-out in a biting cold wind, then I help to wash the white paint on deck. A steamer sighted at 6pm and also lighthouse Sule Skerry on the North coast of Scotland. We the starboard watch make cocoa and coffee at midnight, it was very welcome.
Position 59.56°N - 3.47°W

Day 22 Saturday October 12th

During the port watches watch on deck 4am to 8am they take in all three lower to'gallants. During our watch on deck in the morning 8am to 1pm I wash the fo'c'sle out and midships. The rest clean the white paint. In the afternoon we work during free watch until 3pm taking in the three upper top sails and the fore sail in a terrific gale. One can hardly stand on deck and buckets and boys too go flying into the scuppers. All hands are at this work. During the afternoon the gale increases and sometimes the masts lean over at an angle of fortyfive degrees. At

3pm we 'Splice the Main Brace' i.e. the Captain gives everyone a glass of rum. There is a lot of discussion all afternoon about this taking in of sail, the boys think it unnecessary. I have second wheel 8pm until 9pm and it is very heavy so the Bosun helps me, but while Johansen is at the next wheel the wind suddenly shifts and both the fore and main upper topsails blow out and all hands have a hell of a job making them fast. Then the fore staysail blows out too. Our watch work all night until 12 midnight. Two ships sighted at 11.30pm. We are now sailing along with only two sails. One staysail and the mizzen lower topsail in a terrific gale. We all make coffee again.
Position 60.53°N - 5.22°W Very cold.

Dirty weather off Scotland

Day 23 Sunday October 13th
Our watch from 6am to 8am set the foresail and unbend the blown out fore lower topsail. I carry water to the Galley. We turn the ship again at 8am. I am feeling very tired and have hellish toothache. Our watch (who are all dead beat) sleep soundly all morning. Then in the afternoon our watch work from 1pm to 7pm unbending the torn main and mizzen upper topsails, then we bend the two new ones. At 6.30pm we get a fair wind from aft.
Position 62.4°N - 3.55°W

Day 24 Monday October 14th

During our watch 8am to 1pm the wind again goes headwind and we steer Bi de Vind the wind increases to gale force and at 10am all hands take in the three upper topsails. The ship is rolling very heavily and is steering S.S.W. We wash down the white paint on deck.

I still have this toothache and sore throat. I sleep on my bunk during the free watch in the afternoon. I get told off by the Mate for not being on deck while policeman when he blew one whistle at 11pm. We set the main and mizzen upper topsails again. I overhaul the gardings (buntlines) on the main mast. We wake the watch up at 12pm by playing our famous jazz band and the famous tune Hotsy Totsy.
Position 61.54°N - 5.54°W

Day 25 Tuesday October 15th

Our watch again make tea in the night watch. We are all kept awake by the 3rd Mates shouting during our free watch 12pm to 4am as they set the fore upper topsail and Hussel tells him to "go to hell". At 6am the wind has left us and we are still sailing Bi de Vind.

Before breaky I overhaul gardings on the fore and main masts then take up sea water to the Captain back on the poop. I very nearly fall overboard only a stay preventing me from certainly falling into the sea. The Captain is ill but the boys say he is dead drunk. We clean the white paint on deck all afternoon in pouring rain and we all get wet through. Then at 5pm while I am at the wheel our watch take in the main sail. At 7pm all hands take in the foresail and the port watch take in the fore and main upper topsail between 8pm - 12pm. At 1am our watch take in the mizzen upper topsail. We are now sailing Bi de Vind.
Position 60.32°N - 5.23°W

Day 26 Wednesday October 16th

I carry coal to the galley during working watch 8am to 1pm the rest carry on washing white paint on the deck. Christensen gets two buckets on his head and I get one but we are not injured. There are plenty of seagulls about and at 12pm midday two trawlers come near. We about ship at 1pm and the port watch set the mizzen and foresail during the working watch in the afternoon. The wind is strengthening at 4pm. I chat with Mrs Duff. I don't like the skipper at all, he is ungentlemanly in every way and very bluff. Laurie overhauls the gardings on the mizzen sail, it is a great joke amongst the crew.

I play my ukelele in my bunk during free watch in the afternoon. The port watch set the three upper topsails, foresail and mainsail at 2pm only to take in the mainsail, fore and main upper topsail at 6pm. It is all very crazy. Then at 11pm our watch take in and make fast the mizzen upper topsail and at 12pm all hands take in the foresail in a terrific hail squall. The sea is very high and we have successive hail and wind squalls.

The Mate chats with me at the wheel and tells me that to show Clapperton how to overhaul gardings, the 3rd Mate broke them twice. The ship rolls from side to side at angles of nearly 45 degrees throwing things and people in utter confusion in the fo'c'sle and out on deck. I cannot help but laugh over Christensen doing all he can to stand. Still Bi de Vind.
Position 59.48°N - 5.14°W

Day 27 Thursday October 17th
I carry water to the tanks on the poop before breaky. Johansen (Swede) slips on deck owing to the ship still rolling and hurts himself. The ship is still rolling badly and at breakfast the food and pots etc. go flying about all over the fo'c'sle making the floor a filthy mess. We wash the white paint under the fo'c'sle head in the afternoon but do little work. We have a sing song at night.
Position 61.2°N - 4.51°W

Day 28 Friday October 18th
Our watch during working watch 8am to 1pm unbend the mizzen upper topsail and bend a new one. We turn the ship about and we still sail Bi de Vind but the course is a little better being W.S.W. At 1pm while I am at the wheel all hands take in the mizzen and mainsail, then the port watch take in the fore and main upper topsails. It is blowing a hellish gale and hail and snow comes down. We all get wet through. Two thrushes are on board today.

We "all hands" at 3pm to take in the foresail , it took us three quarters of an hour. Towards night the wind increases even more but comes finer. Our watch stand by all night. Two at the wheel. Christensen falls on deck and hurts his head and he has to lay up.
Position 60.16°N - 5.44°W

Day 29 Saturday October 19th
At 4am there are still two at the wheel but we have course SW.½ W. The wheel is hell and very heavy. At 6.15am the mizzen staysail blows in two and we have a job making it fast. The wind is blowing a real hurricane and we now have three at the wheel. The deck is awash and many boys are hurt including myself. I land against a capstan and hurt my wrist badly, buckets and all things go sliding about all over the deck and the fo'c'sle and the galley are one mess of flying pots and pans. It is especially dangerous out on deck, we batten down the hatches, the 2nd Mate says he has never seen the barometer so low before and Liewendahl

says he has never seen such weather, certainly I never have in all my life. I sleep on my bunk during free watch in the morning. Still three at the wheel in the afternoon and I am there from 1pm to 4pm in a freezing cold wind. Then I wash dishes and overhaul gardings on the main mast and also make the main upper to'gallant sail fast to the yard. At 5pm the wind is getting less strong and only two men at the wheel. A hell of a day. Between 7pm to 12pm the port watch set the fore upper topsail and lower to'gallant.
Position 59.12°N - 9.53°W

Day 30 Sunday October 20th

Between 12pm and 4am our watch set the mizzen sail and the main lower to'gallant. I am sent up to loosen the lower to'gallant. I have a hell of a time with the gaskets, they are all rotten and made fast very badly. The Mate yells hell at me from the deck,and when I get down on deck again he plays up with me for being such a time. So I tell him, nobody could be quicker on a ship with such rotten gaskets. At a quarter to four I am sent up to let loose the mizzen lower to'gallant but after a quarter of an hour I come down as it is hopeless trying to undo such rotten gaskets and I tell the Mate so. The port watch between 4am to 8am set the mizzen lower to'gallant.

It is much warmer and we have a fair wind with a good course. I work all morning what with dishwashing and two hours at the wheel. At 12am our watch set the fore and main upper to'gallants. My watch complain at dinner time about my dish cleaning and I tell them to go to hell.

The port watch in the afternoon set all three royals and all staysails and mizzen spanker. So now we are sailing along at about 12 knots with all sails set. I chat with Clapperton in the afternoon about the ship, the crew and things in general. After lunch we have a sing song, the 2nd Mate playing the drums. Then I sleep on my bunk after coffee until 6.30pm. I feel very tired. Christensen still laid up. The 2nd Mate says we are about on a level with Belfast, so we are going along well.
Position 55.28°N - 13.41°W

Day 31 Monday October 21st

Eriksen has a row with the 3rd Mate owing to the fact that the port light had gone out and he had not looked after it. The 3rd Mate threatened to fight him, so at call over, at 4am, Eriksen offers the Mate a fight. At 6am our watch set first all three royals, as the wind is blowing up strong again and the barometer is dropping. I make fast alone the mizzen royal and take an hour over it and when I come down the Mate plays hell, but I tell him I am not very strong and have a sore wrist and that I tried my best. It is all hurry and to hell with them, I will take my own time. Then I carry water to the galley. Christensen turns out again in the afternoon watch. We continue washing the white paint on deck in the afternoon watch and at night after tea we have a great sing song and it went very well. It is the 2nd Mates "Name Day" and he gives each man two cigarettes. I again have a row with Johansen (Swede) and the only boy I don't like on board the ship. He does nothing but boss about and yet he is another seaman himself. I don't like him he is not true to ones face.

Position 51.54°N - 14.13°W

Day 32 Tuesday October 22nd

While I am at the wheel this morning at 3.30am a steamer comes very close and we morse her and she replies. We tell her whom we are and where we are bound for. She tells us she is the "Orion" from Philadelphia bound for London. We ask her if she has seen any other sailing ships but she replies, no. Again we see another steamer at 8am we are in the track of American shipping. We are down in the hold chipping in the morning watch. The 2nd Mate, at 12am, sends me up to overhaul all gardings, a rotten trick, he seems to dislike me now for some reason, but I don't care at all and take my time. We still have a fair wind, occasionally sailing Bi de Vind. I cut my hand rather badly, I am all over sore places. At 11pm we take in the mizzen upper to'gallant. We speak by morse to a Danish steamer at 10pm.

Position 48.53°N - 15.16°W

Day 33 Wednesday October 23rd

The port watch between 4am and 5am make fast the fore and main upper to'gallants. The wind is strengthening a lot but we have course SW. ½ S. At 6am. Our watch take in the fore lower to'gallant and at 8am the port watch take in the main and mizzen lower to'gallants. The barometer is falling fast. Between 4am and 8am we sail 40 miles.

It is much warmer. I am again cursed by the Mate, this time for being so slow carrying water to the galley. I sleep on my bunk during free watch 8am to 1pm and at 12 midday the port watch set again the three lower to'gallants.

In the afternoon our watch set the three upper to'gallants and three royals. I overhaul the gardings on the main upper to'gallant and the fore royal. I was three quarters of an hour waiting up on the fore royal for them to raise the yard and it was very cold. After coffee I overhaul the gardings on the three lower to'gallants so in fact I spent the whole afternoon in the rigging overhauling buntlines a job I dislike. The Captain seems to be very nervy about his sails, if the barometer drops he always takes in sail. Poor old Clapperton is not very popular in his watch , they call him crazy. I warm myself some coffee in working watch at midnight by holding my mug over the small lamp in the fo'c'sle. It takes roughly ten minutes to warm it up.

Position 45.47°N - 14.51°W

Day 34 Thursday October 24th

Down in the hold chipping during the working watch from 8am to 1pm. While I am at the wheel from 11am to 12am the Mate shows me how to take the sun.

There is one large bird following us. It is a lovely day and most boys wash their clothes. I sleep on my bunk in the afternoon. The Mate tells me he sees a rat in the chart house at night.
Position 42.5°N - 16.46°W

Day 35 Friday October 25th

I carry water to the galley before breakfast. We now have a North wind and our course is SW by South. It is a lovely day and quite warm. I sleep on my bunk during morning watch.

Down in the hold chipping in the afternoon. The wind is now from aft so we are slowly getting our North East Trade wind. An oil tanker passes ahead of us at 6pm, we try to morse her but she does not reply.
Position 39°N - 18.1°W

Day 36 Saturday October 26th

Early this morning the wind shifts to slightly NE. I wash the fo'c'sle out and midships during the morning watch and at lunch time I get into a row with my watch for not having it clean enough, but I don't listen to them because they are a filthy lot of hounds and had it been clean it would have been dirty again in five minutes.

The wind by the afternoon is blowing up fairy strong and we are doing about 11 knots. We have a sing song in the afternoon and Clapperton comes up and sings. Mrs Duff comes out onto the poop to sunbathe. Most of the boys get drunk at night especially the Timmerman, 3rd Mate and Cookie. Cookie is certainly a scream conducting the singing in the galley.

A good many of us are suffering from boils including myself. Between 9pm and midnight we travel 36 miles averaging 12 knots.
Position 35°N - 19.26°W

Day 37 Sunday October 27th

It is a lovely morning and I take some snaps. I carry water to the galley before breakfast and then during free watch I wash some of my clothes. Laurie and some of us chat about sailing ships up in the fo'c'sle. We start the dayman business today at 4pm and Liewendahl, Hussel and Stranberg leave us, so now we are left with four men. I have two wheels this afternoon and later we again have a sing song.
Position 30.27°N - 19.45°W

Liewendahl Hussel Stranberg

Day 38 Monday October 28th

I again have a row with my mate. I don't like him at all, he is not to be trusted and is very two faced. He and Johansen (Swede) do a lot of talking together and cause trouble.

When I am alone the Mate is kind and friendly but in front of the rest of the watch, he is always shouting at me. This time it was about the course and as it happened, I was in the right, but he childishly went up to the fo'c'sle to ask Christensen what course he had given me. Anyway I just don't take any notice.

Except for an hour at the wheel I am down in the hold chipping all morning. Then in the afternoon I sleep till coffee time on my bunk. I have a little chat with Mrs Duff on the deck after coffee. At 6pm we have a sing song.

While I am policeman from 11pm to 12pm the Mate asks me to stand by on the poop while he has a sleep a thing he wont allow us to do.
Position 26°N - 20°W

Day 39 Tuesday October 29th

Johansen has Christensen on at 5am this morning when he wakes him up for look-out he tells him it is muster and old Dansky turns out aft only to find he has been had. I carry water to the galley before breakfast etc. Then during free watch 8am to 1pm I sleep on my bunk.

It is a lovely day and the cat and dog enjoy the warmth and play together on deck. We carry coal to the galley in the afternoon and later we are down in the hold chipping. I chat with Laurie at look-out for a few minutes about the ship and the boys. The daymen play cards at night and at 11pm we definitely get our NE Trade wind.
Position 23°N - 20°W

View N E trade wind

Day 40 Wednesday October 30th
We wake up to a very fine Trade Wind and a beautiful morning. We start bending the Trade Wind sails. Our watch in the morning unbend and bend the fore royal, upper and lower to'gallant. I spend two and a half hours at the wheel in glorious sunshine. Mrs Duff steers with me at the other side of the wheel.

During the free watch in the afternoon she chats with me on the fo'c'sle head.

The port watch in the afternoon change the two fore topsails and Mrs Duff helps them both aloft and on deck, she is quite good up in the rigging. At 7pm a steamer passes us heading northwards, we try to morse her but she does not reply. I chat with Laurie aft while I am policeman at 7pm.

During my look-out 11am to 12pm I fell asleep. I cannot keep awake and cannot ever remember being so tired before. I also have bad toothache.
Position 20°N 20.10°W

View from aloft

Mrs Duff on the capstan

Day 41 Thursday October 31st

I still feel very tired, I think it must be the heat. Between 6am and 8am our watch unbend the main royal and bend the new one. It is a glorious day again and very warm. I see a porpoise this morning but so far I have not seen any flying fish.

I sleep on my bunk during the free watch this morning. The port watch unbend and bend the main upper and lower to'gallants and in the afternoon our watch unbend and bend the main upper and lower topsails. At 5pm I overhaul all gardings on the main mast and it takes me one hour and a half. I go up to the royal three times. The gardings on the royal and upper to'gallant were supposed to have been overhauled by the port watch but they were not and why? I come down and curse like hell in the fo'c'sle not realizing the 2nd Mate was sitting there, it is a good joke.

The Captain and Mates seem fed up with Mrs Duff, she follows them all over and gets in the way. We have a sing song at night on deck, 3rd Mate drunk again. I see some flying fish.
Position 15.56°N 20.21°W

Bending a new fore lower to'gallant

Day 42 Friday November 1st

Between 6am and 8am the port watch unbend and bend the mizzen upper to'gallant. During our watch on deck 8am to 1pm we unbend and bend the mizzen upper topsail and the foresail. I overhaul the gardings on the mizzen upper topsail. A locust comes aboard probably from Africa. We finish changing the Trade Wind sails at 1pm. I have a row with the Cook again he is very moody.

I also have a row with Lund up in the rigging. The dog is not so well and cannot walk properly, most of the boys laugh at it, poor creature. The port watch are again down in the hold chipping in the afternoon. Almost all of the boys, except for myself, are suffering from boils.

This evening, donkeyman, (who is the best of the crew) cuts my hair, as good as any barber can do it. After tea we have a sing song on the fo'c'sle head. Mrs Duff comes for'ard and dances with me and some of the other boys, while other boys dance together.

During free watch in the afternoon our Mate (second) comes up an shows donkeyman and myself types of knots. It is a lovely night and I see the Southern Cross for the first time this trip.

While I am policeman from 8am to 9pm the little black cat comes up and plays with me on deck.

Position 12.19°N 21.5°W

Mrs Duff listens to music, self on ukelele

I take water up onto the poop before breakfast. Mrs Duff turns out for the first time in the port watch and cleans brass.

This morning we see plenty of porpoises also a large whale aft.
We only have a little wind this morning. During the afternoon watch on deck we clean the brass, then we wash down the deck, only two men to do it and I pulled up seawater from over the side in a boiling tropical sun.

Oh, how my back ached and how tired I was. Then straight after I had one and three quarters of an hour at the wheel. We all do stunts on deck after 5pm long jumping and all kinds, we bring in the 2nd and 3rd Mates. Mrs Duff chats with the Captain on the poop in the afternoon. Our jazz band practice again in the evening and we also have the gramophone on. I sleep out on deck tonight with Christensen and most of the other boys. We have now lost the NE Trade Wind and we are definitely in the calm belt. One small swallow is following us.
Position 9.39°N 21.33°W

Day 44 Sunday November 3rd

I am once again dish washer. It is very hot again today. We sit out on deck and have the gramophone on and I play Liewendahl at deck tennis. Then we have a rain squall (tropical) and it came down in bucket loads. All hands collected it including the Mates and most of the boys were running about naked although in full view of Mrs Duff looking out of her porthole. And so is the life on a sailing ship. We fill all tanks up including the donkey boiler. The Chief Mate gives his dog a wash and then clips him like a poodle. I chat with the 2nd Mate at the wheel. We have two small swallows following us and what I take to be a seagul.

We are truly a very happy crew and get on well together. I play deck tennis with Clapperton, the 3rd Mate and the 2nd Mate after coffee, then I referee for them.

Heavy rain sets in at 6pm and goes on all night, we all get wet through and we have to stand by aft. Johansen did not know and the old chap was fast asleep up for'ard.
Position 8.13°N 21.33°W

Day 45 Monday November 4th

It is still raining hard at 4am and at 4.30am a heavy squall springs up and our watch have to stand aft by the mizzen royal halyard. At 6am the fore royal gives way and we start unbending it. I carry water to the galley. The port watch at 8am bend a new royal. It is still raining, when will it cease? We sail Bi de Vind.

Christensen catches a small swallow, poor wee thing was tired out and was dozing on deck. We have now five swallows following us and they all seem tired and wet through. I now have a boil on the wrist, everybody seems to have them.

In the afternoon we commence chipping in the hold , then it rains cats and dogs and we come up on the deck and with the rain water we wash the whole deck down. I have last wheel at 6pm to 7pm and during that time a very heavy rain squall comes up and I get wet through. I have a little row with Christensen over not helping me carry the dishes. I told him I was always doing things for other people but nobody ever did anything for me. Poor old Clapperton, they are always talking about him behind his back.
Position 6.5°N 21.56°W

Day 46 Tuesday November 5th

During our watch 12am to 4am we have to do plenty of bracing and the Captain comes out as it was blowing up hard. I sleep very badly tonight, home is always on my mind and little Honey (Mother). Clapperton told this morning by the Captain that he looks like Judas with his long black beard. At 9am we get a fair wind and we brace and set the mainsail, mizzen sail and also the flying jib and jigger gaff. I am down in the hold chipping and we also commence painting. It is a lovely day what a difference to the last two days of nothing but continuous rain. We see about eight large sharks astern this afternoon. Mrs Duff is now turning out regularly with her watch and the boys say she steers at the wheel very well. The boys have a sing song after tea under the fo'c'sle head and it sounded very fine to hear it from aft. Christensen is caught asleep while policeman. *Position 5.5°N 21.53°W*

Mrs Duff helps with the bracing

Day 47 Wednesday November 6th
I carry water to the galley after breakfast and also onto the poop. The port watch commence tarring the deck, a hateful job. Johansen and I play our music in the hold during our free watch in the morning on special request from the sail maker. We have showers all morning. Clapperton turns out late for muster this morning at 4am and gets into a row. The little dog is better again and goes down into the hold with the First Mate. I then sleep for two hours on my bunk.

During working watch in the afternoon I am down in the hold for half an hour and then I am dishwashing and then on the wheel 2.30pm to 4pm. At 3pm we are given a holiday but it was a poor holiday as the Mate had us putting sail away and then I was look-out from 6pm to 7pm. I have four games of deck tennis with Liewendahl and he beat me in each set 6-0, 6-2, 6-2, 6-3. We have

a lovely SE Trade Wind blowing but we sail Bi de Vind steering SW ½ W. At 7.15pm a conference is held in the sail locker by all those who have crossed the line before including the three Mates. We have sardines and Tomatoed Herrings for tea (how great), I sleep in the sail locker tonight, it is impossible to sleep up for'ard as the daymen make such a noise. A lovely day.
Position 5.9°N 23.32°W

Clapperton after baptism

Day 48 Thursday November 7th

Down in the hold chipping in the morning. At 12 midday we are 2 minutes off the Line so the Captain gives us a half holiday and says we will hold the ceremony of 'Crossing the Line' today at 3pm. Before 3pm we get everything prepared and at 3pm prompt the fun commences and how well the boys dressed especially the Chief Mate as the Doctor and Cookie as the policeman. Mrs Duff is first and is painted and ducked in the bath also shaved

with paint. Then comes Clapperton who is stripped almost naked although Mrs Duff is watching. Old Stranberg made us all laugh, he did not like it and tried to refuse everything but he was forced into it. Our Jazz band plays for the Captain aft at 8pm and we go on until 10.30pm. The Captain seemed to thoroughly enjoy it and the officers, Captain and Mrs Duff dance on the poop.

The Captain gives us all a glass of rum, a glass of Gin and a tin of cigarettes, not such a bad fellow after all. A most enjoyable time everybody was happy. Again I say we are a very happy crew.
Position 0.20°N 26°W

Liewendahl as Queen Neptune

'Crossing the line', Mrs Duff 3rd from right

Day 49 Friday November 8th
I carry water to the poop in the morning between 6am and 8am. Sleep on my bunk during free watch 8am to 1pm. We oil all the deck in the afternoon watch. The 1st and 2nd Mate were helping. The 1st Mate is a great fellow, I like him immensely, a real human kind of chap. I chat with Pedersen about Mrs Duff. I again sleep in the sail locker and I get this hellish toothache.
Position 2.51°S 28.14°W

Day 50 Saturday November 9th
I spend the whole morning watch cleaning the fo'c'sle out. My boil is much better today. The rest of the boys clean the brass on the poop.

I play a few games of deck tennis with Liewendahl and Karlsson. I have yet to beat Liewendahl. I play my ukelele while I am at look-out. I chat with Laurie while I am policeman, he tells me the 3rd Mate (his Mate) has started bullying him but he does not care and will wait his chance to get his own back.

The SE Trade Wind blows strong all day and we steer SSW ½ W. The 3rd Mate seems to be disliked generally, he is far to cocky being only 21 years old.
Position 5.43°S 28.33°W

Day 51 Sunday November 10th

I carry water to the poop before breakfast. I have a row with Christensen, I am beginning to dislike him very much, he does nothing but make a fool of me. While I am look-out at 4am this morning the Mate comes up onto the fo'c'sle head and accuses me of smoking but it was not me it was Christensen. We all take snaps. Clapperton is being continually bullied by the 3rd Mate and was again this morning. He says he is going to report it to the Captain.

I wash some of my clothes. We have a leak in the ship aft and there is plenty of water in the hold so the donkeyman and Timmerman have to go down and cement it up. I play some games of deck tennis after lunch and in the evening.

The 2nd Mate and Liewendahl (Finland) challenge myself and Clapperton (England) they beat us and a certain amount of ill feeling crept into the game. The 2nd Mate also seems to dislike Clapperton. We play our jazz band at night.

I try to make different types of knots in the afternoon sitting on the deck in glorious sunshine. I again sleep in the sail locker. Two steamers pass us tonight, one when I was look-out and the other when at the wheel. The first we morsed and got a reply but she was foreign and could not use English, the other did not reply.
Position 8.58°S 32.21°W

Day 52 Monday November 11th

We chip in the hold during morning watch 8am to 1pm. Pedersen (Dane) and Mrs Duff seem to follow each other about all over the place. It is the talk of the ship. At 2.30pm a steamer is sighted and at 3pm she comes alongside. She turns out to be the German ship "Iolanthie" we signal her and ask her to report us to Lloyds. Then we ask if she has seen any other sailing ships, she replies she saw the "Parma" at 12 midnight last night. Christensen and I are still not on speaking terms, he is a great baby.

I sleep on my bunk from coffee time 4.30pm to 6.30pm. It is a lovely night with a full moon. I have a chat with Laurie while at look-out and he tells me the 2nd Mate has again been nasty with him. He says he is not going to stand it any longer and is going to report the whole affair to the Captain. If there is one thing above all that annoys me very much about the Scandinavians in general they seem (all) to have nothing better to do than discuss people every minute of the day, it gets on my nerves.

While policeman 10pm to 11pm the 2nd Mate shows me some tricks (all sorts) and we both have a shot at seeing who can raise a weight the most times. I lift it 12 and he does 20.
Position 11.58°S 33.12°W

168

Steamer "Iolanthie"

Day 53 Tuesday November 12th
I carry water to the galley before breakfast and sleep on my bunk during free watch.

We chip in the hold all afternoon in baking heat. I am so hot I look just as though I have been swilled with water. The cat sits by the wheel while I am steering and once actually gets on my shoulders.

Clapperton tells me he has been to the Captain about the Mates so we must await results. The Mate plays up with me for washing before going to the wheel, unnecessary.
Position 15.15°S 34.15°W

Day 54 Wednesday November 13th
We are again down in the hold chipping during the morning watch, the 1st Mate being down with us all the time. During free watch I clean my bunk out and find some red bunk bugs. I also air my shore clothes which are full of green damp owing to the weather.

It is again a lovely day and very warm. At 11am we get our course South by East. The 2nd Mate tells me this morning while I am at the wheel, that this morning we have passed the sun. That is, the sun instead of being directly ahead of us before, that is to say South, it is now North of us and will be all the time until we cross the line again 'homeward bound'. Johansen (Swede) whom I considered

169

'no good' is quite a good fellow at that but just a little weak willed. This afternoon he gave me a packet of tobacco, mine had all gone damp and mouldy.

Christensen is caught asleep at look-out by the 2nd Mate and is ticked off and told to go up aloft and overhaul all the gardings. Then the Mate, who seems to be in a very bad temper, goes into the fo'c'sle and tells the daymen, who are playing cards , that they must turn the lamp out. They refuse, so he comes up again and turns it out himself. The crew seem very angry with him. Our watch have now to 'stand by' until further notice.
Position 18.15°S 33.28°W

Day 55 Thursday November 14th

I carry water to the poop before breakfast. All the crew are very annoyed with the Mate and he has now given orders for no oil to be given to the fo'c'sle today. He plays up with me for allowing salt water to flow into a fresh water tin which happened to be empty.

I sleep on my bunk in the morning and write a few letters. In the afternoon we are all again down in the hold chipping rust, the Mate keeping us down there right up until 6pm. I chat with Laurie at look-out between 7pm and 8pm about what the Captain said when he reported the Mates. He tells me the Mate came up to him (2nd Mate) and said he had better be careful what he said in future.

The Southern Cross is plainly visible now and for the first time I see the two pointers.
Position 21.36°S 31.48°W

Day 56 Friday November 15th

During our watch on deck between 12am and 4am the South East trade wind leaves us during a heavy rain squall and we brace four times, the wind being more aft. I have a row with the Mate, because he does not tell the look-out to come and help so I shout a little and he asks me what I mean and I tell him it is impossible for two men to brace alone. Also I don't obey the order to 'stand by'. I sit in the fo'c'sle and make my usual cup of coffee.

In the morning watch 8am to 1pm I am in the coal hole getting coal for the galley. It is hellish hot and I spend three hours down there very tired and hot. In the afternoon I again write letters. I play deck tennis with Liewendahl and Christensen after coffee. The Mate chats with me at the wheel at night. I make myself a cup of cocoa during night watch on deck.
Very little wind but we still hold our course South by East ¾ East.
Position 23.51°S 30.30°W

Day 57 Saturday November 16th

Carried water to the tank on the poop before breakfast. Slept on my bunk during free watch and again wrote a few letters. In the afternoon till 4pm we cleaned up the deck. Then all of a sudden the fine weather left us, the wind changed around and began to blow strong. Our watch of three men with the Chief Mate turned the ship. This took us until 6pm, very heavy work. Then Christensen and I made fast the jigger topsail the Mate playing hell because we took so long. It rained in torrents from 4pm until 7pm and we all got wet through. At twenty to twelve our watch were roused up to turn the ship again and we worked continuously in pouring rain and a gale until 4am. We took in all three royals, only nine men and actually tightened up the braces by applying them to the capstan.

The Mate plays hell with me on the poop in front of the Captain for missing his commands but I just tell him to go to hell whereupon we have an argument. While I am holding the rope around the capstan, Lund, who is hauling round with a capstan bar comes into collision with me, I cut my left eye very badly and the Mate, who is now very friendly, apologises and bathes it for me. The deck is very dark and it is hard to see anything. Everybody seems to be in a bad mood. The 2nd Mate I cannot make out at all one minute he is the best fellow you could wish to meet then suddenly he plays hell.

Good-bye to the Tropics.
Position 25.19°S 27.43°W

Hussel as sail maker

Day 58 Sunday November 17th

I wash my shirt and clothes this morning. I see my first albatross this voyage and stormy petrel. The 2nd Mate is very friendly again today. I sit on my bunk and read during free watch in the afternoon also I write a few more letters. We turn the ship again at 7pm all hands turning out including the daymen. At 7pm Hussel, Karlsson, Stranberg and Orlander are ordered to return to watches. I have hellish toothache again tonight.
Position 25.51°S 29.43°W

Day 59 Monday November 18th

Before breakfast I carry water to the galley then I have wheel 7am to 8am, the rest of the watch commence changing the tropical sails for the stronger ones. They unbend the main lower topsail in terrific wind and rain and it takes a very long time. At 8am the port watch bend the fresh sail. Then on account of the wind and rain the 1st Mate stops the changing of the sail and they chip rust. At 10am the wind dies away altogether and we have brilliant warm sunshine for the rest of the day, so in our afternoon watch we unbend and bend the main royal and upper topsail. I overhaul the gardings in each case. The Mate plays hell with our watch for taking so long with the royal. At 6pm while I am at the wheel we go course S by E ¾ E but at 8pm we are becalmed again and the port watch take up the mizzen and mainsail. We later take up the foresail. Clapperton and the 3rd Mate have a terrific row in front of the Captain and Mrs Duff and they call each other all the swear words under the sun. Albatross still here.
Position 25.52°S 28.51°W

Day 60 Tuesday November 19th

In the morning watch 8am to 1pm our watch change the mizzen royal, upper to'gallant and lower topsail and the fore upper topsail. I overhaul the gardings in each case. There are two albatross following us today. Mrs Duff helps the port watch after lunch. They change the foresail and so we finish changing the tropical sails. Clapperton is now given all the dirty jobs by the Mate, such as carrying water and cleaning the lavatories out but he does not seem to mind. I sit out on deck in the afternoon in glorious sunshine as we are completely becalmed.
Position 26.29°S 27.39°W

Making fast the main royal

Day 61 Wednesday November 20th
I carry water to the galley before breakfast and overhaul the gardings up the fore mast. It is again a glorious day with hardly a cloud to be seen. We are completely becalmed the sea being just like one large piece of ice. Down in the hold chipping again in the afternoon, this time on the port side, the Chief Mate has now commenced chipping in the bilges. I chat with Clapperton in the evening, poor fellow he seems fed up with everything. Towards night we get a little wind and set the mainsail, mizzen and foresail and we sail Bi de Vind steering SW ½ W
Position 27.55°S 27.51°W

Day 62 Thursday November 21st
We chip rust in the hold all morning. The wind is stronger now than last night but we still sail Bi de Vind steering South West to South. I have hellish toothache again all morning. Two albatrosses still following us. There is a fairly calm sea today. I sleep on my bunk all afternoon during free watch from 2pm to 6.30pm. The boys play cards at night and I play my ukelele.
Position 29.28°S 29.13°W

Johansen and self

Day 63 Friday November 22nd

I carry water to the galley before breakfast, then down in the hold chipping. We have a sing song during free watch out on deck the 2nd Mate coming up and playing with us. I sleep for one and a half hours on my bunk. Down in the hold chipping again in the afternoon. I have a row with Johansen over the lamp, he thinking he could go to the wheel , come back and claim the same lamp, ridiculous, so I said next time take the lamp to the wheel with you. We have ten albatross here with us today and we feed them. The Cook catches two and to the disgust of Mrs Duff and myself , kills them. Typical of his character. We have a sing song at night. We have been completely becalmed all day.
Position 30.21°S 29.30°W

Two dead albatross

Day 64 Saturday November 23rd

I clean the fo'c'sle out and midships. The rest first of all clean filthy, smelly wheat from the aft hold and what a stink, then they are down in the hold chipping. Mrs Duff comes aft in the morning and chats with the boys of the port watch, she takes photos. I wash two shirts in the afternoon. Two albatrosses here today and a very large Blue Whale keeps on swimming round the ship. Most of the boys work with their models. It amuses me the seriousness they put on when working on these models. I play my ukelele out on deck in glorious sunshine. Our jazz band plays before the Captain aft again tonight, it is a great success. Mrs Duff joins in and sings with us. The Captain gives us cigarettes and cigars. Poor old Pedersen, he is very lovesick over Mrs Duff, it is the talk of the ship.
Position 30.5°S 29.30°W

Donkeyman with his model

I carry water onto the poop before breakfast. We had a lovely sunset and it is a lovely day with a fair wind and course South East. Johansen who is a real comedian amuses the fo'c'sle after breakfast with his antics. Pedersen is still lovesick this morning. I sleep on my bunk for one and a half hours. Clapperton takes a photograph after lunch of the whole crew. Some of the boys play cards.

Mrs Duff and Pedersen go up the mizzen mast to the royal taking snaps. The Bosun is laid up with tropical fever and then Timmerman with a badly cut hand. We average 12 knots all day. Liewendahl and I often tease each other, this fellow has a sense of humour which a majority of Finns do not. We have a special dish tonight tomatoed herrings.
Position 31.7°S 27.5°W

The whole crew, Mrs Duff 1st on left

Down in the hold chipping rust all morning watch, five hours! The Chief Mate I like very much, he has a sense of humour and is a great comedian. He is continually joking in the hold. I hear today that Mrs Duff was signed on as an apprentice and is to work for money on the trip home. We average 12 knots all morning. The sea is beginning to get quite rough. It rains bucket loads between

5pm and 7pm and the port watch fill up all the water tanks and the donkey boiler. At 7pm, our watch on deck, we take in all three royals, upper to'gallants, jigger spanker and gaff. The flying jib blows out, I am at the wheel at this time. It rains like hell at 10.30pm so we take in and make fast all three lower to'gallants. I make fast the fore upper to'gallant with Lund, it is a hellish job with the sail flapping about madly and twice I am saved from falling on deck by catching hold of the upper to'gallant footrope. We all get wet through although we have oilskins on.
Position 33.23°S 23°W

Day 67 Tuesday November 26th

At twelve midnight all hands clew up the mizzen and main sail and our watch make fast the mizzen sail. This takes us one hour, so by the time we get into our bunks it is 1.45pm only giving us two hours sleep. At 4am this morning we are again working this time bracing, the wind is now blowing from aft. We brace again at 5.15am and at 6am we unbend the main upper to'gallant sail which was torn in the gale last night. Then we bend a new one and the port watch finish it at 8am. We are all very tired and all sleep all morning during free watch.

The course now is SE by E ½ E. Down in the hold chipping all afternoon. I have last wheel 6pm to 7pm and the little cat comes up and plays near me. It is the most playful cat I have ever seen. Liewendahl, myself, Stranberg and Orlander play the jazz band after tea. I see my first Cape pigeon this afternoon and a stormy petrel and about five albatrosses. Lovely sunset.
Position 35.20°S 18.24°W

Day 68 Wednesday November 27th

At 1am our watch are called out to turn the ship. The Mate plays up with me because I let loose the Bi de Vind sheet and says how many bloody times have I told you not to do so. I argue saying never, he tells me to be quiet and I say I won't. Then later I have an argument with Johansen and the Mate hears me and then, the low kind of chap he is, he starts on to me again and calls me a "Bloody Englishman" and asks me who I think I am and tells me not to argue with him.

Whereupon I butt in and tell him he is the biggest two faced person I have ever met, always my friend and chatting to me when none of the crew are about then yelling at me in front of them. I cannot weigh his character up. Down in the hold chipping all morning, the 3rd Mate is down with us being a dayman now. I sleep on my bunk in the afternoon free watch. At 3pm it starts to rain again and by 7pm the wind has increased a great deal and at 8pm our watch take in the two jigger sails the spanker and upper gaff. I make fast the latter with Lund. The Mate is trying his hardest to make friends with me again but I refuse to have any of it.
Position 35.40°S 17.37°W

Shipwright at work

Day 69 Thursday November 28th

We turn the ship at 4am in pouring rain and I get wet through. Then I carry water to the tanks on the poop, later overhauling gardings on the fore and main masts. We are now sailing Bi de Vind again. Down in the hold chipping again during afternoon watch. The 2nd Mate is trying his hardest to be friends again. Mrs Duff helps us to set the spanker. I let loose the gaff. I note a number of albatrosses about today. The rain clears up at 2.30pm. In the evening Cookie tries to harpoon some big fish which are following the ship just below the bowsprit but does not succeed. Mrs Duff gives me two tins of cigarettes. We have a fair wind and tonight I hear we are only 95 miles from Tristan de Cuna, so we should be there about 4am tomorrow.

Position 36.36°S 15.14°W

Day 70 Friday November 29th

We keep a sharp lookout for Tristan de Cuna during look-out all night but through very poor navigation we miss it and are supposed to have passed it a long way back at 4.30am. I spend five hours in the coal hole in the morning. There are a lot of shore birds about all day and plenty of Cape pigeons and a few albatross. Mrs Duff comes up fo'ard in the afternoon and chats with us. I get a bucket on my head in the coal hole and it knocks me out for a few minutes. I wash some clothes in the afternoon and then sleep on my bunk. Hussel pinches some coffee beans from the galley, getting in by means of the sky light and we all have a coffee at midnight a real good coffee too.

Position 38.5°S 10.42°W

Day 71 Saturday November 30th

Just after we had started work at 6am the bosun slips into the hold from the half deck, he slipped over a sail. He seemed to be in agony and has cut both his wrists and the left side of his chest very badly, in fact raw, but as to whether he has broken any bones or not nobody seems to know. I carry water to the galley and fo'c'sle before breakfast.

Down in the hold chipping rust until 3pm then we brush the deck finishing about 4.30 pm. then I overhaul gardings on the fore royal afterwards. We have the wind bearing aft, at 5.30pm it becomes overcast and the wind blows up. It looks like we are in for a rough night. At 6.15pm we take in and make fast the jigger spanker and gaff and the outer jib, inner jib and upper to'gallant staysail on the bowsprit. I help Lund to make them fast and we also take in the main and fore staysail. My hat blows off the second one I've lost this trip. We have pancakes again for tea, the third day running, we are all fed up with them. It is not enough for us when we are working all day and night.

The ship is rolling badly. The policeman in each watch has to stand by the Bosun all night whom I hear is very poorly and the Chief Mate has discovered he has broken ribs.
Position 38.23°S 7.31°W

Day 72 Sunday December 1st

At 1am this morning our watch brace, the wind now coming from the South, so we set all the bowsprit staysails, the main and mizzen staysails while the port watch later on set the two jigger sails. We have a black albatross following us all day, it is very rare to see a black albatross. Laurie comes up for'ard and chats with us after lunch. I read my book, "My Crowded Solitude" after coffee time in the afternoon. Towards evening the wind gets stronger and a very heavy sea comes up making the ship roll very badly and she is very hard to steer. Nobody can make out why the officers, all of them, don't take more interest in the poor old Bosun who actually is worse than people think.
Position 39.31°S 2.1°W

Day 73 Monday December 2nd

I carry water to the galley before breakfast then overhaul gardings up the fore mast, going up to the royal. I have now toothache on the other side of my face, what agony I am suffering. I try to work in the afternoon going into the hold for one hour but the pain is agony and at 2.30pm I have to come up being unable to stand it any longer. I go to the fo'c'sle and lie on my bunk but cannot sleep. I spend a restless night from 7pm to 12pm with perhaps a few minutes sleep at times. Laurie comes up and chats with me in the afternoon.
Position 40.16°S 3.16°E

Day 74 Tuesday December 3rd

I turn out at 12 midnight with the rest of my watch but the pain is still agony. However, I do it to save my watch extra wheels etc. Down in the hold all morning chipping rust. The 2nd Mate, who is very friendly, shows me how to steer as it is very rough and the ship is rolling badly. I try to talk to Christensen but he refuses. Honestly he is the biggest baby and most impossible creature to get on with I have ever come across. But what do I care? Not two hoots. The Bosun is a little better but still looks very poorly.

At night the wind strengthens considerably and I have a very anxious time at the wheel between 10pm and 11pm it being so hard and once I was actually 2 points off, the mate ordered another man up (Hussel) but it was unnecessary. At 10.45pm our watch took in all three royals and at 11pm we take in all three lower to'gallants, I and Johansen making fast the fore upper to'gallant which was very easy. It rains heavy and the Mate tells us the reason why we took in sail was because the barometer was falling fast.
Position 40.47°S 9.47°E

Day 75 Wednesday December 4th

I am unable to sleep one minute last night having hellish toothache caused chiefly through the rolling of the ship. I carry water to the galley before breakfast then overhaul gardings up the fore and main masts. We set the main staysail. We have heavy showers all morning.

Down in the hold chipping all afternoon. The Captain very kindly asks me how my toothache is while I am at the wheel. We average 9 knots once in 32 minutes and do 15 knots in one hour. There are a few Cape pigeons about. The Mate is very friendly nowadays. My toothache ceases at 7pm for the first time in three days.
Position 41.9°S 16.5°E

Day 76 Thursday December 5th

Down in the hold chipping rust all morning. Mrs Duff comes up onto the poop while I am at the wheel and chats a little. Again I have a quarrel with Christensen over nothing at all. The port watch between 4am and 8am set the three royals and all staysails. We brace at 9am the wind being dead aft. I read a letter on my bunk during free watch in the afternoon, then help Hussel with his model.

Mrs Duff comes up forward after tea and chats with me for about 15 minutes. The boys play a prank on Pedersen. There is a peculiar ring around the moon tonight, probably a sign of bad weather.
Position 41.57°S 21.57°E

Day 77 Friday December 6th

The Captain gives us a whole holiday in commemoration of Finlands freedom from Russia. I carry water to the tank on the poop before breakfast. There is a strong wind blowing and two men are at the wheel.

I sleep on my bunk in the morning. We make 32 miles in 2 hours and 56 miles in one watch, which the Mate tells me is a record. The port watch take all three royals in, two having torn sails.

During the morning watch 8am to 1pm there are two at the wheel but at 1.30pm we again only have one. It rains most of the afternoon. I have almost a free night except for one hour.
Position 41.59°S 27.31°E

Day 78 Saturday December 7th

I clean out the fo'c'sles and midships and the Mate rows me for not taking my wheel and says in future I must take my wheel on a Saturday.

There are one or two albatrosses about, some Cape pigeons, a stormy petrel and about six sea swallows. I wash a shirt and towel. It drizzles mainly all morning but clears up in the afternoon. Laurie takes a snap of me and Lund up the fore

rigging and of a number of us round the capstan and the fo'c'sle head. I chat with Mrs Duff aft while policeman.

We brace twice between 7pm and 12pm the wind now coming from the North. A small shore bird is following us tonight and flies over the poop. A wonderful moonlit night.
Position 42.11°S 31.59°E

Up the fore rigging

Day 79 Sunday December 8th

I carry water to the tanks on the poop before breakfast with Johansen. I clean my bunk out during free watch in the morning, then sleep on my bunk.

The wind increases gradually all day and at 1pm it becomes cloudy with the likelihood of rain and we now sail Bi de Vind. The wheel is heavy but easy.

At 3.15pm we take in the jigger gaff and I make it fast but it is so hard that Johansen, who is at the wheel, comes up and helps me, the Captain taking the wheel. We also take in the two royals, Main and Fore, Stranberg and Christensen make them fast. There are a lot of albatross and a few stormy petrels about today. At 5pm we take in the jigger spanker and then the three upper to'gallants. Then the inner and outer jib which tore in two. I make fast the fore upper to'gallant with Christensen and the outer jib with Stranberg.

The wind still increases and the port watch at 8pm take in all three lower to'gallants.
Position 42.20°S 37°E

Day 80 Monday December 9th
At 2pm while I am at the wheel "all hands" (free watch being called out) take in the mainsail and the mizzen sail in drenching rain and very cold. I spend two hours at the wheel. I again have toothache.

Down in the hold chipping rust all morning, I have no wheel. It is still rainy and blowing hard, we set no sail and later fog comes. I sleep on my bunk during free watch in the afternoon.

The port watch make fast the fore and main upper topsails. The wind is blowing a perfect gale and the ship is rolling about at fortyfive degrees and everything in the fo'csle is flying about all over. The wheel is very hard but I manage to keep within half a point. It rains hard too and it is bitterly cold more so than the North of Scotland and I cannot even get warm in my bunk. We square up a little again and go course NE by E ½ E.
Position 44.32°S 42.53°E

Day 81 Tuesday December 10th
It is bitterly cold again this morning. There are scores of Cape pigeons flying about today and some albatross. I am starving cold at the wheel. I carry water to the tanks on the poop before breakfast . I clean my shore suit out during free watch in the morning, then sleep on my bunk.

Down in the hold chipping all afternoon. Johansen goes up sick at 3pm with a bad stomach ache. At 6pm we heave up the foresail as there is no wind and at 6.45pm while I am at the wheel, we turn the ship, the wind now blowing from the South.
Position 44.48°S 47.36°E

Day 82 Wednesday December 11th

At 2am this morning we set the foresail, fore upper topsail and mizzen upper topsail. I overhaul gardings in the mizzen mast and I am up the rigging for one and a half hours in a biting cold wind and rain and am so cold that I cannot feel anything.

*View Looking down
from mizzen mast*

Down in the hold chipping in the morning watch. We set the mizzen and main sails and the three lower to'gallants. Johansen again having to overhaul gardings which he does not like and plays up with the Mate but the Mate tells him to shut up.

While I am at the wheel the Captain orders another man up on account of having to keep on turning the ship first to port and then to starboard to help the crew to set the sails. The wind gradually strengthens all morning and the rain ceases thank goodness. The port watch in the afternoon set the 3 upper to'gallants and the jigger spanker.

During the morning watch we do 37 miles in three hours that equals 12 Knots. I sleep on my bunk in the afternoon. Mrs Duff is helping the sail makers every day now. The little cat comes up forward into the fo'c'sle tonight and comes into my bunk, it sleeps all night on Johansens bunk.
Position 44.57°S 50.7°E

Day 83 Thursday December 12th

The port watch at 2am this morning set the fore and main royals, the mizzen royal being unbent and repaired by the sail makers. Before breakfast we set the mizzen and I carry water to the poop and overhaul gardings. I sleep on my bunk during free watch this morning.

Down in the hold all afternoon chipping rust. The Mate plays hell with Johansen over slacking with his chipping and at 6pm sends him up the fore mast to overhaul gardings and I go up the main and mizzen. The food on the ship is getting worse and worse and tonight we have some disgusting dish which no one will eat. Hussel dumps all the pickles on the top and takes it back to the Steward just as it is. The Steward plays hell. There is very little wind and it is much warmer.
Position 43.30°S 56.35°E

182

Day 84 Friday December 13th

Down in the hold chipping for one hour during working watch in the morning. Then for the rest of the time I am down in the coal hold filling tins up with coal which Christensen carries to the galley. There are a lot of sea birds of all kinds about today. I chat with the chief Mate for a few minutes up forward after lunch.

I sleep on my bunk after coffee. While I am at the wheel from 8pm to 9pm the Mate comes and chats to me about how long we must spend at a navigation school in England. I and Johansen make some toast at night over the lamp. We have plenty of bracing.
Position 42.10°S 60.19°E

Day 85 Saturday December 14th

I carry water to the galley and to the tanks on the poop. I am not feeling so well this morning being very hot although the weather is still cold. I think it is a cold I have. At one time I am so exhausted I very nearly fainted. We square the yards at 6am the wind being dead aft. The 2nd Mate comes up forward after breakfast and views some of the boys models.

I sleep on my bunk for a while but as usual Eriksen, who never seems to do any work, is in the fo'c'sle gassing away. In our working watch in the afternoon, we bend a new mizzen royal, I going up and giving a hand and then I overhaul the gardings on all three masts.

It is a lovely day and much warmer. Mrs Duff gives me two tins of Kensitas cigarettes. We brace at 5pm the wind now coming from the North.
Position 42.21°S 63.41°E

Day 86 Sunday December 15th

There is a strong wind blowing from the North this morning it had gradually got stronger during the night. At 10am we brace a little the wind now being more aft and it begins to rain. The wheel is very hard and I am a point off nearly all the time. We take in the outer jib and the inner jib and the main and mizzen staysails, also the spanker and the gaff.

We have a great political talk up forward after dinner, chiefly about Communists who seem to be disliked thoroughly and we have discussion again after tea, Clapperton joining in. At 6pm the wind shifts aft and at 7pm it blows up from the South, the rain and mist immediately clear and we have a fine moonlit night but plenty of wind. The boys again play a trick on Pedersen who is with Mrs Duff on deck a long time between 7pm and 12pm.
Position 42.58°S 69.42°E

Day 87 Monday December 16th

I carry water to the galley before breakfast then overhaul gardings on all three masts. Just before 8am we have a very heavy squall with rain and it blows hard.

The wheel is again very hard to steer swinging a point each side .

We have three albatross still following us and a few Cape pigeons. At 12.30pm the Captain orders two men at the wheel there is a very heavy sea but at 1.30pm we have one man again. I find the wheel very hard indeed but the Mate kindly helps me. Then I am down in the hold until 6pm chipping rust. There is a tremendous sea at 6pm and the Mate and some of the boys take snaps from the top of the charthouse. At 6.20pm while Hussel is at the wheel we nearly get pooped. A wave rushes at the stern and comes completely over the ship (poop) wetting Hussel through and the Mate calls for two men at the wheel.

Everything all over the ship is in tremendous disorder owing to the tremendous roll she gave at the time. Up in the fo'c'sle pots, sea-chests and cases fly all over, while aft in the sail locker paint, sails etc are spilt all over the floor and we set about cleaning it up. At 6.30pm we take in all three royals I and Johansen making fast the mizzen royal, while at 6.45pm we take in the three upper to'gallants but the port watch go aloft at 7pm and make them fast. They also take in the main sail. At 9pm once again we have one man at the wheel. Hussel told me later that the compass went wrong when we got pooped and that he had never known water on the poop before not even off the Horn.
Position 43.16°S 76.42°E

Day 88 Tuesday December 17th

This morning we still have one man at the wheel although there is plenty of wind and a heavy sea and I find it hard to steer.

During our morning watch we set the three upper to'gallants, I going aloft to overhaul the gardings up the main mast. We later set the spanker and the main staysail. I clean up the rope room aft under the wheel box it was in a terrible mess owing to yesterdays weather. It is a fine sunny day with occasional showers.

I found it impossible to sleep last night owing to the continual heavy rolling. I sleep on my bunk a little during free watch in the afternoon.

We brace twice in the watch 7pm to 12pm. There is very little wind now and again we set the outer and inner jibs and the main staysail. I feel ill tonight having drunk a mug of tea with salt in it instead of sugar.
Position 42.36°S 82.49°E

Day 89 Wednesday December 18th

I carry water to the galley before breakfast and onto the poop and overhaul gardings on all three masts. I sleep on my bunk during free watch in the morning. Down the hold chipping in the afternoon. After 2pm the wind begins to get strong and at 6pm we take in the jigger spanker and gaff. The wind increases as the night goes on and at 11.30pm the port watch take in and make fast the three royals.
Position 52.50°S 88.26°E

Day 90 Thursday December 19th

At 2am our watch take in the three upper to'gallants and I spend two hours at the wheel which later gets so heavy that we have two men at the wheel, Hussel joining me. At 3am we take in and make fast the three lower to'gallants. I and Lund making fast the fore upper to'gallant. I have another row with the 2nd Mate over going into the fo'c'sle to take off my coat when I came from the wheel. He always goes for me.

The wind still increases and at 4am the port watch take in and make fast the mizzen sail while at 8am all hands take in and make fast the main sail. Down in the hold chipping for an hour in the morning. Dish washing this morning is almost impossible. Our watch are then told to come out of the hold and stand by. We make fast all holds. We then take in and make fast the mizzen staysail, the fore staysail and inner jib. We now have three men at the wheel and while I am up there and steering with Johansen and Christensen, I have a tremendous row and offer to leave the wheel.

Meanwhile all sails go back and we nearly get pooped. All the watch, the Captain and the 2nd and 3rd Mates helping to turn the wheel. At 2pm all hands (we being called out from free watch) take in and make fast the mizzen and main upper topsails. The mizzen topsail was a devil the sail kicking about like a madman nearly chucking all hands onto the deck. Then later the port watch take in and make fast the fore upper topsail. There is a lot of water on deck big waves continuously coming over and also on the poop, very unusual. At 4.30 pm the fore sail blows out on the port side and once again we are called out from free watch to help to take it in all in a biting cold wind and rain. There are now five men at the wheel (4pm) and it is blowing a hurricane. We now have only four sails up. There is a tremendous sea. I have a very difficult job dishwashing at night, it is almost impossible.

I have a row with the port watch over the dishes not being clean enough. At 8pm we have two men at the wheel, the weather cheers up and the barometer is rising.
Position 42.57°S 95.38°E

Day 91 Friday December 20th

The barometer again drops this morning but while I am at the wheel 5am to 6am there is only one man at the wheel but as the wind and sea has increased considerably by 8am once again we have two.

I heave up water for the tanks on the poop, an almost impossible job with the ship listing at an angle of almost 45 degrees. Twice I nearly go overboard. It rains hard all morning. In the afternoon watch we carry coal to the galley. We still have two at the wheel but at 5.45pm we get course NE ¼ E and we now have one at the wheel. The Captain and the 2nd Mate repair the compass in the afternoon. The port watch in the morning set the mizzen and main upper topsails and the foresail, the starboard side only. We later set the fore staysail and main staysail. At 11.30pm at night the port watch set the mizzen and main lower to'gallants.
Position 44.15°S 101. 11°E

Day 92 Saturday December 21st

At 2am our watch set the fore lower to'gallant Johansen going aloft to overhaul the gardings, while at 3.30pm we set the main upper to'gallant and I overhaul the gardings. I get up at 5.30am to commence cleaning out the fo'c'sles a good job too or else I should never have finished by 1pm. We unbend the torn foresail and bend a new one in its place. Then our watch set the mizzen and fore upper to'gallants, the three royals, the spanker and gaff and a few staysails and also the mizzen sail, while later the port watch set the mainsail in the afternoon.

There are albatrosses following us today. Hussel and Eriksen have poisoned hands and cannot take the wheel. It is still very cold weather.
Position 42°S 106.46°E

Day 93 Sunday December 22nd

I wash a few things during free watch in the morning, then sleep on my bunk. It rains nearly all day.

We still have three albatrosses following us. I have another row with the 2nd Mate, this time at the wheel. I was only half a point off yet he told me to be quiet. I am fed up with things in general and may possibly think of working my way back home on a steamer.

We have very little work this Sunday for a change. Hussel and Eriksen laid up with sore hands. Stranberg, while look-out tonight strikes the bell thinking there is a steamer but it is the moon and it is a great joke amongst the crew.
Position 42.20°S 112.22°E

Day 94 Monday December 23rd

We commence soda washing the white paint again on deck, a job all of us hate. The Mate again plays up with me for nothing at all. I nearly get dragged overboard this morning when a bucket I am hauling up water with gets dragged by the ships wash aft. It is a lovely day but there is a strong wind and heavy sea a few waves lop overboard. Just before dinner time we set the fore staysail and outer jib and the main and mizzen staysails. A few boys wash their clothes on account of the fine weather. I take Hussels wheel and policeman at night, so that I have two wheels in three hours.

The weather is much warmer.
Position ---------

Day 95 Tuesday December 24th

Before breakfast we carry on washing white paint, then I wash Hussels and my bunk during free watch. In the afternoon we are free at 2.30pm after washing down the deck. There are two black albatross following us today. The boys put on clean clothes for Christmas. We have a wonderful tea tonight all fresh food and cheese and later the Finnish boys sing Finnish carols and then we have a sing song.
Position 39.30°S 123.54°E

Day 96 Wednesday December 25th Christmas Day

We have a whole holiday for Christmas Day and we have truly some very fine meals we find it too much to eat. Hussel is very bad all day and in the evening the Captain gives him some Opium to relieve his pain and help him to sleep. He absolutely writhes in agony and has not slept for three days and three nights.

We have a sing song in the morning. Our watch turn the ship round in the morning but all day we have very little wind and only five hundred miles from Port Lincoln.

A few albatross still following us. It has been much warmer all day.

I sleep a little on my bunk during free watch in the morning. We are sailing Bi de Vind and the wind shifts continually from South to East-North-East.
Position 37.51°S 125.58°E

Day 97 Thursday December 26th Boxing Day

Again we have a holiday. I feel very tired all day. Hussel is a little better and has had a little sleep. We have a tiny bit of wind. The Mate plays a gramophone on the poop in the afternoon while I am at the wheel. Mrs Duff comes up forward in the afternoon.

A whale seen today, very large. I fall asleep again on my bunk after coffee missing the muster at 7pm but luckily the Mate did not notice. We again have a sing song after tea but it was not a success. Later on in the evening we are becalmed again.
Position 38.42°S 126.1°E

Day 98 Friday December 27th
I spend five hours washing the white paint during the morning watch and my hands were quite raw afterwards with the soda. Mrs Duff lends us her gramophone records in the afternoon. I sleep on my bunk after coffee. Hussel much better. We have little wind most of the afternoon.

A steamer sighted low down at 7.15pm but I think it is a sailing ship.
Position 39.27°S 126.13°E

Day 99 Saturday December 28th
I help with washing the white paint during working watch before breakfast then sleep most of the watch in the morning. During working watch in the afternoon we wash white paint until 3pm then just brush down the deck finishing about 4.15pm. While I am at the wheel from 5pm to 6pm the 2nd and 3rd Mates leave the gramophone in the charthouse and sing and dance. The Whale is still following us.

After tea we have a great sing song and Johansen, as usual, is a scream. Mrs Duff and Pedersen spend a long time on deck with each other again at night.
Position 39.26°S 127.58°E

Day 100 Sunday December 29th
A little more wind now but instead of getting warmer it seems to get colder. I have a rotten Sunday as it was to me just like a work day. At 8am we turn the ship, then I spend an hour dishwashing, then policeman, then wheel, then at 12.30pm carry dishes to the port watch. Some of the boys, including myself, wash clothes.

We are now sailing by our compass E.N.E. but by the standard compass SE to E. Whenever shall we get to Port Lincoln? God only knows. The compass swings quite frequently from S by East to East. Everybody is fed up with this head wind.
Position 36.23°S 128.23°E

Day 101 Monday December 30th
I carry water to the galley and to the tanks on the poop before breakfast. Plenty of albatross about and they often sit on the water in batches. Still a head wind and very little wind at that. We again wash white paint on deck with soda during

the working watch in the afternoon. We are back again in the Roaring Forties and we know it too because it blows up strongly at night. Mrs Duff and Pedersen again spend a long time together on deck at night.
Position 39.23°S 128.6°E

Day 102 Tuesday December 31st

We again wash the white paint on the deck during morning watch but thank goodness now we have finished. We are still Bi de Vind and sailing East. I pull Clappertons leg while he is washing paint in the afternoon as he and the 1st and 2nd Mates have real beards now. In the afternoon, I play poker with some of the boys but it is very hard to understand, although they all say it is easy but they talk in their own language and so I don't understand.

The port watch wash the deck down after coffee and then finish about 5pm. After tea we all play cards and have the gramophone on , Laurie comes up too. The port watch only have about one hours sleep. At 12pm midnight (New Years Day) we play our jazz band Auld Lang Syne as we muster aft and then we play aft for the Captain. The Officers and Mrs Duff can be seen dancing and jumping about like a three year old on the poop. We turn the ship at 7pm.
Position 40.10°S 130.7°E

Day 103 Wednesday January 1st New Years Day 1936

Poor old Tony (the dog) slept in the fo'c'sle with us, all night, he was terrified out of his life last night with the rockets the Mates sent up. I carry water to the galley before breakfast. The Cook looks very angry today over the food that was all returned to him last night made up into a terrible mixture.

It is a lovely day, just like an English Summers day, it makes me long for home. The last few days I have been feeling very nervy due to the lonely life I think. A few albatross still with us but of the smaller type.

We have a whole day holiday. I play cards (Poker) in the afternoon and the 3rd Mate joins us. We have another sing song after tea. At midnight we take in the three royals while the port watch took in the spanker, gaff and mizzen sail. The barometer is dropping. We turn the ship at midnight too. We have a better wind steering NE ½ North.
Position 39.21°S 129.42°E

Day 104 Thursday January 2nd

Laurie and I have a great argument with the 2nd Mate who seems to thoroughly dislike the English. He says it was a most unfair war and the English are always saying we won the war, so Laurie and I get at him and he cannot answer all our questions.

I wash the rails near the poop and one davit up forward during the morning watch and I overhaul gardings on the main mast which we set at midday. We go course NN.E ¾ East the wind being from aft.

I sleep all afternoon being very, very tired. The port watch in the afternoon brace twice, the wind now being from the other side. During our night watch from 7pm to 12pm we heave up the mizzen sail but don't make it fast. The port watch in the afternoon make ready the anchor chain.

I am feeling fed up with everything in general. I get ticked off by the watch for not hearing two whistles. I explain to them I am deaf but they only laugh.
Position 37°S 128.12°E

Day 105 Friday January 3rd
At 4am all hands heave up the main sail. We have a wonderful wind this morning and doing about 12 knots. Most of the night we have a great thunderstorm with forked lightning.

I carry water to the poop tank before breakfast, the rest of the watch clean up the davits on the fo'c'sle head. At 8am the port watch make fast the main and mizzen sails. We have 230 miles to go now.

During afternoon watch I polish brass in the chart house while the rest of the watch get the anchors ready and while I am at the wheel 6pm I see my first seagull and the albatrosses are still with us. Neptune Lighthouse sighted 7.15pm.

The port watch between 7pm and 12pm make fast the three royals. We pass the "Abraham Rydberg" homeward bound at 8pm and morse her.
Position 36°S 134.44°E

Day 106 Saturday January 4th
I have the wheel at 12 midnight and steer the ship into Port Lincoln. We arrived here at 1.23am 89 days from Deal. After hauling up the log I help aloft making the sails fast. The "Pommern" is here too 83 days from Copenhagen.

We sleep until breakfast 8am then I wash midships and the fo'c'sles.
Position Arrived Port Lincoln

"Ponape" at anchor

[Editor's note

There seems to have been some adjustment to the crew before the return voyage and Geoffrey is now the only Englishman on board. Since Geoff did not speak Swedish this put him at a distinct disadvantage and left him feeling very lonely at times. Depression settles over Geoff like a cloud and he seems to be out of sorts with the world a lot and experiences more ill health than on any other voyage. There is no further mention of the Jazz Band which so lifted his spirits either, or of Mrs Duff who was supposedly to be taken on as a paid crewman for the return journey.

There are no entries in Geoffrey's log about moving to Port Germein though the ship sets sail from this Port for the return journey to England after being fully loaded.]

*Johansen watching the Ketch "Yalata"
loading wheat*

Log of the Finnish Sailing Ship

Filling water tanks

"Ponape"

From Port Germein Australia to Falmouth England
The Return Journey 1936

Thursday February 13th

We leave Port Germein at 10am bound for Falmouth. The tug leaves us at 2pm. I was asleep when we left but was just able to see the last of Germein before it was out of sight. We anchor because of a headwind and we have the sea watch system. I turn out at 4pm.

Friday February 14th

Still anchored off Wallaroo. I and Svenska carry coal from deck into coal hole. We make steam in the donkey boiler in the afternoon as we have a fair wind for five minutes but like when we were back at Deal we get a head wind again. Port Germein can be clearly seen this afternoon.

Saturday February 15th

Still anchored but we try in the morning, getting wind for about an hour. Then again we heave up the anchor at night only to drop it again as soon as we had the sails all set. Our watch worked again during free watch from 7pm to 10pm. What a life. We have three cats on board.

Sunday February 16th

We again get a fair wind this morning, this time only for half an hour. Our watch work the sails all morning first setting the sails and then making them fast. Three steamers pass us this morning one is Swedish the "Ellerman City". It is a very hot and tiring day.

Monday February 17th

We set sail again at 3am and again we are called from our free watch. We work continuously until 9am as we anchor again at 7am only to heave up again at 8am. We have head wind again at 1pm so anchor again opposite Port Broughton and the "Parma" can clearly be seen loading there. Our watch make fast all sails. Rain sets in at the end of the day.

Tuesday February 18th

We heave up the anchor again at 2am this morning and work continuously till 1pm except for one and a half hours. We are all dead beat and all the crew are full of curses. The 2nd Mate has started to be off hand with me again he seems to dislike the English. We are opposite Wallaroo at 1pm and anchor.

A steamer "Pundalla" passes alongside us at 10pm and drops her ensign to us. Our little black cat while fighting on the fo'c'sle head with another cat falls overboard and I go over on a rope and rescue it after it had been in the water 10 minutes. It is quite alright again after half an hour but if it had not been calm it would have drowned.

194

Day 1 Wednesday February 19th

I sleep on my bunk all morning. We turn the ship at 1pm and are sailing Bi de Vind but only one point off. In the afternoon I help Stranberg with filling fresh water into the lifeboat then I overhaul gardings. A small motor Ketch comes alongside at 7pm.

Stranberg and Liewendahl

Day 2 Thursday February 20th

Soderstrom and myself clean the deck house tops and poop which were covered with sand. A few small islands to be seen. It is a lovely day and quite warm. We have a sing song in the afternoon and again in the evening. We turn the ship at 12 midnight and go course South by West ¼ West.

Day 3 Friday February 21st

There are a lot of islands to be seen at 6am this morning. I carry water to the galley before breakfast. I clean out my bunk during free watch in the morning. In the afternoon we are on the fo'c'sle head making fast the anchors. We see Kangaroo Island at 1.30pm and at 2pm our watch take in and make fast the mizzen sail, mainsail and three royals as we have a strong head wind. I make fast the mizzen royal. At 4pm all hands turn the ship. At 5pm a four masted Barque sighted, the Captain thinks it is the "Moshulu". We turn the ship again at 7.30 pm and again at midnight. Soderstrom has a very badly poisoned foot.

Day 4 Saturday February 22nd

Neptune Island still in sight at 4am.I have two hours at the wheel this morning. A steamer is sighted. One albatross, first one this trip, and one stormy petrel sighted. We clean up under the fo'c'sle head. I have hellish toothache again. We are sailing for the Cape of Good Hope and not the Horn. In the afternoon during free watch we have a sing song. Then about 5pm I suddenly get a terrible sick pain which goes on all night. An English steamer passes close to us in the afternoon and dips her ensign and sends us a message but as usual we never replied until she was past and had taken her pennants in.
Position 35.30°S 135.32°E

Day 5 Sunday February 23rd

A large liner passes us at 5am and a small coastal boat at 9am. We have hardly any wind all day. I still have that beastly sick pain. Most of the boys get drunk this morning having bought rum from the Captain and they are all very merry, especially Svenska who is a scream. We turn the ship about five times in the day. I am sick all day and eat nothing.
Position 35.21°S 134.32°E

Day 6 Monday February 24th

It is a glorious day and very hot. I oil all the wires during the working watch. I discover that my bunk is overrun with those bunk bugs and I have been bitten very much lately. The Captain is hardly ever seen now, he sleeps all day and night it seems. The Steward and I are great pals nowadays. Towards evening the wind strengthens and at 9pm we are going along at about 9 knots.
Position 35.22°S 133.25°E

Day 7 Tuesday February 25th

The wind is blowing strong this morning and we are going along at a great speed and occasionally a little water lops aboard. I wash some clothes in the morning. We have no fresh water left now, except for drinking water and this is rationed, only three buckets a day for fourteen men. My pain has almost gone now. The three cats are a little seasick today on account of the rolling. I paint the rigging with Soderstrom in the afternoon watch and later overhaul gardings.
Position 36.11°S 130.23°E

Andersen and Soderstrom

Day 8 Wednesday February 26th

Our watch work continuously from 12am to 4am turning the ship twice, at 3am we get a little wind, this increases as the day wears on so that by 8am it is at gale force and a head wind too. Our watch at 9am take in the three royals. I make fast the main royal and it is very hard 165 feet up there with the mast swinging at 45 degrees and the yard kicking. Then we take in the mizzen and main sails and later take in the three upper to'gallants. I and Svenska make fast the fore upper to'gallant. I nearly fell on deck the sail was kicking about and knocked me off my hold for a minute. Then we take in the three lower to'gallants and at 1pm turn the ship. There is plenty of water on deck all day and seas break over the fo'c'sle head. In the evening we go course and between 7pm and 12pm our watch set the mizzen sail, main sails and three lower to'gallants. I overhaul the gardings.
Position 37.1°S 128.51°E

View to deck from aloft

Day 9 Thursday February 27th

Between 12pm and 4am the port watch set the three upper to'gallants and at 6am our watch set the three royals, outer jib and spanker. An oil tanker comes fairly close at 5.30am and morses us but evidently our lamp was not strong enough for them to see. I sleep all morning on my bunk and dream of Honey and Ada.

There are quite a number of the larger type of albatross about today. During the afternoon watch I scrape the rust off the anchor winch forward. I have a big boil on my left leg it is very painful also I still have my stomach trouble and today also toothache, so I am a wee bit out of sorts. Life is extremely lonely here at times, not that the boys mean anything, but sometimes it is days before I ever am spoken to especially as I cannot join in their conversation, and so I just sit there and try to make out as much as I can. I like this new fellow Andersen very much, a genuine fellow. It looks as if we are in for a long trip. During afternoon watch I again scrape rust off the anchor winch forward. I am feeling very tired.
Position 36.33°S 127.35°E

Andersen and self

Day 10 Friday February 28th

I have a very restless night only sleeping roughly two hours on account of the boil on my leg. Today I am feeling extremely ill and it is only my will power which makes me work and my thoughts for the other boys not having extra work. I am thoroughly run down in all ways and have now a head cold. In the morning watch I help Liewendahl in the mizzen rigging to put a new buntline to the upper to'gallant sail. Then I scrape rust again on the anchor winch. It is funny the way the Mate always gives me the dirty work, any old job, I had about five different jobs this morning but he hates the English as he has told me. I shall be pleased when I am home again and then, never again. The sailing ship and the work is good but the people, like the world over, are rotters. I sleep on my bunk in the afternoon. We are still without water and none of us have washed for a week now. It is a dark, cloudy night and it is going to be cold.
Position 34.46°S 126.12°E

Day 11 Saturday February 29th

I carry water to the galley water tanks and to the tanks on the poop and clean the pig house out and yet the Mate calls me a "Bloody Englishman" and hurry up etc. I am sick and told him so but the cur that he is, after all that I did for him in Port Germein. He acted like a baby then with his sore hand. One night I actually had to dress him. I get all the dirty jobs! We expect to pass Cape Leeuwin tomorrow night if this wind keeps up. I clean our fo'c'sle in the afternoon. The wheel is very hard today. Stranberg has a pain now in his stomach and does not turn out during the night watches but I notice I never got such privileges. We have a good wind blowing all night. I eat very little all day.
Position 36.44°S 122.46°E

Day 12 Sunday March 1st

I am still sick and sleep on my bunk in the morning, then again in the afternoon and I refuse to turn out at 3pm for turning the ship in free watch. Of course I hear about it from Svenska, but let anybody else lay up and nothing is said. It blows up hard towards evening and the port watch take in and make fast the main sail, foresail and mizzen sail and all three royals as we are Bi de Vind. At 7pm we go course and set the three big sails again. It rains and is blowing up squalls.
Position 36.17°S 118.28°E

Day 13 Monday March 2nd

I explain, or try to explain, to the 2nd Mate that I am very ill and would he try to understand things (me being a little slow etc.) but the cur only just laughs. We start that hellish job before breakfast of washing the white paint on the poop. I am a wee bit better today. We are still going course and we have a fairly strong wind with a fair amount of water on deck. At 8am The port watch set the three royals. I sleep on my bunk all morning. We continue washing the white paint all afternoon and I was dead beat, as I had the last wheel from 6pm to 7pm. My boil is almost finished on my leg but it has been a bad one and now I have one on my left arm. I am free all night and make the best of it too.
Position 35.56°S 116.13°E

Day 14 Tuesday March 3rd

We commence in the morning watch washing the paint again, but at 9am we start changing the strong sails for the tropical rags and our watch change the fore royal, upper and lower to'gallants. I spend two hours at the wheel. There are a few albatross following us still, although it is very warm and we have a SE Trade Wind. We see from the fore royal a school of bonito round the bowsprit. We start the dayman business again and now we have only three men in our watch. The Captain orders myself and Stranberg aft at 8pm to be examined as to whether we have appendicitis or not. After being examined the Captain says I have a swollen gland and I think Stranberg has the same. We do 9 knots and 36 miles in one watch.
Position 34.55°S 113.23°E

Day 15 Wednesday March 4th

A flying fish comes aboard with a large wave and the cat eats it up with relish. We start changing the sails on the main mast today. There is a little water on deck today. The port watch finish changing the sails during this morning watch except for the foresail. I help Stranberg in our working watch to unshackle the flying jib. Then we haul up coal and I am down in the coal hole and I take plenty of time , in fact, once I nearly went to sleep. I still have a very bad cough and my stomach is a little better but I have a bad boil on my right arm now.
Position 33.27°S 109.30°E

Day 16 Thursday March 5th

It is Honey's birthday and I am thinking about her a lot and wishing her luck and health. We carry on washing the white paint. I tell Svenska he ought to be a Mate because he does nothing but boss, boss, boss. He thinks he is a fine seaman but in my opinion the worst I have come across, a baby and fit only for his mothers knees. He is the only fellow I dislike on the "Ponape" a most annoying and childish creature. I try to sleep on my bunk in the afternoon but as usual it is impossible owing to Svenska (noise) and the daymen. Stranberg has to come down from look-out between 11pm and 12pm owing to his pain and lays up. The crew fuss him and tell him to go to his bunk. I have had the same pain and a good deal worse but he still eats, I never did, yet not once did anybody ask me to lay up.
Position 32.30°S 106.44°E

Day 17 Friday March 6th

Stranberg still laid up on his bunk this morning, meaning extra work for our watch, only four men now. A great fuss made of him at coffee, people giving it to him in his bunk. Finns help one another but never outsiders. Pedersen also laid up this morning with a badly poisoned foot. I have my arm boil attended to this morning by the 1st Mate. God it nearly killed me, he plucked at it and squeezed it, pulled the inside out with his nails and then poured Iodine into the hole. Talk about pain.

We set the spanker. Where is the SE Trade Wind? We are sailing Bi de Vind and going North whereas we should be sailing NW. I chip rust on the bowsprit all afternoon in brilliant sunshine, a good job.

I now have pain in one of my balls it is swollen like hell and pains considerably. We are becalmed at night.
Position 30.55°S 105.44°E

Day 18 Saturday March 7th

I am again chipping on the bowsprit with Lund in the morning watch. The Cook kills one of the sheep, so good, fresh meat tomorrow I hope.

The pain in my ball is very bad today and making me feel ill. We have only a little wind. Stanberg still laid up but seems better.

It is very warm today. Certainly a fine trip so far as regards the weather. I work continuously from 7pm to 12 midnight, feel very tired. Go to the Mate about my ball and he gives me some stuff to rub on.
Position 30.32°S 104.48°E

Day 19 Sunday March 8th

I still have terrible pain again this morning. A good wind and doing about 9 knots. I sleep on my bunk during free watch in the morning. We have fresh meat for lunch today but I think most of it must have gone "aft" as we had very little.

I hear that the Captain has thrown the rest of the rum overboard to stop himself from drinking but what about us? He never thinks of anybody but himself. I chat with the Bosun on deck while policeman about sailing ships etc. he says he will never go on another. We have a sing song after tea and I get so hot. I cannot sleep one minute in free watch 7pm to 12pm.
Position 29.19°S 102.4°E

Day 20 Monday March 9th

I am feeling heaps better this morning. We still have good wind from aft. I commence chipping up on the bowsprit and then on the mizzen mast but finish up on the anchor winch. The Chief Mate has cut Tony the dog like a Poodle again and the poor thing looks very unhappy. We have fresh meat again for lunch. I try to sleep on my bunk in the afternoon but as usual there is a hell of a row, chiefly from Svenska and it is impossible to sleep, so I have a sing song at 5pm with Ike. I am feeling very tired and find it impossible to sleep at night on account of the bugs in my bunk.
Position 28.53°S 99.37°E

Day 21 Tuesday March 10th

I clean out my bunk during free watch in the morning and discover heaps of bugs eggs. I am a little better today but still have a swollen ball. We only have a little wind but at any rate we are moving. I chip rust in the afternoon out on the bowsprit and also the anchor winch. I feel very faint and tired at 7pm. I can hardly move and wish to sleep and sleep but cannot. There is something very wrong with me. I hope I reach home safely and Honey. Stranberg says that if the black cat shits any more in the fo'c'sle it goes overboard.
Position 28.49°S 97.16°E

Day 22 Wednesday March 11th

I am very weak again all day and feeling very much like just sleeping all day long. I am again out on the bowsprit chipping rust in really glorious sunshine and very warm but on account of my weak feeling I cannot work well. Tony has got some more hair off his back, poor dog. I sit on deck a little during free watch in the afternoon in glorious sun and chat with Ike, one of my best of friends, about going to Mariehamn with him and to his home etc. I work continuously from 7pm to midnight and am very tired. We square up at 11.30pm. Svenska does not hear the two whistles and gets into a row.
Position 28.37°S 95.27°E

Day 23 Thursday March 12th

I don't sleep one wink during the night. The bugs get at me like a piece of meat and in the end I try sleeping on the floor but fail. My intestine is extremely large this morning and I can just crawl about. In fact, I find it impossible to work but carry on till breakfast, then I go to the Captain and show it to him. He asks me if I have ever had any venereal disease but I never have, so he cannot say what it is but tells me to rub this ointment on which the 1st Mate gave me. I lay up all day and the boys are very good to me, telling me to rest up for two or three days, it is all right with them, but I hate to lay up. It is much better at night time and has gone down considerably.

We have a very good wind blowing at present and it is getting warmer.
Position 27.44°S 92.55°E

Day 24 Friday March 13th

I lay up on my bunk all day but turn out in my night watch at 7pm although not well yet, but in order to help my watch mates. But when I am at the wheel, all the Mate can do is curse me about my steering, so that's the way he treats a sick man. I might just as well have stayed in my bunk. It is no earthly good being sick or injured on a sailing ship because you will get neither help nor sympathy. I have found that to be true.

The wind dies away at 6.30pm and we sail Bi de Vind.
Position 27.33°S 90.18°E

Day 25 Saturday March 14th

At 1am we go course again, the port watch turn the ship and the wind gradually strengthens so that at 8am we are doing 10 knots and the wheel is inclined to be hard. Everybody now (just because we have a good wind) say Cape of Good Hope in fourteen days, but I don't believe it, this wind wont stay long. The Steward kills the other sheep this morning, poor wretched animal, it seemed to know what was coming by the look in its eyes. I sleep on my bunk all morning.

During working watch in the afternoon I clean the fo'c'sle out and have the wheel from 5pm to 6pm then look-out from 6pm to 7pm, so I worked all through a Saturday from 1pm to 7pm. One albatross seen while I am at the wheel.
Position 27.27°S 88.18°E

Day 26 Sunday March 15th

At 1pm, while I am at the wheel the Collar of the mizzen lower to'gallant snaps and the yard falls and is only prevented from falling on deck by the alert Mate who rushes up the mast and makes it fast by wire. Then at 2pm when I come from the wheel we take in the royal, upper and lower to'gallant sails to relieve the pressure. Then by means of ropes we make fast the lower to'gallant yard to the upper to'gallant to prevent it falling on deck. So our watch work continuously from 12 midnight till 4am. Then at 7.30am The port watch heave up the foresail, it has a big tear on the starboard side. I have two hours at the wheel. Then I help Stranberg on the fore yard to sew up and patch the torn foresail. Then we help to fix the collar to the mizzen lower to'gallant again which has been repaired by the daymen who work all day from 6am to 5pm and seem very angry especially old Timmerman.

It is a glorious day and hardly a cloud.. The Danish boy discovers six flying fish on board this a.m. and has them for his breakfast. We are still doing about 10 knots. I am feeling very tired but in health a little better. I sleep on my bunk until coffee time then I take a snap up on the broken lower to'gallant of the 1st Mate up there, he jokes with me and tells me I am making a movie picture up there. The job is finished at 5.30pm and the port watch set the three sails, the mizzen royal, upper and lower to'gallants. The daymen are told they can have a holiday tomorrow.
Position 27.32°S 84.42°E

Chief Mate Karlsson
repairing the yard

Day 27 Monday March 16th
We brace at 5.15am the wind now coming from the side but there is very little wind. I grease a wire before breakfast. I sleep on my bunk during morning free watch.

In the afternoon I chip rust on the anchor winch and have two hours wheel. Johansen is laid up with a bad stomach owing to the food. A beautiful sunset and a lovely day. We work until 6.30pm. I still have some bugs in my bunk. We have a sing song at night, we make strings for the instruments from cotton.
Position 27.27°S 82.56°E

Day 28 Tuesday March 17th

We brace (our watch) at 12am and spend two hours at it as the wind is now coming from the side, so we set the spanker and three jib staysails. The Mate gets on to me again, this time for not letting loose quickly, he pushes me and tells me I never do (absolutely untrue) so I tell him I am not the only one in my watch. He says I am a Bloody Englishman. So, I tell him to wait until we reach England and then I'll show him something. The only person I dislike on the ship, about the worst two faced fellow I have ever met. Then later on I try to give Lund a little help and all I get is a fist in the chest. These Finns are the limit, morose creatures.

We now have a good wind, for God's sake let it blow like hell and let us get home. I scrape rust all morning on the anchor winch under the fo'c'sle head, except for an hour at the wheel. During free watch in the afternoon I try to sleep as I have now a bad stomach but as usual there is a hell of a row and it is impossible. The Mate plays hell with our watch tonight as he caught Lund sleeping when he was policeman and tells us this is the last chance. It has been a glorious day all day. My stomach is very bad at night and I can hardly stand up. We have not had a drop of rain since leaving Port Germein, 33 days, but tonight we have a little shower. We are doing about 9 knots but towards midnight we slacken down to about four.
Position 27.22°S 80.46°E

Day 29 Wednesday March 18th

While I am at the wheel at 6am I sight a steamer coming up towards us from aft, she comes up very slowly and at 8am she passes very close astern. She is English the "S.S. Ranauld" and we ask her to report us to Lloyds. She dips her ensign and we dip ours. At 9.30am she is out of sight. She has come miles off her course to see us. At 8am we turn the ship and go course N.W. to N. We have rain squalls all morning. This is the first steamer we have seen for 16 days.

I sleep on my bunk during the free watch in the morning. I am chipping again under the fo'c'sle head until I have to take the wheel at 4pm and after being at the wheel I help the 2nd Mate to paint the jigger mast. We square up at 6pm. I have a very bad night as regards sleep, the bugs keeping me awake. A beautiful sunset.
Position 27.46°S 78.45°E

Day 30 Thursday March 19th

We get up to a lovely sunrise, all golden in the sky. I paint all morning the anchor winch under the fo'c'sle head giving it its second coat of red lead. I am feeling a little ill again and very tired owing to having no sleep. We have a very good wind blowing from aft all day. I sleep on my bunk after coffee only I am woken up by bugs eating me again. We square up at 10pm our watch always

seems to get the bracing, the 3rd Mate never seems to watch the sails at all. I have another perfectly foul night as regards sleep, hardly getting a wink. The bugs in my bunk are simply awful and tonight I am bitten all over, so I sleep on the floor but here again the bugs find me.
Position 27.26°S 75.46°E

Day 31 Friday March 20th
It rains a little this morning but we still have our fair wind. We brace a little at 5.15am. I carry water to the galley before breakfast. I sleep all the free watch in the morning on my bunk. In the afternoon I chip rust near the anchor chain all the working watch, a hell of a job, as it was a very awkward position and gave me cramp. I am again feeling very much better. We heave up the mizzen and main sails at 6.15pm as there is no wind. It rains steadily all afternoon and we have put out barrels at all points for catching water. The port watch fill the tank aft between 7pm and 12pm. Tonight I sleep in the sail locker and what a difference, peace from the bugs, I sleep soundly.
Position 27.34°S 73.25°E

Day 32 Saturday March 21st
I again chip near the anchor chain in the working watch this morning then later with Lund, I wash with soda the lamp locker. In the free watch in the afternoon I wash a lot of my clothes, in fact everybody is busy washing now we have water. In our working watch last night from 12 to 4am we brace no fewer than five times and there is hardly any wind too, but at midday this morning we again get a good wind and at 3pm we are again doing about 8 knots. The three cats and Tony the dog are still thriving and all look very fit. The cats are never out of the fo'c'sle and sleep on our bunks and they now always come at meal time, it seems as if they understand the bells. I get wet through at the wheel between 11pm and 12pm. It rains cats and dogs. We have a good speed now of about 8 knots.
Position 27.21°S 71.51°E

Day 33 Sunday March 22nd
We square up a little at 6am. I again sleep in the sail locker and very sound too. There is a very fine wind this morning and we are doing about 10 knots and we have a lot of water on deck. The boys are all again busy washing clothes. The poor sad and quiet little Black and White Whisky cat is killed today and chucked overboard, by Andersen. It shits in the fo'c'sle and he catches it and hits it over the head with an iron. Talk about blood. The poor little thing was still alive when tossed over the side. There is an albatross following us today very unusual for these regions. I have a terrible Sunday, it is more like a workday what with two wheels, dishwashing and two policemen. I again sleep in the sail locker.
Position 28.7°S 68.16°E

Day 34 Monday March 23rd
I wash the starboard lighthouse, a hell of a dirty job, in the morning watch on deck and I am given caustic soda with which to wash the rust off. My poor old hands, there was hardly any skin left on at the end of the morning and all my nails went brown.

The ship is rolling badly as there is a fairly heavy sea but we are still doing about 10 knots. I read a little on my bunk in the afternoon. Towards evening the wind increases and the wheel gets very hard so two men are placed at the wheel. So, with dishwashing I work five hours continuously.
Position 27.49°S 64.5°E 222miles.

Day 35 Tuesday March 24th
Between 7pm and 8am I only have three and a half hours sleep, so you can imagine I am dead beat. We still have two men at the wheel at 8am and it is still blowing hard. The lights of a steamer are seen on the starboard side at 4.30am and we morse her but evidently she does not see us. A small sea swallow is with us today. There is a lot of water on deck again.

These sailors are a queer lot to weigh up. They can be decent, well behaved and real gentlemen at times and then, at other times, they are immoral and filthy fellows, all talk about girls. Then again they are some of the dirtiest people I have ever met yet they fuss over a speck of dirt on a plate.

 I am again scraping the anchor chain guide under the fo'c'sle head in the afternoon. I again sleep in the sail locker, so also Andersen.
Position 27.36°S 59.35°E

Day 36 Wednesday March 25th
I rise up at 5.30am (although free) and commence to clean out my bunk first of all borrowing the 1st Mates "Flit". I give the bunk a thorough dose of the "Flit" all over. Then I wash it with soda again, all the boys clear out their bunks. The fo'c'sle seemed to be chock full of them. Let us hope we have no more bugs.

We brace a little in the morning. There is very little wind now but at 11am we get a fresh strong breeze again and a good speed. Talk about meanness certainly Erikson and his Officers are so. The way they make you get every little speck of rust off on deck and paint like hell. Yet, they will not give us any paint for the fo'c'sle for our bunks. All for the ship and nothing for the crew.
Position 27.43°S 57.8°E

Day 37 Thursday March 26th

I sleep all free watch in the morning on my bunk. My ball is again very big and painful. There are two men at the wheel all day and even then the wheel is heavy to turn.

I am scraping again under the fo'c'sle head and later paint it with red lead. It is quite dangerous to be on deck today as there is plenty of water and with the ship rolling a lot from side to side we walk on the gangway and not on the deck.

I manage to take look-out and policeman at night but cannot take the wheel on account of the pain. There is a tremendous sea running all day and big waves sweep the deck all over.
Position 27.43°S 53.1°E

Day 38 Friday March 27th

I am laid up again all day with this terrible pain in my stomach. All my watch are very kind to me and tell me to stay in my bunk until I am better but as regards the Officers, of this sailing ship, they are a disgrace. None of them came to see me and the 1st Mate actually came into the fo'c'sle to look at the blooming paintwork. I suppose a poor human being can go to hell and just die in his bunk, or so it seems aboard these sailing ships. Honestly! I do truly think a boy could die on one of these ships without an Officer ever even seeing him. All for the ship and nothing for the crew, that's my opinion and also of most of the crew.

We are opposite Madagascar at midday.
Position 28.21°S 48.18°E 250 miles.

Day 39 Saturday March 28th

I am still laid up and in fact feel a little worse. Nobody again comes to see me and the 1st Mate again actually comes into the fo'c'sle to see how his beastly painting is going along but not even a turn of the head at poor old me. God help me if I was dying.

It is very hot all day and it is the very devil to be laid up in such a stuffy place.
Position 29.18°S 44.40°E

Self after illness

Day 40 Sunday March 29th

I turn out again at midnight in my watch although far from fit but I don't think I shall get any better than I am now and anyhow, what is the good of laying up with no one to help you. I do honestly believe Svenska is a real twister. To your face he is all fuss, 'stay in your bunk' etc but instead last night he did his best to rise me up at 12am so that it would benefit him. He is one of those too fussy people who are never true.

I take my wheel as usual again this morning and it is beautifully hot.

Actually the 1st Mate and the Captain when they saw me, asked me if I was better, only because I have turned out again. I still suffer from those bug pests in my bunk at night and last night I again slept in the sail locker.

The wind is still from aft but at 1pm we brace and the port watch, between 1pm and 5pm, brace no fewer than 5 times and even turn the ship twice, what a Sunday. There is very little wind and between 1pm and 4pm we go four miles but at 5pm we again get a good wind and all sails (stays) are set again.
Position 27.23°S 41.24°E

Day 41 Monday March 30th

I sleep all morning on my bunk. I still feel a little ill and have pain and also feel very tired but I do my best. I am chipping in the wash house in the afternoon watch. The Steward catches a bonito at 4.30pm and we all have fresh fish for tea, it was delicious and tasted like Halibut. It weighed 9lb and was caught from the bowsprit.

Two steamers sighted this morning. The first at 6am and the other at 9am. At 7.30am we get a fair wind again and we once again set all staysails. In the afternoon we bend a new jigger gaff not having used one since Australia. The wind gets more aft towards evening and we once again take in all staysails and make fast all on the bowsprit.
Position 29.8°S 40.45°E

Day 42 Tuesday March 31st

I have a terrible night as regards sleep, actually not sleeping above fifteen minutes. My bunk is again overrun with bugs. Where they come from God only knows. I am again chipping rust in the wash house. What a ship for rust, heaps worse than the "Olivebank" and what a fuss the Chief Mate makes about it, every bit has to come up. We have heavy showers all morning. I am feeling much better but very tired and just long for home. It rains cats and dogs all night and once again the tank aft is full. We brace and square up at 10pm.
Position 29.24°S 37.13°E

Day 43 Wednesday April 1st

We have very heavy showers all morning from 4am to 8am thus causing the wind to shift continuously and we have four hours almost continuous bracing and we also fill up the donkey tank with fresh water so now we are once again well supplied. I also carry water to the galley and onto the tanks on the poop.

There is one fairly large black bird following us today. I am again chipping in the wash house in the afternoon until coffee and then we bend a new foresail, as the old one will not be strong enough for the winds of the Cape. I am feeling heaps better.
Position 30.24°S 34.52°E

Day 44 Thursday April 2nd

I am chipping all morning, five hours, in the washhouse and we have two bracings with only two men, the rest are in the rigging painting. What a hard job for just two men. It is very hot and a glorious day. At 12am we brace for a side wind and set all staysails again. Two of the boys have made harpoons for catching fish.

The wind gradually strengthens as the day wears on but the weather remains wonderfully clear and fine and it is a lovely starlit and moonlit night. The wheel is very hard but I manage to keep course. At 10pm we take in the jigger gaff and inner jib the latter I make fast. At 11.15pm the barometer begins to drop, so we take in the three royals but the port watch make them fast. Between 12am and 4am the port watch take in and make fast the three upper to'gallants and spanker.
Position 31.55°S 32.46°E 100 miles.

Day 45 Friday April 3rd

The wind is blowing a hurricane early this morning and at 4am we turn the ship sailing By de Vind direction NW. At 6am our watch make fast the mizzen and mainsails and at 8am all hands take in the 3 lower to'gallants, the port watch make them fast. There are big waves coming overboard especially up forward and while we are taking in the upper to'gallants all hands get wet through with the water. The fo'c'sle is flooded and in a very dirty state. Thank goodness the weather is fine. Tony the dog seems to dislike this weather very much but the little black cat is quite at home. Between 8am and 1pm the port watch take in all three upper topsails, the fore upper topsail blows out and the fore staysail blows out very badly at 2pm. Our watch are called out of free watch to help to break the buntlines of the upper topsails.

There are heavy rain squalls all afternoon and at 1pm all hands get wet through turning the ship. We are now sailing with only five sails and even then doing 5 knots, (the sails being the 3 lower topsails, foresail and jigger staysail). I chip rust off a block under the fo'c'sle head all afternoon and being wet through I am very cold. We again turn the ship at 12 midnight. The deck is awash all day and it is extremely dangerous to walk on the deck. The ship is rolling very badly and taking heavy seas overboard.
Position 32.65°S 29.57°E

Day 46 Saturday April 4th

The wind gradually dies down between 12am and 4am. The Mate is very thoughtful, he allows us to stand on the flying bridge while taking our turns at look-out. Between 4am and 8am the port watch set the mizzen and mainsails and we are nearly going course sailing By de Vind but direction WSW ½ W. They also set the inner jib and main and mizzen staysails. At 7am the East African coast is sighted and at 8am we again turn the ship. Our watch between 8am and 1pm unbend and bend the fore upper topsail and fore lower to'gallant. There is very little wind now and we are sailing along the coast about fifteen miles out. We again turn the ship at 1pm.

The Mate is very friendly nowadays and seems to like me much better now.

The port watch in the afternoon set the main lower to'gallant sail and spend nearly all afternoon bracing right up until 6.45pm they all look very tired. Then we spend a whole five hours, 7pm to 12pm setting sails. We set the three upper to'gallants, a lower to'gallant, three royals, jigger gaff and foresail and mizzen sail. I overhaul gardings on the main upper to'gallant and royal and foresail.

We are all very tired but I sleep badly again owing to the bugs. There are three albatross and some stormy petrels following us today. Land still in sight and a steamer and lighthouse are picked up.
Position 32.27°S 30.10°E

Day 47 Sunday April 5th

We brace three times between 6am and 8am the wind continually shifting.

Then the port watch also brace about three times between 8am and 1pm. It is a glorious day and the land (South Africa) is very clear. At 1pm my darling little English black cat is killed and thrown overboard for shitting under the bunks. Poor little soul. Andersen killed it, he hit it on the head with a belaying pin and chucked it overboard. I watched it fight for its life in the water. These fellows just laughed. What really cruel souls they have got. They seem to delight in cruelty.

Funnily enough this morning I had a dream that Eriksen had kicked it and made it die and then chucked it overboard so evidently dreams come true sometimes.

The boys play cards and have the gramophone out on deck in the afternoon.

We brace three times again between 7pm and 12pm and at 10pm I go up and overhaul the buntlines on the foresail which had been clewed up all afternoon and which we now set, having first turned the ship and gone course again. We also set the mizzen sail and jib staysails. At 6.30pm we sight Port Elizabeth light and a steamer (English) comes along. We morse her and she morses back she is homeward bound from Hong Kong to New York. We ask her to report us. She morses us for at least an hour wishing us Good Luck and wanting to know our Captain's name.
Position 33.27°S 28.1°E

Day 48 Monday April 6th

I chip rust under the fo'c'sle head all morning. Two boys spend the morning sewing up the torn mainsail and at 12 midday we once again set it. It is a glorious day and we have course doing about 5 knots. I sleep on my bunk a little in the afternoon then at 3pm I clean my bunk out also Johansen and we paint our boards. We have a sing song at night.

It is still very warm. There are a large number of albatross about including a large black one.
Position 35.16°S 25.46°E

Day 49 Tuesday April 7th

I fix up my bunk again and it smells so fresh with paint. I sleep a little during morning free watch. In the afternoon watch I am chipping rust out on the bowsprit again but underneath in a hell of a place. It is again a glorious day and very hot. Liewendahl tells me that at midday we had only 160 miles left to the Cape of Good Hope and that we need go no further South now. We do 56 miles between midday and 4pm. I sleep on my bunk between 7pm and 12pm but God if those damn bugs are not there still.
Position 35.38°S 22.30°E

Liewendahl as sail maker

Day 50 Wednesday April 8th

Between 3am and 4am Andersen catches a fish with his harpoon which he chucked from the bowsprit only the harpoon snapped and he lost his catch. There are scores of these fish playing about under the bowsprit. I again sleep in the sail locker. Until 10am I chip rust up on the bowsprit then I have a dirty job clearing coal etc. out of the donkey room. There is very little wind all morning and twice we turn the ship. The Steward catches a large albatross but after about an hour on deck, on which it is sick, he release it. There must be at least 100 albatross about today. There is a strong wind in the afternoon only we must sail By de Vind going South. The wind blows up very strong towards night

but the weather remains fine and a clear moon.

Position 35.39°S 20.29°E

212

Day 51 Thursday April 9th
I again sleep in the sail locker. Between 12am and 4am the port watch have no
fewer than 6 two whistles. They took in and made fast the spanker, inner jib,
three royals, three upper to'gallants, mizzen and mainsails and at 4am we turn
the ship. They are all tired out. No one can understand the 1st Mates action. The
wind was not as strong and the glass was no lower than at 2pm. All of his watch
are very annoyed with him. At 6am our watch set the mizzen and mainsails.
I overhaul gardings on the mainsail. Then we set the three upper to'gallants
but I carry water to the galley and clean out the pig house. I sleep on my bunk
during free watch in the morning. In the afternoon I chip rust for an hour on the
bowsprit and then I overhaul gardings on the fore and main masts.

It is very cold and we still have head wind and sailing By de Vind. We finish
work at 3.30pm (Easter) and we have a sing song. I again sleep in the sail locker.
Position 36.35°S 19.56°E

Day 52 Friday April 10th
The port watch turn the ship at 6am and set the mizzen and mainsails, spanker
and gaff and all hands again turn the ship at 8am. donkeyman cuts my hair after
breakfast.

There is very little wind all morning but as the afternoon wears on the wind
strengthens until at 5pm it is gale force and the port watch take in and make fast
the gaff and spanker. At 8pm our watch take in and make fast the three upper
to'gallants, I making fast the main upper to'gallant with Andersen. At 9pm we
take in and make fast the mizzen and mainsails and at 11pm we take in the fore
lower to'gallant, I, Svenska and Sandstrom make fast and at 12pm all hands turn
the ship.
Position 36.19°S 19.19°E

Day 53 Saturday April 11th
All through the night the wind is gale force. Tremendous seas sweep the ship
from stem to stern, reminding me of Cape Horn seas. It is extremely dangerous
to go on deck , many of the boys ,including myself, are sent flying headlong
into the scuppers by the waves. The ship rolls heavily from side to side making
things still worse. Honestly landlubbers have no idea what the sailors have to
go through. Last night, in my opinion, was just one long hell. We were all wet
through and our watch only managed to get two and a half hours sleep. At 6am
the wind has died down considerably but there is still a heavy sea running and
at 7am we go to course NW ¾ W and consequently we set the mizzen and
mainsails. I overhaul gardings on the mizzen sail. At 8am the port watch set the
fore lower to'gallant. The Steward is in a very bad temper this morning as his
galley has been flooded out during the night. I have hellish toothache all night.

We see land at 4.15am this morning, the rugged and mountainous coast of Africa. I clean out the fo'c'sle and midships in the afternoon, there is only a little water on the deck. We are going course, NW and doing about 7 knots. We finish work at 3.30pm and at 6.30pm a steamer passes close to us. We morse her and she replies, she is the Englishman "Anglo Australian" bound for Cape Town. *Position 35.14°S 17.42°E*

Day 54 Sunday April 12th

Another steamer sighted at 4.30am this morning. We spend a very fine Sunday with no bracing, what a change, and we have fresh meat Pork.

I take a few snaps and one of the Captain taking the midday position of the ship by the sun. He looked very angry at me, why I don't know. We still have course with a good wind dead aft. There is still a little water on deck. I sleep on my bunk till coffee time. The wind strengthens towards evening. *Position 33.45°S 15.4°E*

Captain Granith taking the midday fix of the sun

Day 55 Monday April 13th Easter Monday

We have a whole day holiday as it is Easter. I sleep on my bunk all the free watch in the morning. At coffee time we start the dayman business again and God what a shock we all got. The watches are reduced from seven men to three men. God what slave work. This means continuous work in the night watches from 7pm to 12pm and 4am to 8am with only 3 ¾ hours for sleep. Is this fair? No. They never think of fairness on this God damned ship "Ponape". I shall be only too thankful to sign off and "Never again as long as I live". We start the dayman business at 4pm so that we did not have much of a holiday. I worked continuously from 4pm to 7pm. I am again pestered by bugs in my bunk. *Position 30.47°S 12.4°E*

Day 56 Tuesday April 14th

I chip rust all morning on the roof under the fo'c'sle head and actually I am given a painting job, one block! What an angel I must have been to the Chief Mate this morning.

I sleep from 2pm to 5.15pm so it shows how tired I am. Nobody back on shore can guess what slave work we three men are having now. Just imagine three men to turn and manage a big four masted Barque, absolutely crazy.

I might mention now that since Gravesend the ship, as regards rigging ropes, foot ropes that we stand on aloft and owe our lives too, rings that we hold on to aloft on the yards, blocks etc. have been in a miserable state. Yet, so near the end of the voyage everything is being overhauled. Surely no thought for the life of the sailors, only just to make the ship look fine and safe in port.

Day 57 Wednesday April 15th

I am feeling very tired, so I sleep all the free watch in the morning. We change sails, putting up the "Tropical Rags" in the afternoon. Our watch change the foresail, lower to'gallant and upper topsail. I overhaul the buntlines in each case. Our three man watch is very much overworked and we all feel very tired. It is continuous work almost all day and night.

Tony the dog is very friendly with the two white pigs and he is ready at the pighouse every morning at about 7am when they are cleaned out and let out on deck. He plays with them and chases them about the deck. I chat with the 2nd Mate in the night watch about books and poems, especially poems. He is very friendly and kind to me nowadays. Why I don't know.
Position 26.12°S 5.47°E

Day 58 Thursday April 16th

We carry on changing sails in the morning and our watch change the main lower to'gallant, lower topsail and also the main royal, then later the mizzen upper to'gallant. It is hot tiring work running up and down the rigging. We have fresh meat again for dinner. There are two albatrosses with us today exceptionally far up for this kind of bird. I do not sleep at all during free watch in the afternoon. I decide to take my cases down into the hold as there are so many bugs always in them.

Svenska is a nuisance and keeps turning his mattress over so I get all his bugs down on my bunk.

We finish changing the sails in the afternoon. There is very little wind now.
Position 24.32°S 3.52°E

Day 59 Friday April 17th

I sleep on my bunk during free watch in the morning. In the working watch I chip rust on the fo'c'sle head until 2.30pm then myself Lund and the 2nd Mate (only three men) turn the ship round. Heavy work? I should say so. It is very heavy work to turn a four masted Barque I can tell you and it took us three quarters of an hour. After my turn at the wheel I polish brass on the poop.

It is a glorious sunset. Until 3.30pm when we go course again NW ½ N we have been sailing By de Vind all day. I again sleep in the sail locker. The ship is over run with rats and this afternoon Tony, the dog, catches a big one.
Position 23.28°S 3.2°E

Day 60 Saturday April 18th

During the working watch in the morning I clean the compass brass on the poop and spend two hours at the wheel, which was nice as it is a lovely day and hardly a cloud about, but very hot. The Captain has started to clean his cabin out and he is actually working this morning scraping his teak wood.

We are almost becalmed all morning but in the afternoon we get a little wind. I try to sleep on my bunk in the afternoon but it is impossible on account of the always noisy day men. I am dishwasher again and what a job with all these daymen about it is an impossibility almost. The day men take up half of the table as soon as they have eaten and start to play cards.
Position 22.25°S 1.5°E

Day 61 Sunday April 19th

I am feeling very tired at 4am this morning and we work continuously till 8am. We brace at 5.15am the wind now coming from aft. The 2nd Mate who has been wonderful truly and helped us in our overwork plenty of times goes up aloft to take over the mizzen gaff, as the two boys who were doing it he had told to go and drink coffee. The Captain sees him and tells him to come down and send me up. What a Captain, nothing but a drunk disreputable creature. I sleep a little on my bunk during free watch in the morning but as usual the selfish daymen made it impossible with their unholy noise. I work continuously, except for half an hour, in the afternoon from 1pm to 7pm, although a Sunday, having two wheels, dishwashing, look-out etc.

It is a glorious day and the boys sit out on deck in the sunshine.

The Steward and Andersen catch one bonito each and we have fresh fish for tea, it was good. I commence writing a story of my cycle journey last year through the Yorkshire Dales. The 2nd Mate lends us his gramophone.
Position 21.27°S 0.32°W

216

Day 62 Monday April 20th

I sleep in the sail locker again all last night and very well too. During the working watch in the morning our watch carry coal to the galley. The 1st Mate without doubt seems to dislike our watch as he arranges all dirty jobs for us. These Finns cannot see a joke for their dear life, I gave Svenska a mouldy old loaf at dinner time when he asked for bread and Karlsson who was in the fo'c'sle at the time, serious and interfering as usual, told Svenska to tell me to get some bread. He could not see the joke and that I would get one anyway.

I wash a few clothes in the free watch in the afternoon then I sleep on my bunk until tea time. Another glorious day. While policeman at 8pm to 9pm I chat with the Bosun and he says another 6 weeks to Falmouth but I think at least 8 weeks.
Position 19.53°S 0.23°W

Day 63 Tuesday April 21st

At 6am we bend the tropical mainsail. For two weeks we have been sailing without a sail on this yard owing to it having to be unbent for repairs. I see what I thought was a black albatross but the Steward says it was a mollyhawke, there is very little difference and I cannot see it.

The way we start chipping rust in different places all over the ship then leaving off and starting somewhere new amuses me, why not finish one place first. I feel sure the 1st Mate is going perfectly off his head. Svenska is not feeling so well today he has a pain in his stomach but he keeps on working, what else can he do poor fellow with only three men in the watch. We commence chipping rust on the pin rail starboard side. It is quite warm in the daytime but still cold at night.
Position 18.42°S 2.34°W

Day 64 Wednesday April 22nd

We are again chipping rust on the pin rail in the morning watch. We are now on the Plymouth to Cape Town shipping route and the Mate tells us to keep a sharp look-out during my look-out between 12pm and 4am. There is a little sea water coming on deck today due to the rolling of the ship.

I read a book the Steward has lent me "Sunny Tomorrow" during the afternoon free watch. Then after coffee I sit on a hammock on the fo'c'sle head. I have a row with the day men after tea as they will take up the whole table in the fo'c'sle for model making and playing cards and leaving me only a little room for dishwashing. Svenska and I brace at 9pm. I have a very deep cut in one of my feet due to the salt water.
Position 16.22°S 4.11°W

Day 65 Thursday April 23rd

While I am at the wheel at 6.15am we pick up St Helena Island on the starboard side roughly twenty miles away. It is not very clear as there is a mist about but it appears very small and very hilly. The day men are still painting the mast and yards. Tony is always waiting by the pigs every morning for his little game. He does enjoy it poor old soul.

We are again chipping rust on the pin rail midships in the afternoon. We have now started to wet the decks at 6pm at night. God we poor watch men have never finished it seems and we do not even seem to have a minute for a smoke. What a wonderful worker the Chief Mate is, he works just like a slave. I do really wish some of those work grousers at home could see him, it would open their eyes a little.
Position 15.1°S 5.31°W

Day 66 Friday April 24th

We are again chipping rust on the pin rail midships but this time we have started underneath in the scuppers. The daymen have now finished painting the masts and are chipping rust with us.

What a poor South East Trade Wind we have had this time barely doing above 3 knots all the time.

Our big tiger cat seems to live in the hold these days, he knows where the rats are. It is a glorious day without hardly a cloud to be seen. I sat on the fo'c'sle head in the afternoon sunning myself and making knots. Orlander plays hell with me for taking some of his ropes.
Position 13.47°S 6.58°W

Day 67 Saturday April 25th

At 7am the Steward catches a bonito from the bowsprit. There are a large number swimming about under the bows. After breakfast our free watch try to catch some more but fail. Then I sleep a little on my bunk. In the afternoon working watch I clean midships out, the other two brush up on deck and at 3.30pm we finish only at 6pm to wet the deck. We are never finished, there is always work. Most of us try in vain in the afternoon to catch more bonito but fail. We have fresh fish for tea, oh, how good.
Position 12.45°S 8.19°W

Day 68 Sunday April 26th

It is a glorious day and very warm. Our watch brace a little at 9am. Up until 9am we have caught three bonito, the Steward caught one and Andersen caught two. Most of the boys sleep out on hammocks at night now, we poor wretched watch men spend a Sunday working, what with two wheels, two policemen and bracing. It turns out very hot. Another bonito is caught in the afternoon by Andersen who is getting crack at it now, having caught three today. There are two small sea swallows following us . At 6pm we have no more drinking water left in the fo'c'sle and the Mates will not give us any more. Only three buckets a day for fifteen men worse than the French Foreign Legion. I see a steamer far down on the port horizon at 5pm.

A star falls tonight almost right onto the ship, very near.

The Mate rows me and Svenska for allowing the port light to go dim, it was not our fault but the lamplighters.
Position 11.40°S 10.12°W

Day 69 Monday April 27th
The Mate rows me for spilling water in the sail locker while carrying it to the galley. I could not help it with the ship rolling. He seems to dislike me now.

Large schools of flying fish about today and one huge bird with a black head.

We have fresh fish for breakfast and fresh fish for tea last night. Two more bonitos caught this morning before 8am, the Steward one and Andersen one. I try to sleep on my bunk during free watch this morning but fail except for one and a half hours.

We are again chipping rust on the pin rail underneath but now aft. The port side is almost finished now.

Another glorious day. We again work continuously from 1pm to 7pm except for half an hour for coffee. We are all three very tired, no wonder too. It is slave driving work.
Position 10.25°S 11.37°W

Day 70 Tuesday April 28th
It is exactly ten weeks ago today that we last heaved up anchor off Broughton. I go into my bunk at 6am to sleep but within five minutes I have been bitten all over and I kill at least fifteen bugs. The fo'c'sle is absolutely overrun with them.

All hands are chipping the fresh water tank back aft today. At 8am this morning we have huge rain squalls for about half an hour and we fill the donkey tank up half full. Two white Cape pigeons flying around the ship today. Large schools of flying fish about and it is a terribly hot and depressing today.

Liewendahl has started painting the Captains saloon. He is always favoured by the Captain. I sleep on my bunk until coffee. The Captain very kindly gives me a book to read.

Two large birds with black heads and a lot of white Cape pigeons about this afternoon. At night they chatter away like magpies.

We look out for Ascension Island all night but never see it, bad navigation again.
Position 8.55°S 13.20°W

Day 71 Wednesday April 29th
The Mates and Captain are still looking out for land this morning. But they might just as well look out for Falmouth because we are nearly away to the West.

I have a big row this morning breakfast time. I forgot to fill the tub in the crews heads with water (it was ¾ full) and nearly all the hands get at me and play up, especially the three usual, Lund, Karlsson and Svenska. Then somebody also had the dirty trick to go and tell the other crewmen that I am always telling the mates about them. Never making trouble for me as usual! I say to Eriksen I wish I knew who the devil it was and lo and behold if he doesn't go against me and wants to fight me. Honestly, what a crowd.

We are again chipping rust aft. Not a bad job really but in this heat very tiring.

There are still a few Cape pigeons about.
Position 7.22°S 15.27°W

Day 72 Thursday April 30th
In the morning we are again chipping rust aft. The 2nd mate has started to chip the mizzen winch on the poop, the Captain also did a little. It is very hot again but we have a very good wind and doing about 7 knots.

 I again catch about 20 bugs in my bunk. Between 7pm and 12pm I have no fewer than 3 wheels, one look-out, one policeman and bracing. There is a lot of water on deck and boys found 5 or 6 flying fish at night and they set them on wood.
Position 5.16°S 17.41°W

Day 73 Friday May 1st
It is May Day and I think of home and all the beautiful spring, the trees, the countryside and everything. I wish I were home. The 2nd Mate says another forty days. God can I stand it. We have a few drops of rain early this morning but not enough to collect.

Poor Tony the dog is ill, poor soul he looks so sad and he was turned out of the 1st Mates cabin last night, why I don't know. He is so faithful to the Mate for what kindness he gets. The Mate never thinks of giving him a drink in this hot weather, so I often do so. Yesterday the poor dog got hit by him for rubbing up against the paint. How is the dog to know where fresh paint is? It strikes me the Mate only has him for a play thing.

We again chip rust on the pin rail but this time forward. We do not wet the deck tonight.

There is a lovely sunset and a lovely moonlit night.

A small land swallow has followed us all day, evidently making for the European summer. I have a row with Svenska. He is always downing the English, so I tell him he must not speak to me like that about them.
Position 3.27°S 20.29°W

Day 74 Saturday May 2nd
I spend three hours at the wheel today in the morning and enjoy it as the weather is glorious and not too hot owing to the fine breeze blowing. We are averaging roughly 8 knots.

I chip rust aft and then the pin rail on the midship house. I sit midships during the free watch in the afternoon and chat with the Bosun. Then, after coffee I sit on the fo'c'sle head in lovely sunshine.

We had a lot of water on deck today owing to the heavy sea running.
Position 1.4°S 22°W

Day 75 Sunday May 3rd
Between 4pm and 8am we have the wind coming strongly from the NE and we do about 8 knots but it rains hard and it is very miserable. I again sleep in the sail locker. I work continuously from 4am to 8am.

There are heaps of fish playing around the ship at 7am and the boys try to harpoon them from the fo'c'sle head. I sleep in the sail locker between 8am and 1pm as I am very tired. No wonder, God what work.

The 1st Mate gives me some magazines to read. Most of the boys have boxing matches in the afternoon with socks for gloves. The 2nd and 3rd Mates also come up and box. I also have a shot against Karlsson and Eriksen and I did fairly well considering my size.

We brace at 1.45pm the wind again coming from aft. It is terribly hot and I am very tired. Except for one hour free I again work continuously from 1pm to 7pm but thank goodness, starting tonight, each watch has two more men. We cross the line at 1.15am this morning with a good wind.

It rains cats and dogs from 4.30pm until 7pm and we are kept busy catching it. We fill up to the top the donkey tank and all barrels. At 4.30pm we again brace, the wind being from aft again and we all get wet through. What a Sunday, only just time for a smoke.
Never again on a sailing ship.
Position 1.17°N 24.22°W

Day 76 Monday May 4th
At 2am we brace, the wind coming from the side again and for a few minutes we steer By de Vind. In the morning watch 8am to 1pm we bend and furl and set the flying jib, outer jib, inner jib and jigger topsail and it rains nearly all morning except for one hour while I am at the wheel.

I chip rust for an hour aft under the pin rail. The port watch square up at 1pm in drenching rain. We have heaps of fish eating now. I hear today the Captain has no soap left. What are we to do without soap for possibly 40 days or so.

I read a magazine in the afternoon given to me by the 1st mate. We brace two times between 7pm and 12pm
Position 2.56°N 25.46°W

Day 77 Tuesday May 5th
At 6am we commence to wash the fo'c'sle out with soda. Thank the Lord! Now we have made a start, perhaps we shall now get rid of the bugs. In the free watch between 8am and 1pm I sleep on ropes in the sail locker and not badly too. In the afternoon we carry on and finish washing the fo'c'sle. Under the fo'c'sle head the boys have put up hammocks, and all manner of cases, trunks, sea chests, sea bags, clothes etc. are all there too. It resembles the Black Hole of Calcutta, nobody knows where any of their things are. I overhaul gardings at 5.30pm on the mizzen and main masts.

It rains cats and dogs all day. I am fed up with getting wet, I never seem to be dry now and we brace no fewer than 3 times in the end. Sailing course N by W
Position 3.16°N 26.4°W

Day 78 Wednesday May 6th
We begin to paint the fo'c'sle but only A.Bs. get this job, we scrape and chip rust in the passage way. We brace twice in the morning watch. At 1.15pm the wind

comes from the other side and in absolutely drenching rain the port watch and day men brace. They brace another four times before 7pm. It rains all afternoon and up to midnight. We brace three times in our watch. We are absolutely becalmed.
Position 4.26°N 28.4°W

Day 79 Thursday May 7th

I clean out the pig sty, the heads (lavatory) and sweep the deck before breakfast. The Mate plays hell with me for letting the pigs out and yet they come out every morning with the other boys and never anything is said. I sleep on the midships hold top in the morning and well too. In the afternoon I am again chipping rust aft under the pin rail. We have a little sing song in the fo'c'sle in the evening.

The fo'c'sle has now had its second coating of white paint. It has been a much better day and only a little rain.
Position 4.45°N 28.35°W

Day 80 Friday May 8th

It is terribly hot today hardly bearable, at least it takes me all my time, I am thoroughly exhausted and wet all over and on top of that we are again chipping rust off aft under the pin rail. It is stifling and the side of the ship is red hot with the heat.

A steamer passes us a long way off at 1pm. We are now on the South America to Europe route. I ask the Mate when free this morning if I can paint my boards but the stingy beggar refused. Yet, after lunch and in our free time we have to scrape wood. He sees that we do that alright. The meanness of this filthy ship is terrible. The "Winterhude" was a palace compared to this. Svenska as usual in his sly way gets me to get more food and then just as I finish he jumps up and grabs my scraper and sets to work. I have to wait as usual. Swedish Finns are mean to the core.

We are becalmed once more. A little wind in the afternoon. Another steamer sighted at 6pm.
Position 5.42°N 24.43°W

Day 81 Saturday May 9th

A foreign steamer comes very close aft heading Northwards and we morse her and she answers. We have now definitely got our NE Trade Wind and the weather, thank goodness, is fine again.

When I take the sugar tins to the Steward this morning he plays hell with me for bringing them at coffee time and picks a shovel up as though to hit me. I suppose somebody has upset him and he replies by going for poor me. What beggars these Swedish Finns are, never trust them any further than your little finger. After all I did for him in Australia too, saved him from court proceedings over his gaff episodes. Then the Mate plays hell with me for cleaning glass when he told me to tell the look-out to come down. I replied it is better I do not go to sea again. Given a fair wind these fellows are o.k. but if no wind or headwind, no good. What a lot.

I sleep for four hours up on the fo'c'sle head in glorious sunshine tempered by a nice NE breeze and when I wake up one side of my face is scorched.

I clean midships out in the afternoon and then at 5pm I paint my bunk boards and clothes box. The fo'c'sle is now finished and we shall be back again in a day or two.
Position 6.52°N 28.35°W

Day 82 Sunday May 10th
It is a glorious day again without a cloud in the sky. I sleep on the hatch midships in the afternoon. Svenska is the most annoying creature I have ever come across. He is continually making a fool of me in front of the boys and he and the 2nd Mate tell each other everything I do and say. We are back to three men in a watch again.
Position 8.1°N 30.24°W

Day 83 Monday May 11th
The mizzen royal sheet breaks at 1am this morning and so the port watch make fast the sail but in the morning watch 4am to 8am we repair the damaged sheet and again set the sail.

There are a large number of flying fish about today and it was a glorious sunrise watched by me from look-out. In the morning free watch I bring up my cases from the hold and give them a thorough cleaning and inspection and then I sleep on Pedersens hammock in the donkey room.

Chipping rust on the pin rail midships in the afternoon. We have now almost completely finished chipping rust and soon we shall commence painting all over.
Position 9.31°N 32.5°W

Day 84 Tuesday May 12th
Another nice day and a good breeze blowing too. Doing roughly 6 to 7 knots and we are sailing most of the time N ½ W. In the working watch in the afternoon I just commence chipping rust again midships and then scrape the fo'c'sle floor. A hell of a job down on ones knees all day.

I chat with the mate while at the wheel 12am to 1pm about how old in their years sailors are compared to landlubbers and he agrees.

I saw the Southern Cross very plainly last night although it is said you cannot see it North of the Equator. I also see for the first time my old friend the North star.

A big bird with a long neck following us today. I think a land bird. I sit out again on the midships hatch and read my book in lovely sunshine. The Steward is most unfriendly with me, why I don't know. Just another moody Scandinavian.
Position 11.10°N 33.23°W

Chips on deck

Day 85 Wednesday May 13th

I clean out the pig house and fill up the water tanks and then chip rust midships before breakfast. Svenska, as usual annoying, paints his cupboards, so late too, also his bunk just above mine and all the paint falls down onto my clothes etc. Just like him, no sense at all.

We went course NNE nearly all night doing about 8 knots. Most people, including the 2nd Mate ascertain 30 more days. God I hope so.

I sleep on number three hatch during free watch in the morning but did not sleep very good for when the sun went it was very cold. Chipping rust on blocks, bolts, etc. on the starboard side in the afternoon. The fo'c'sle is now quite ready for us coming in but so far nobody is sleeping in. The boys have a sing song at night.

We go course almost all day. The 2nd Mate says he has been at sea on sailing ships for 52 months but has never known any ship before to go course with a NE Trade Wind, most unusual.
Position 13.18°N 34.22°W

Day 86 Thursday May 14th

I am still sleeping in the sail locker and very well too. We have still got a good wind and go course NNE all morning.

I chip rust aft just by the steps of the poop then later, on number two hatch. At 1pm the Norwegian oil tanker "Vanja" comes off her course and almost passes along side aft. We ask her to report us to Lloyds and she replies, "Yes". Another nice day but it is getting a little colder now. At 1.45pm we experience a heavy squall and consequently for the rest of the day we go at a fine pace holding course except for one hour when it went to NNW. Spray from the waves comes continuously over the fo'c'sle head and at look-out we all get wet through. Heavy showers in the afternoon, doing about 7 knots, waves come on deck too. At 9pm our watch take in and make fast the jigger gaff.

The wheel is very hard.
Position 15.22°N 34.49°W 136 miles today.

Day 87 Friday May 15th

We hold course all through the night and keep also the wonderful speed up, about 7 knots. It rains very hard between 4am and 5am. At 7am we take off the wheel box (all hands) and rotten, like the rest of the ship, it collapses immediately it is raised.

What a wreck of a ship the "Ponape" is. I clean the tarpaulin cover that collects the oil under the wheel box, a very dirty job. It has been a hard nights work for three men and I am feeling dead beat. Some of the boys are beginning to get on my nerves but this is only natural after so long at sea.

I sleep in my bunk for the first time for about a month but believe me there must still be bugs there because I was bitten again. In the afternoon working watch I am up on the poop cleaning the paint on the wheel with soda, getting the oil away. While I am at the wheel 5pm to 6pm it begins to set in a drizzle and becomes foggy, true north Atlantic weather, this later sets in to heavy rain and the wind strengthens considerably. While I am at look-out from 6pm to 7pm I have to work the fog horn as the fog is thick. At 7.30pm the wind is blowing a hurricane and the night is looking very black and dirty. Suddenly the fore and mizzen royals split in two and the day men are called to help in taking them in and making fast. They also take in the mizzen upper to'gallant. Later the flying jib has to be taken in owing to a tear. The Captain during all of this is terribly nervy shouting and prancing about like a madman. At first I thought the ship was going down with his shouting.
Position 17.55°N 36.5°W

Day 88 Saturday May 16th

I again slept in the sail locker but for the last time as I found two bugs there last night. It is still blowing hard and there is a lot of water on deck, while heavy spray continually comes over the fo'c'sle head. It rains every now and again in the morning but clears up around midday.

I am again cleaning the paint on the wheel. We have course NNE nearly all morning. The wheel is very hard to work and turn and every so often the Mate has to help us to turn it. The day men unbend the fore royal and bend a new one and later they wash white paint with soda. They cursed but it will do them good.

I must truly say that except for four men out of the whole crew the rest have no true ounce of decency in them. I, being the smallest, they are continually getting at me all day for one thing and another and then when I am dishwasher they always make me go for more food etc. and treat me just like dirt, but when Sandstom, a big boy, is dishwasher and a Swede they go themselves. Rotters, just because I am small. Give me the English people every time, you can trust them but these people you cannot, friends one day and not the next.

I sleep until coffee time on my bunk and try to sleep afterwards but there is so much noise it is impossible. We keep up our fine speed.
Position 21.5°N 37°W 199 miles.

Day 89 Sunday May 17th

It rains very hard between 4am and 8am but we are now going at a fine speed, just over 8 knots.

I clean out the pig sty before breakfast. I see my first Sargasso weed so now I suppose we are in the Sargasso Sea. I sleep on my bunk in the free watch in the morning. The port watch and the day men set the main royal and after lunch our watch and the day men set the fore and mizzen royals, jigger gaff and flying jib. I overhaul gardings on the fore royal.

There are heavy showers nearly all afternoon but towards evening it clears up. The wind is not so strong but we still do about five knots.
Position 24.36°N 37.58°W 214 miles.

Day 90 Monday May 18th

I sleep in the sail locker at first but bugs there force me to come to my bunk. It is a glorious day and quite warm.

I chip rust on blocks and the hold port side. Lund has returned to our watch and Karlsson to the port watch, making both watches four men each now. I sleep on my bunk until coffee time then I read and look at snaps. I am again bitten very badly by bugs tonight in my bunk.

The one I hate most on the ship plays up with me tonight when I am dishwasher and says the table is dirty and gets my hand and rubs it on it hard. He is a perfect devil, treats me like a bit of dirt and thinks he is a great fellow because he is an ordinary seaman and orders me always to get more food and when I was trying to talk nicely with him he just sneers. I wish old Bob was here he would make some of them sit up.
Position 27.9°N 32.15°W

Day 91 Tuesday May 19th

I carry water to the galley before breakfast and also clean the heads and pig pen then scrape rust on number three hatch. We have good wind and go "full and by" going round about NE.

The poor cat that I feed was absolutely nervous this morning, I think it gets very little to eat. I am chipping rust on three hatch in the afternoon. While I am policeman from 6pm to 7pm the 2nd Mate comes down onto the deck to me and chats. He shows me his navigation book. It blows up hard towards night.

The 2nd Mate is like the rest of them, should anybody be against me in front of him he will immediately turn against me too. What a crew.
Position 29.4°N 39.11°W

Day 92 Wednesday May 20th

I again chip rust on number three hatch midships in the morning watch and I spend two and a half hours at the wheel in glorious sunshine, which I thoroughly enjoyed. The wind kept on shifting the whole time from between NE and NW. Where is the west wind we should have by now. God I wish we could get it and then be in the last stage.

The whole crew row me this morning, all shouting at me at the same time and all because I finished dishwashing in half an hour and they said the dishes were not clean enough. They are the dirtiest people I have ever come across and yet they dare to row like this. I hate the ship and everybody in her. Oh, to be away and at home. I have terrible pain in my right side all evening and I can hardly stand up.

We are almost becalmed all evening going between North and West.
Position 31.26°N 40.15°W

Day 93 Thursday May 21st

We have a whole holiday today but I did not know, nobody told me. At 4.30am our watch turn the ship the wind now comes from the West so perhaps at last the West wind has come. It comes light at first and then strengthens as the day goes on. At 9am we are going East by South.

There is a small bird like a pigeon flying about all day. The 2nd Mate rows me this morning first because I did not release a wire quick enough, he came and tried and hardly moved it a fraction. I said to him, "It is not so easy is it?", he said "Shut up" and I said "I won't". Typical of him and the rest, friends and chatting with you one minute and against you the next. He is continually sniggering about me to the boys, like he did to Clapperton. Dirty work because I don't understand the language.

We have now no soap, no potatoes and no cigarettes left. We are eating Danish tinned potatoes.

I have terrible pain in my right knee just by the joint and I go to the 1st Mate and he gives me some tincture to rub on. It is very painful. While I am at the wheel from 3pm to 4pm it rains very hard and I get wet through.

We are sailing all day with a fair breeze about NE. Two more have come back to each watch making six in each now. The wind continues to shift about all over the place all day. Most of the boys have returned to their bunks now.
Position 32.39°N 40.26°W

Day 94 Friday May 22nd

While I am at look-out from 12pm to 1am I sight the lights of a steamer on the port side but she does not come near enough to morse.

We commence to change sails this morning. In our working watch 8am to 1pm we change the mizzen upper topsail, lower topsail and later the main upper topsail. We also put back the buntlines to the mizzen and main upper and lower to'gallants. I spend three hours running up and down the rigging, as I have no wheel, I can tell you I was tired. The wind is still playing tricks all day changing from NE to NW.

I sleep on my bunk a little in the afternoon and then I read and played the ukelele.

Fine weather and a little warmer.
Position 33.50°N 39.2°W

A fair wind fore mast and fore sail

Day 95 Saturday May 23rd
An oil tanker bound South comes off her course and passes very close at 4.15am while another one bound South also is seen away on the horizon. Two birds are flying about this morning a black and white one and a white one. I clean the pig house and overhaul gardings before breakfast. The 1st Mate catches me sitting on the topsail yard doing nothing just smoking and he is very angry making me carry coal. The Captain comes up to the fo'c'sle after breakfast to examine the models. I wash a few clothes. I clean the midships out in the afternoon. At 12.30pm we again go course but there is very little wind. As the day wears on the wind strengthens up and by 9pm we have a fairly strong wind. Karlsson and I have a sing song after coffee.
Position 35.2°N 39.43°W

Day 96 Sunday May 24th
The wind is still with us all morning and we do about 5 to 6 knots. There is a small sea swallow flying about aft today. The sea has a typical grey North Atlantic appearance today making it seem much more like home.

What a set of people the Swedish Finns are. The 2nd Mate walks about today with a face as drawn and angry as possible. Why I don't know, with a fair wind like we have. Moody. I sleep on my bunk until coffee time and then I read my book, "Further Adventures of Jenny Dale", very good. Between 9pm and 12pm we average 9½ knots. Soderstrom asks me to change first wheel with him, which I kindly do, only to find out he is another low down dirty rotter, because instead of my first police, I have to take his last look-out.
Position 37.43°N 38.40°W

Every sail straining to the wind 10 knots

Day 97 Monday May 25th
A glorious sunrise, typical of those only seen at home in England, a lovely red horizon flanked with a light green sky. Before breakfast I fill the tanks on the poop and have again another dirty trick played on me, this time by the 2nd Mate. He told me (although I am not dishwasher) to fill the tank up in the heads while Soderstrom, the dishwasher, helps him to paint and chip. Favouritism and I certainly get none of it. I sleep on my bunk all morning. At 12am a Danish oil tanker the "Jane Maersk" passes close, bound South, while at 6.30pm a Greek tramp steamer passes close aft bound from the States to the Mediterranean. In the afternoon working watch I scrape rust just forward of the pig house. We have a fair wind all day and towards night it strengthens.
Position 40.18°N 35.41°W

Day 98 Tuesday May 26th
Between 12am and 4pm we touch 12 knots for three hours, the lee rail at times being under water while the deck and fo'c's'le head are awash with sea spray. At 3.30am a steamer passes us close by, a pretty sight all lit up. This morning Cookie kills the 2nd pig, only one remains now. At 8.30am while I am at the wheel we have to go from course to "full and by the wind" but most of the morning it is only a quarter point off course. I chip rust on number one hatch forward all morning. Two birds seen today one a large whitish thing and the other looked like a hawk. We have now commenced to scrape the teak wood on the poop. I sleep on my bunk until coffee time and then I read my book again until tea time. At 8pm we are six points off the course. It is much colder tonight and not at all like summer time up here.
Position 43.5°N 32.47°W

Day 99 Wednesday May 27th

I carry water to the galley and clean the pig house out before breakfast. The boys are still scraping teak wood on the poop. The black and white hawk is still following us. This morning we are one point off the course and a fairly strong wind.

We have fresh meat for breakfast and how good it tasted. I sleep on my bunk all morning. In the afternoon I and Soderstrom spend five hours under the wheel scraping the teak wood deck, my legs were very tired at the finish.

There is a very yellow and stormy looking sunset.

A large four masted Barquentine passes us bound South East she looks very pretty.

Still sailing By de Vind and a long way off course.
Position 45.35°N 32.5°W

Day 100 Thursday May 28th

At 3.30 am a fairly large passenger steamer passes fairly close to us bound SW but in the light of dawn I think she could neither see us nor our morsing because she cut right in front of us. I again spend four hours scraping teak wood under the wheel.

Again favouritism comes to the fore, Soderstrom is given a painting job although he is only the same rate as me, but, I am an Englishman and "never to be given a good job" seems to be their slogan.

I sleep on my bunk until coffee. Just after coffee I have a hell of a row with that filthiest and lowest of all curs on this ship.

As it happened I took the fresh water jug up to the wash house and forgot to bring it back. He comes for it and plays Cain and Able with me. Calls me a "Bloody Englishman" (not for the first time) and says he will fight me and kill me in another minute. I ask him what is up between us two for over a week now. He says "I have been with you for 8 months now, I know what you are and what you say to the boys about me."

Fancy, what cowards they are on this ship. Obviously some cur who dislikes me is putting it on me by making out to people I say this and that about them. What a set of real sly cowards nearly the lot of them are on this ship.

At 5.30pm a four masted barque is sighted and as she comes nearer we see she is painted white, therefore either "Viking", "L'avenir" or the "Hertzogin Cecilie".

At 6.45pm she is alongside and turns out to be the "Viking". At 7pm she turns round and comes North with us.

It is a very cold night with showers.
Position 47.55°N 30.45°W

We race the
S.V. "Viking"

Day 101 Friday May 29th
We turn the ship at 6.30am as the Viking is nowhere in sight and having turned we sail By de Vind still and going South by East. At 8.30am the Viking is seen far down on the starboard horizon.

I clean the pig house out before breakfast. I shook hands last night with Eriksen (as a Britisher and a sport) but this morning he still has a hellish sneer on his face when he passes me. They are not sports these Swedish Finns they don't know what it means to be a sport undoubtedly.

I chip rust under the fore mast all afternoon. It is very cold, one cannot get warm even working.

The Viking is in sight all day, down far away on the starboard horizon and towards evening we seem to be gaining on her. There are a large number of fair sized birds about today as well as a school of sea swallows.
Position 49.20°N 30.22°W

Day 102 Saturday May 30th
We are still assing about with a head wind and today we are almost becalmed. God help us, it is driving me mad this being so near and unable to make any headway. The Viking is out of sight today. A fairly large steamer passes us a long way off bound West probably for the United States.

Again I am given a dirty job this morning while the rest paint. I wash the white paint on the port side ready for its second coating. A whale and a very large shark seen today. I sleep on my bunk until coffee time and then I lie on my bunk

and read a magazine. It is very cold all day and towards night it gets colder still. At 9pm for twenty minutes we go course East to South and then suddenly in five minutes we are back to South ½ East steering Bi de Vind again.
Position 47.42°N 29.46°W

Day 103 Sunday May 31st

I clean the pig house out and carry water to the galley before breakfast and then I sleep all morning till dinner time.

At 1pm the British oil tanker "Athelviking" comes off her course and passes close aft. How nice to see a Britisher for a change and what a fine sight, as she left, in true British spirit, she lowered and dipped her flag three times and as she did so she gave three blasts on her siren, truly a fine bit of sportsmanship on her part. At 1pm we turn the ship and then steer Bi de Vind going NE but while I am at the wheel from 3pm to 4pm in one hour we come up from NE½N to, East by North, and not so far off course.

Another steamer is sighted at 3.45pm low down on the starboard horizon. It is much warmer today. A lot of sea swallows about and one big bird. Also I again see that very big shark.

After my wheel at 4pm I go into my bunk and read the magazine again. Between 7pm and 12pm we are only one point off course so perhaps soon we shall at last have it.
Position 46.30°N 29.56°W

Day 104 Monday June 1st

We have a whole holiday today as it is Whit Monday. At 8am an American steamer bound East for Europe called the "Black Hawk" passes close by puts her flag up but never dips it as she leaves which makes the crew very angry. An oil tanker (home and nationality unknown) passes on the port side at 10.30am bound East in ballast.

I wash some clothes in the morning while most of the boys get on with their models. The 2nd Mate lends us his gramophone.

We are becalmed between 3pm and 7pm but still hold course. Two large birds soar about.
Position 47.8°N 29.31°W

Day 105 Tuesday June 2nd

Today it has been fifteen weeks since we last heaved up the anchor. God what a time and here we are so near home and yet unable to get there what with head

234

winds and then calms. At 6.30am this morning we again go Bi de Vind, two points off. A large three funnelled liner seen at 4am this morning making East for Europe. A big shark and another large fish with two fins seen swimming aft while I am at the wheel, also the two large sea birds are still with us, and two small sea swallows. I carry water to the galley, clean the pig house and carry coal to the galley before breakfast.

Everybody on board is beginning to get bad tempered, a fed up feeling, being so near port and unable to get there. It will drive me crazy soon if we don't get a fair wind. In the afternoon while I am at the wheel 3pm to 4pm the wind changes from a head wind to almost aft and we set the three sails again, fore, main and mizzen and square up the sails a little. I chip rust forward on the anchor.

We have the gramophone on all night and we who are free watch have a job trying to get some sleep as the grammy is played until 11 o'clock. I sleep just one hour. The wind strengthens a little towards night and we still hold course. *Position 47.26°N 28.31°W*

Day 106 Wednesday June 3rd
When I am look-out 2am to 3am a large tanker comes close to us bound West. We morse her and she replies but her morsing thing will not work. I again chip rust on the anchor chain guide all morning.

A few sea swallows and two large white birds still with us. A steamer sighted starboard horizon at 12am and another at 4pm. We have a very nice wind now and doing almost five knots. The port watch square up at 2pm. I sleep on my bunk until coffee. I have a row with the 2nd Mate as usual in front of other boys. I was policeman and he blew two whistles, not heard by me, and he says all manner of things to me. Had it been a Finn nothing would have been said. *Position 47.46°N 25.27°W*

Day 107 Thursday June 4th
I offer Eriksen some tobacco and all he says is "Go to hell." Think of it, offering a fellow some tobacco and that's the kind of reply. God what a crowd. I loathe this fellow, he is sly and false. Soon he will be coming up to me and in a sweet voice, "Can I borrow your razor." etc. etc. This time the answer will be "No." Again I wake the Steward and when he comes on deck he shouts and yells murder at me. Why God only knows. Only half an hour later , like the rest of them, he was pals again. I will never trust them one yard these Swedish Finns.

I see an oil tanker away on the horizon at 6.30am bound East. The wind shifts a little from aft to the port side, so we brace a little and take over the staysails. I have a thorough fed up feeling and just longing and longing to be off this truly perfect hell of a ship and hellish people.

I chip rust up forward near the fo'c'sle head on the port and starboard sides and then, what a wonder, I was actually allowed to paint it afterwards.

We have a fine wind from aft all day but towards night it shifts more to the port side.
Position 47.54°N 22.30°W

Day 108 Friday June 5th
The 2nd Mate this morning is in one of his disgusting moods. He does nothing but find fault with me whatever I do and always only in front of the other boys. He says nothing to Soderstom ever about his rust chipping which is never good, it's slack work, and yet I truly work like a slave and get nothing but this again. If I were to go up to the fo'c'sle for ten minutes or so like Soderstrom did this morning there would have been hell playing but he only received smiles from the Mate. I am really treated just like a piece of dirt. Whatever I do there is always sniggering between the 2nd and 3rd Mates.

There is a mist all day, a little rain and cold. It comes in foggy towards night and we have to use the fog horn.
Position 48.19°N 18.30°W

Day 109 Saturday June 6th
We still have course at 6am this morning and doing about 4 knots. It is rain and drizzle all morning and inclined to be foggy. We commence to wash the white and brown paint under the fo'c'sle head. I don't think it had been cleaned out for years because there is a lot of Guano about and it is 6 years since "Ponape" took Guano for cargo.

Eriksen is laid up with a poisoned hand and leg. I sleep on my bunk during the free watch in the morning. An English motor ship passes us at 11am bound West. I clean midships out in the afternoon and I hope to God it will be my last dishwashing etc. I tried to make the Timmermans place nice and clean but like the rest of these cads on this ship he plays hell with me for taking so long. Honestly the people on this ship will drive me perfectly crazy if we don't reach Falmouth soon. I am tired and fed up with everything in general.

It is still very cold and there is a damp mist about all day.
Position 48.36°N 15.3°W

236

Day 110 Sunday June 7th

We have a look-out all day being Sunday of course, if a week day like yesterday and fog, no look-out. We see a few trawlers for the first time today 2 in the morning and 4 in the afternoon.

A lot of wood and ship wreck are floating about in the water. I chat with Liewendahl at look-out in the morning about the ship and people on the ship in general and he agrees that Svenska is a hell of a nuisance and teases me too much. He also says he will be pleased to leave.

I wash a few clothes again. We have a look-out all day though the weather is clear.
Position 49.3°N 11.4°W

Day 111 Monday June 8th

We commence at 6am to get the anchor chain up from the chain locker and this is completed by 8am. The port watch paint the anchor davits and commence chipping rust on the port anchor. God only knows why but in my opinion a waste of time. The look-out has to chip rust too, what a dirty trick.

Three trawlers pass close by at 9am. I sleep on my bunk until dinner time, then in the working watch we get up the landing step and the donkey funnel from the hold. Terribly heavy work for three men but we managed it. Then we heave up the anchor (port wires) from the hold onto the fo'c'sle roof top and oil it. While I am look-out from 4pm to 5pm I am the first to see the first land, Bishops Rock.

Two large steamers and a few trawlers bound West pass us between 5pm and 7pm.

The Scilly Isles become quite clear at 6.30pm. We have scores of seagulls following us all day and their screeching sound all day seems so homely. The Mate chats with me at the wheel from 6pm to 7pm about Finland. I have terrible toothache all night.

The last pig is killed this morning, poor old soul, it had got so tame and friendly.

We very nearly collided with a steamer at 10pm our starboard light having gone out, a very near squeeze.
Position 49.20°N 7.17°W

Day 112 Tuesday June 9th

While I am at look-out from 3am to 4am a large oil tanker suddenly appears out of the very thick fog directly ahead of us and she is nearly upon us before

237

she sees us. We think we must be opposite the Lizard because we hear the lighthouse fog horn. When we rise at 8am we are opposite the Manacles, land can just be seen. The first I have seen of England for 9 months. The fog lifts as the morning goes on and we slowly wend our way in when suddenly, when we were opposite about Coverack or so we met a head wind and we had to ask for assistance from a private yacht and motor boat to tow us round. Two four masters in Falmouth, the "Olivebank" 108 days, and "Archibald Russell" 104 days. We hear "Herzogin" has run ashore near Plymouth and "Abraham Rydberg" collided with a steamer in the channel. We have a head wind all day and turn the ship no fewer than five times between 2pm and midnight, first over towards Fowey and then back towards Coverack, only gaining a little ground each time. We stare open mouthed when at 7pm along came the "Viking" hugging the coast and goes straight in to her anchor.

"Olivebank" at anchor, Falmouth

Day 113 Wednesday June 10th
We turn the ship several more times between midnight and 6pm when we at last anchor and our eyes nearly fall out for lo and behold, there is not only the "Viking" but the "Penane" also. We make fast the sails and then have the rest of the day free.

Home at last thank God, Falmouth.
118 days from Australia.

[Editors note:
This was the last voyage of the "Ponape" as she was sold to Latvian ship breakers in September 1936. However, her memory lives on, not only in print and photograph but in poems, particularly by Isabella Kiernander in her book "Songs of the Tall Ships".

The sight of the "Herzogin Cecilie" aground and broken affected Geoffrey greatly as she had been so beautiful.

Perhaps these sad photographs and a poem written to Geoffrey by Isabella went, in part, to encourage him to answer once again the restless song of the sea.]

"Beauties

Soft is the gentle breeze that comes a-sighing,
Serenity to heal the troubled night
It sings its own sweet melody, then dying,
Is lost again, as birds are lost in flight.

Gracious the fragrant beauty that is kept
Within the hush'd flower garden of the past,
Here many sad and lonely souls have crept
Found sanctuary amid its peace at last.

More blessed still the sanctuary you keep
Within the secret places of your soul
Who toil with gentle hands and eyes that weep
To bind the broken things and make them whole."

Isabella Kiernander

239

Voyage of the Finnish four Masted Barque

"OLIVEBANK"

From Glasgow to Port Victoria

1938 - 1939

_____

Day 1 Friday October 28th

We heave up the anchor at 7am and the tug comes alongside at 8am. We commence to tow away from Greenock at 10am prior to doing so the C.P.R. "Duchess of Athol" salutes us by going all round us. We see coast on each side and at 3.30pm pass close to the Isle of Arran.

A small fishing trawler comes alongside to enquire our destination. There was plenty of shouting by the 1st Mate. Tug leaves us at 5.30pm and I am sent up to overhaul buntlines on the lower to'gallant and mizzen royal. I have two hours at the wheel steering by the tug. I do it well. Len seems unhappy. I am fed up. We have a passenger off Scotland.

Day 2 Saturday October 29th

Len tells me he is sent down from the wheel and also that the 2nd Mate called him because he could not get up to the royal yard. Len says he is fed up and wishing he had not come. So do I. The 1st Mate this morning orders me to overhaul all the buntlines on the mizzen mast and then sends me down the coal hole. He dislikes me. I am also in the hold hauling on wires and making fast ballast.

We steer "By the Wind" all morning and all hands about ship at 1pm. The wind increases during the afternoon. The donkeyman dislikes sailing ship life. It still often can be fun. A few steamers about.

Our watch are called out again at 4pm until 6pm and we square the yards. All hands make fast the mizzen, main and fore sails. Head wind increasing only just after bracing.

We again set the three large sails. Why? Ask me another. The starboard watch make fast the three royals. Nobody can understand the Chief Mates action. He shouts a lot. He plays hell with me at the wheel and just because he changes the course and I cannot understand his Finnish. At 8pm all hands are called out and we get the anchor ready for anchoring off Belfast. It is raining hard. I have no oilskins. We make fast all sails the new main sail took one hour with all hands to make fast. We finished at 2.30am all the boys tired out cold and grumpy and as I was without oilskins I was wet through and frozen stiff.

For some unknown reason I and another boy were the only two to make fast the fore upper to'gallant a hell of a job and when it was finished, no nice hot cup of tea. I am fed up and what a damn fool I am to have come. Len also thinks he has been a fool. Donkeyman dislikes it the Steward, Cook and heaps of the boys say this is their last trip. A very hard ship.
Anchored off Belfast.

Day 3 Sunday October 30th

We have a free Sunday and I sleep a lot in my bunk. I play the ukelele and sing songs in the evening. Quite a friendly party. Len asks me to look out for a rowing boat if one happens to come. Len finds it not so rosy as in port.
Anchored all day off Belfast.

Day 4 Monday October 31st

I sleep all night having no policeman job during the night. Down the hold all morning making fast the ballast. We go for tobacco after dinner. The 2nd Mate dislikes me and Len (English) that is certain for when we go for tobacco, all the boys and I stand in the Captains cabin corridor but he orders me out. Why? God only knows, he orders no Finns out and I land up with four packets of tobacco and no papers.

What a stingy ship and we get the same food day after day, pie, soup, etc. Len still wishing he could get off the damned ship. At 7pm our watch come on deck and immediately the 1st Mate has us out to let go the port anchor, quite rightly so as there was a lot of wind and heavy sea and then he orders us up aloft to make fast the mainsail better. I then go into my bunk and half an hour later our watch are again called out to make fast the fore upper to'gallant but I am in my bunk and pretend to be asleep and can't be bothered with doing this every God damned time. I chat to my pal the 3rd Mate.
Still anchored.

Day 5 Tuesday November 1st

The starboard watch in the morning have a hell of a time in a hail storm making fast better all sails on fore and main masts. Len included. Our watch are down in the fore hold all afternoon shifting wood. The hold is a mass of foul smelling dead rats. This will cause disease unless cleaned. The "Bull" one of the strongest and nicest fellows on board comes into our fo'c'sle in the evening as jolly as ever and up to his old tricks. The wind blows hard all day and we still have two anchors. I have a sing song in the evening.
Still anchored all day.

Day 6 Wednesday November 2nd

Down in the hold all morning sweeping up and tightening wires, also we hauled in the port anchor and a few links in of the starboard also. Why? Well just ask me another. God only knows. In the afternoon rain comes and more wind so we let go the remaining links of the starboard anchor. There are tons of dead, smelly rats in the hold and we haul them up. I expect tonight we shall again let go the port anchor.

The Finns are a funny lot never use their brains, all rush and shriek about things. The Steward tells me the Captain has now been drunk for two days and eaten no

food and the passenger is nearly as bad. Stupid man the Captain often is, so it is his own God damned fault. Len has all his hair cut off so also all boys bar two, myself and another boy up forward. We drink cocoa every night.
Still anchored.

Day 7 Thursday November 3rd

The Irish mail steamer passes this morning bound in for Belfast. I wish I was on it. Bjorkman says he will leave the ship in Australia, probably I shall and Len too and a few others. From 7am to 8am we are down in the hold and do nothing. An Ellorman City boat passes close to us this morning and hoists a flag but we do not reply. I sleep a little on my bunk in the morning.

Our watch is down in the fore hold in the afternoon shifting wheat water. Filthy stinking stuff and we find one rat. I speak to the 2nd Mate about the wind, he says it is going more Southerly. A small fishing boat comes out in the evening and the Irish fellows kindly bring us some papers out, (English) which are eagerly snatched up by the aftergaurd and they tell us "Moshulu" left two weeks ago. They wish us luck and take the Stewards letter. We have a sing song in the evening and chat after tea.
Still anchored.

Day 8 Friday November 4th

At 1am the starboard watch let more anchor cable out and the 2nd Mate was loudly cursed by the Chief Mate for letting too much out, which Len thoroughly enjoyed. From 8am to 1pm we wash all the white paint on the port side, a hell of a job. A small schooner comes close steering South. I think she is the small well known "Brooklands". A small coastal steamer passes close aft. Called the "Straide". Johansen (starboard) I do not like, an evil looking fellow never smiles and always very uncouth.

The wind has now gone West. It looks as if we shall be anchored here at Christmas. I am fed up with the whole damn job. I here the Cook killed and threw overboard the large black and white cat. Poor thing it should have been allowed to go in Glasgow. Still the same God damned food, pea soup and pancakes for lunch. We at last get some matches from aft. We have had none in either fo'c'sle since Greenock.

A family of shrimpers are seen at coffee time close to the ship. Sontag and Kanerva come up into our fo'c'sle in the evening and we discuss the usual sailing ship topic, women, and we all have some cocoa. Quite a family gathering and it looked very picturesque with one oil lamp low and swinging. I am hungry at 11pm and find there is no food in either fo'c'sle. What a starvation ship.
Anchored.

245

Day 9 Saturday November 5th

The fore and aft lamps keep going out throughout the night due to rotten kerosene and this morning a steamer only just sees our poor lights in time. A Cunard liner passes us at 7am and an American liner at 9am From 7am to 8am we again soda wash the white paint but Kanerva does not seem to like the work and pretends he is sick.

I hear this morning that when we get to sea one tin of milk must last each man one month. I sleep on my bunk in the morning. In the afternoon till 3.30pm we carry on washing white paint and finish. I feel sorry for the 3rd Mate a decent lad but nobody works hard for him. A trawler M253 passes close and all the crew waves, also a Finnish steamer very close. We are free at 3.30pm. At night donkeyman visits our fo'c'sle and I and Borje Kullberg and Bjorkman play cards. *Anchored.*

Day 10 Sunday November 6th

I am free all night and sleep the sleep of death. Salt bacon for breakfast again. I wash a lot of clothes as they were very dirty. So also some of the other boys.

A small coastal boat passes close astern bound for England. Len and I wish we were on her. The Cook seems to like me and always allows me warm water. The passenger is a real snob and never speaks to either Len or myself. He and the 2nd Mate are very childish. Sonntag shows Len and I how to splice a wire in the afternoon. At 5pm a motor boat comes out from Donaghadee County Antrim with men and girls and they take letters for us, I had one for Jack (brother). They bring us papers and this time I grab two instead of them all going aft. A sweet little red headed Irish girl speaks to me, they come into our fo'c'sle and chat with us but have to leave again in an hour. I teach donkeyman and Bjorkman English at night with my dictionary.
Still anchored.

Day 11 Monday November 7th

We wake up to a Southerly wind and we hear we shall sail, whether or not, I do not know. From 7am to 8am we wash down the deck. After all we do not sail, wind changed again at 8.30am to West. I sleep on my bunk in the morning and we are down in the No.4 hold all afternoon clearing bilge water away and God, what a stink.

The motor boat again comes out but the Officers did not seem to want them aboard. Some more papers which I grabbed and cigarettes for Len. Captain and Mates watch carefully for any hands going ashore.
Anchored.

Day 12 Tuesday November 8th

At 8am we sail. The wind is North. We are not allowed any breakfast until 9.30am. Why I do not know. I overhaul gardings on the main royal and then all the buntlines and gaskets on all the yards in the morning and get very wet as the yards are wet. There is no shrieking from the Mates today, all is quiet. A large number of cargo boats pass us close by. We all clean up forward and after all is in order and after putting oil into the oil drums in the oil room we have salt beef for lunch. Len is again sent down from the wheel, but kindly, by Captain Granith.

The seagulls are still with us and some sit on the yards. I try to sleep on my bunk in the afternoon but this was impossible as the starboard watch braced no fewer than six times and there is a winch just outside our fo'c'sle door. What with this, capstan bars, shouting etc. sleep was impossible so we play cards instead but we are all called out at 6.30pm to help to turn ship, we are now sailing "Bi de Vind" with the English coast abeam. The starboard watch heave up the main and mizzen sails but don't make fast. At 8pm we take in the royals. Sonntag and I go up the fore mast and we complete the job first, a proud effort. I am very pleased and Sonntag says I am good. He is a real fine fellow and my best pal. We then take in the flying jib and outer jib. I have two hours at the wheel from 10pm to 12pm but the wheel is hard over and there is no work for the watch themselves, at 10.30pm we about ship. I make fast the main and mizzen sails. I am very tired.

Day 13 Wednesday November 9th

I overhaul gardings first thing before breakfast. The 1st Mate (whom I loathe) plays hell with me in a catty way over a rope that had got twisted. I never see anything of the passenger now-a-days but in any case he never speaks to Len or myself nor any of the crew, a real snob. I sleep on my bunk all morning. Down in No.4 hold again shifting wheat in the afternoon. At 8am the hills of the Isle of Man are in sight and we turn ship. At 10am we go course with a Southerly wind to pass the North of Ireland. I have more lazy wheel from 4pm to 5pm and lookout from 6pm to 7pm.

Two small Bullfinches are on deck all day. I overhaul gardings at 5pm up the fore mast. The wind increases at 6.30pm and we take in the three royals. At 7pm the starboard watch make them fast. At 6.30pm we pass between the Irish and Scottish coasts (narrowest point) and both light houses can be seen. The wind is stronger at 8pm and the starboard watch make fast the three upper to'gallants. Len and Blomquist go up the fore mast and Len tells me, that because he is not very good, Blomquist is angry. They seem to think anybody can be a seaman first thing. The flying jib and outer jib are also taken in and also the jigger gaff sail. We steer West ½ North and expect to be in the North Atlantic tomorrow morning. I am very tired and fed up with the job.

Off Northern Ireland

Day 14 Thursday November 10th

At 8am a lighthouse can be seen on the port side, presumably our last landfall and it is Northern Ireland. We set the three upper to'gallants and the flying and outer jibs at 10am and I go up the fore mast to loose the upper to'gallant sail. I have wheel from 10am to 11am very lazy and we steer West ½ South I keep the course one whole hour. Down in the hold the rest of the morning clearing bilge water.

The two little bullfinches are still here and look well but, poor souls they wont last long. A large number of seagulls are following us all morning. Henriksson in our watch is disliked by the rest and so is teased and, I hear, because he tells tails to the 2nd Mate. He looks fed up and I feel sorry for him.

It rains fairly hard in the morning. We actually have coffee at lunch. What a treat!

A trawler on the starboard side at 11am fairly close. I sleep on my bunk until 3.30pm and at 5.30pm we have a sing song in our fo'c'sle but the 2nd Mate did not seem to like it for he called his watch out to heave up the mainsail and mizzen sail. We go course sometimes and Bi de Vind others.
In the North Atlantic.

Day 15 Friday November 11th

At 4am the wind is getting strong and we are called out to make fast the three upper to'gallants and myself, Borje, Bjorkman and Lindroos make fast the fore upper to'gallant. It took us three quarters of an hour fighting hard to make it fast and Borje was nearly knocked down on deck when the sail suddenly blew backwards and hit him. He fell backwards but luckily fell against the backstays. Had he not done so he would have been dead now.

Our watch later take in and make fast the three lower to'gallants (wind increasing). Myself, Sonntag and Allonen make fast the main upper to'gallant. At 7pm the wind is gale force and the full watch is called out and all hands take in and make fast the mainsail, foresail and mizzen sail and then the main jib, mizzen and main and fore staysails and then all hands make fast the three upper topsails. I am out on the yard arm in each case working like hell on hard canvas especially the main upper topsail as the buntlines broke and the sail was kicking and flapping like hell nearly chucking all hands off the yard. It took us a time to make it fast. We have a heavy hail storm too. Eventually we sail with storm canvas set, that is, three lower topsails and fore staysail jib. Our watch are eventually free at 10am and have our long lost breakfast, having worked with sails for six hours continuously. Len is fed up and tells me Blomquist is a bugger after all. I am pleased that he has at last found him out, a very moody bugger.

248

The little birds seem to have left us, probably blown out to sea. Big sea and strong wind all day. In our afternoon watch we are all out on deck splicing and putting new buntline wires through the blocks. I help to splice one wire with the 1st Mate and he was very friendly and chatted to me but later on, moody devil that he is, he curses me loudly for a thing that he actually did, not me. Namely measuring a new buntline wire too short and the devil kept us working until 6pm although we had worked all morning and I was dead beat. She is definitely a hard ship and the Chief mate is both a nervy and hard driver. Len and I talk about running away in Australia.

Mid Atlantic

We took in sail

Day 16 Saturday November 12th

While I am at look-out from 3am to 4am the wind is terrific and the hail showers too. The wind in the rigging whistles and shrieks, it is very eerie and is just like on the films only here and in reality.

Lindroos and I carry coal to the galley in the morning watch from 8am to 1pm. The wind is less now but still strong and the sea rough but we set the foresail, main staysail and mizzen staysail. Then we go down in the bilges again, but nobody works.

We are all tired and hungry especially as the clocks have been set back ¾ of an hour so the hold we were down in resembled a pub smoking room. All the boys sat around smoking pipes and chatting, a lovely sight and I laughed. It was worth a laugh. Then we all came up into the fo'c'sle and sat down smoking and chatting until the 3rd Mate comes and heaves us all out. What a mangy ship. Owing to the shortage of Kerosene we have not been allowed any in our fo'c'sle for two days and so we are in the dark. So we pinched some. Then there's the food again, foul, rotten stock fish for lunch today, which nobody eats, and for tea last night simply cake with raisins in it. A real starvation ship and floating coffin.

The starboard watch "about ship" twice between 4pm and 6pm they set the main upper topsail, there is very little wind now and the ship rolls like hell.

A lovely sunset the sun sinking in a fiery ball . The Moon came up making a golden pathway from the bowsprit. At 7.30pm our watch set the mizzen and fore upper topsails and mizzen sail, the main jib and fore staysail. I overhaul gardings with Bjorkman on the mainsail. Bjorkman is a long time letting loose and the Chief Mate asks him if he wants to sit on the yard and have his bunk up there. At 12pm all hands turn the ship. All our watch are tired out. We appear to get all the work.

Day 17 Sunday November 13th
At 4am all hands again "about ship". At 6pm our watch turn ship alone, a hard job as the winches are no good. The Captain comes out at 7am and orders the mainsail and the mizzen sail to be hauled up. We now have no wind. I am ordered up to tie up gaskets and overhaul buntlines on the mizzen upper topsail which I left undone last night, the Chief Mate plays hell. At 8am the Chief Mate musters all hands and plays hell with our watch for not having overhauled buntlines and gaskets last night. He orders Bjorkman up aloft before his breakfast but Bjorky comes first in for breaky and the Chief Mate, like a mad bull, comes and orders him out from breakfast to overhaul gardings. He shrieks at Bjokman like a madman, which I think he is. Kanerva is ordered up to the Captain for swearing at the 3rd Mate, the 1st Mate having reported him, the baby that he is. He certainly is the biggest baby I have ever seen. There is going to be some trouble on this ship I can see, all the boys are now keyed up.

The sail maker cuts my hair this morning. The little black cat often comes into our fo'c'sle now.

Although Sunday (day of rest) I work between 1pm and 7pm all the time bar twenty five minutes for coffee. At 1pm we set the three lower and upper to'gallants and I overhaul the gardings on the mizzen mast. I am up there an hour fighting damn hard to overhaul buntlines which would yield no slack. The Chief Mate yells and plays hell with me and I come down the mast to slack off the buntline ropes which he said were let go but were not. These buntlines on this mast are devils. In the finish I come down and play hell about the buntlines and say bugger them. TheChief Mate hears this and plays hell and orders me up again to overhaul one on the lower topsail and one on the big mizzen sail. As I go up the mast again I say alright twice, to which the Chief Mate shouts something but I do not hear him and tell him to go to hell and I will see him in Australia. I will kill this devil if he goes on much longer, working us like slaves. I have wheel from 3pm to 4pm and look-out from 5pm to 6pm.

250

No sooner had we again retired to the fo'c'sle when two whistles again comes, this time to set the outer jib and flying jib. Then later another two whistles to set the jigger and mizzen staysails etc. and later again the jigger gaff then later still the main royal.

So we had set all sails (our watch) bar two royals. Mock if you like. At 8am the starboard watch set the mizzen and fore royals. I am fed up and Len also.

A slave driving ship.

So we set all sails

Day 18 Monday November 14th

Between 8am and 10am our watch make fast the two anchors onto the fo'c'sle head and then we put all halyards, mooring ropes and wires down in the fore hold but greasing wires first.

We have the same old pea soup for lunch and uncooked fish for breakfast, not enough, and so I was famished at 1pm and could work no longer. I wash some clothes in the afternoon. A lovely day. She is a very damp ship and all my things are mouldy and my trunk is always wet and damp.

The wind has strengthened considerably by 7pm and is still getting stronger. At 8pm we take in and make fast the gaff topsail and from then until 12pm we take in and make fast the flying jib, outer jib and spanker, jigger staysail, three royals and three upper to'gallants. I and Sonntag make fast the fore royal and fore upper to'gallant. A devil of a job as the wind up there was terrific and I was nearly blown down. At 12pm, although our watch was free we (all hands) take in and make fast the mizzen and main sails and then break the lower to'gallant buntlines for the starboard watch and they "back" just the sails.

Our watch get all the work. The 2nd Mate seems useless and a big baby. The 1st Mate is a crazy madman all night.

Day 19 Tuesday November 15th

I get just two hours sleep last night, that is all. By Jove! The romance of the sailing ship. This is definitely a slave ship and the Chief mate a "bucko" Mate and a slave driver. I have look-out from 6am to 7am and the starboard light goes out. I tell Kanerva, who is policeman, but prat of a boy that he is, he says "ok that doesn't matter". I try to sleep on my bunk in the morning free watch but am too tired for sleep. From 1pm to 3.30pm I sit by myself in the hold and shift two pieces of wood and am very happy. After coffee we set the three lower to'gallants and I overhaul those in the fore.

What a ship, we have only three brushes on board they are like pieces of gold to find. A lovely afternoon sunny and warmer, no wind. I hear most of the boys are playing merry hell with the way I, correctly, tie gaskets and they don't. We have a sing song at night and it sounded very nice as it was a lovely night.

Day 20 Wednesday November 16th

Between 1am and 4am our watch set the spanker and the fore and main upper to'gallants and I am ordered aloft to let loose the mizzen upper to'gallant. I go up let loose the port side when the 1st Mate orders me to make fast again. What organisation! In fact none at all and this was at 3.30am. At 4.15am poor Len is ordered out of his bunk to let it loose. What a way of carrying on. From 9am to 11am I am down in the aft hold cleaning away bilge water and this we finish at 11am. I then have wheel till 12 midday. The rest of the watch set again the jigger gaff, flying jib and outer jib. Old Kullberg is ordered up to let loose the gaff and bring the sheet over. He has never been up before and consequently does not know how to do it. The Chief Mate shouts at him and makes him look a fool and made matters worse. All the rest of the crew were down on the deck laughing. Poor Kullberg, I felt sorry for him.

To show how stupid the Officers really are, at 12 midday I ask the Chief Mate if I should wait making eight bells until after the sun has been taken. He just simply puts the clock back ten minutes. Then up comes the Captain Granith and he begins to take the sun. Later up comes the Chief and he begins to take the sun again and it finishes up with not ten minutes wrong as the chief expected but twenty minutes.

While carrying food to our fo'c'sle Borje slips and the food flies all over him and the deck too. At 1pm the wind has increased considerably and the starboard watch take in and make fast those sails we only set at 12 midday. Namely the jigger gaff, flying jib and outer jib. We now have course South by West ¾ West. I read in my bunk in the afternoon. The wind increases all afternoon and the starboard watch take in the jigger and mizzen staysails. Frankly by 7pm there was very little wind and at 10pm our watch again set the jigger staysail, flying jib and outer jib.

A nice starlit night and warmer. I have very bad stomach ache due to the rotten food. I get along fine with all my watch mates and they seem to like me.

Day 21 Thursday November 17th

At 6am I have the wheel and we steer Bi de Vind going South by East. The watch heave up the mizzen and mainsails but at 8am the starboard watch set them again as we are course. In the afternoon watch we are down in the hold shifting wood and at 4pm the wind is no more and we heave up the mizzen and main and foresails to the yards. At 7pm we are completely becalmed. After tea we have a sing song again.

Day 22 Friday November 18th

At 12 midnight we are still becalmed but at 2am when I go to the wheel a little wind comes. By 3am it has gone to gale force and at five to three our watch take in and make fast the three upper to'gallants, the flying jib, outer and inner jibs. The fore staysail only remains. The main and mizzen staysails we make fast too and we take in the spanker and set the storm spanker. At 4am all hands make fast the mainsail, mizzen sail and fore sail and at 5am after three hours at a very hard wheel I am relieved and our watch too. So again we miss an hour of our free watch. I eventually get to sleep at 7am but have to rise again at 7.30am.

The starboard watch make fast the three lower to'gallants. There is a terrific gale and high sea. We now only have set the three upper and lower topsails and the storm spanker, jigger staysail and fore staysail. She rolls like hell sending boys, pots, etc. flying.

At 9am I am sent up to make fast the port side of the fore royal and upper to'gallant, they had come loose due to few gaskets, although this fact I have mentioned twice to the Mates. There is no organisation here. I have a devil of a time being up there for an hour. I loose my second hat and the sail is completely mad and hits me on my nose making it bleed and nearly knocking me on deck.

A steamer is seen aft at 10am. A lot of white swift flying birds are seen following us all day. We are down in the hold all morning stacking up the ballast again which had shifted. At 12am the wind is slightly less and we set the fore, main and mizzen course sails also the main and mizzen staysails as we now go course South by West ¾ West. All hands about ship at 8am and at 1pm the starboard watch square up the wind being from aft. It is very hard to stand up and walk on a very wet and slanting deck.

It turns out a lovely day but cold. I am feeling very tired, hungry and cold. All afternoon until 12 midnight we have two men at the wheel. At 10pm we brace the yards right onto the back stays as we are sailing Bi de Vind and so we set the spanker and outer jib.

Day 23 Saturday November 19th

At 5.30pm an oil tanker passes close by us bound for the English Channel. How I wish I was on her. I am suffering from rheumatism in my legs, hips, back and shoulders. No wonder! My bunk is damp and unsuitable. From 7am to 8am I overhaul gardings in the mizzen mast.

A Lamport and Holt ship passes fairly close aft at 10am bound East. I sleep a little during the free watch from 8am to 1pm. At 1pm our watch brush up the whole of the deck. We are free at 3.30pm but I have my turn at the wheel from 4pm to 5pm and then I am policeman followed by look-out. At ten to seven a rather strong but short squall springs up and for some entirely unknown reason "all hands" take in and make fast the mizzen and mainsails. Bjorkman and I make fast the outer jib. It was the very devil to do as it was not properly taken in. Our watch again work in our free watch but this time only half an hour. Captain Granith chats to me while I am at the wheel. There are heavy squalls all night up till midnight.

Day 24 Sunday November 20th

At 12 midnight all hands take in and make fast the fore upper topsail. Why just the one? Ask me another. At 2.30am our watch take in and make fast the mizzen and main upper topsails. There are heavy squalls and evidently the Captain is nervy. We have a very nice Sunday morning again. Although there is still a strong wind, at 9am we again set the mainsail and mizzen sail. Bjorkman and I overhaul buntlines on the mizzen mast and I cut one of my fingers very deeply. I shall refuse to overhaul any more buntlines today.

A steamer bound West passes us aft at 3am. I have two hours at the wheel as my watch again set the mizzen and main upper topsails. Again I say, what a slave ship. Poor Kullberg is sent up to the top of the jigger mast to make fast the wireless aerial which had come loose due to the strong wind. He is a fine fellow and yet the Mates dislike him giving him all the rotten work. To send him aloft on a day like this with the ship rolling badly was just rotten hell.

Rotten food again for lunch. I am fed up, tired hungry, dispirited and nervy due to the heavy work and no sleep. The 2nd Mate borrows my hair clippers, they are friends when they require something, but only then. The starboard watch at 1.45pm set the fore upper topsail. At 5pm the wind turns very warm and so for the first time I sleep on my bunk without any blankets on.

Day 25 Monday November 21st

At 7.30am we set the three lower to'gallants and I, out of luck as ever, get the mizzen mast to go up and overhaul gardings, the worst sail. It was an impossibility with my cut finger and Allonen comes up to help me but the winch gets fast in a rope and we both have to let loose but the Chief Mate shrieks at both of us. At 8am (free watch) I have overhauled the port side but the starboard side I refuse to do and come down and inform the 1st Mate about my finger. He plays hell but I refuse to go up again and so it stood. Be firm, they don't like it. Our watch also set the outer jib at 8.30am and the starboard watch set the jigger staysail and three upper to'gallants. At 1.30 pm we set the flying jib and jigger gaff and then we go into the hold and commence, for the first time, the never ending Knniken Rosst (knocking rust). We do very little. We sit down talking and smoking nearly all afternoon. Kanerva, as usual, is full of fun and takes half an hour to sharpen his scraper and Allonen lies full length on a stanchion smoking a pipe. At 5.30pm when we should have finished work that slave driver, the Chief Mate, has us setting the three royals and he sends me up the mizzen mast to overhaul buntlines! This I finish at 6pm having again cut a finger on a bad and torn wire. I shall have no hands left at this rate. I sleep in the sail locker, impossible in my bunk, what with winches, hammering and the 2nd Mate pacing the roof above. We pass a steamer at 10.30pm.

Day 26 Tuesday November 22nd

For the very first night our watch never has one "two whistles". We are down in the hold all morning watch 8am to 1pm chipping rust. I don't do much work nor anybody else. It is a lovely day and very hot. The sailmaker is out on deck for the first time sewing sails. We square up the yards at 10am. All the boys clean out the fo'c'sle and air all clothes, which are so damp they are covered in mildew. We have a sing song after coffee time. There is no wind all day and we are just waiting for the North East Trade Wind.

Sail maker on deck mending sail

Day 27 Wednesday November 23rd

This morning we start work at 6am and it was barely light. When going out for two whistles I jump down from my bunk and by chance land on the poor spot on my bad leg and the cartilage goes again and this time badly. I am in such pain I cannot go out to brace . At muster, that sly dog Henriksson comes past me to see if I am there and then giggles, damn cur that he is.

I take water to the Captains tank on the poop before breakfast then overhaul buntlines in the main rigging. I manage to go up only slowly with my poor leg. Then we are down in the hold chipping and then commence to paint. I sleep on my bunk all morning free watch.

We are down in the hold again chipping in the afternoon. In the evening we have a sing song and I visit carpenter and sailmakers cabin and chat with them and Len about Finnland etc. Our watch get wet through while bracing in the afternoon.
Position 36.19°N 17.0°W.

Bracing

Day 28 Thursday November 24th
Down in the hold again all the morning working watch scraping rust. The boys tease the 3rd Mate poor lad, he is a decent sort but some how disliked.

We have a good wind from aft and are doing about 12 knots. The course is South South West ½ West. Whether this is the North East Trade Wind I don't know. Kullberg gets around the Cook and so gets another tin of milk.
I wash some clothes in the afternoon free watch. Borje, Lindroos and Bjorkman play cards. I help Len at the wheel from 3pm to 4pm and show and explain how to steer. A lovely starlit, moonlight, tropical night.
Position 35.6°N 18.5°W.

Day 29 Friday November 25th

Len and all his watch get wet through at 1am while setting the jib boom staysails, that is the flying jib, outer and inner jibs and fore staysail. At 6am I overhaul gardings on the fore and main masts and up to the main royal which I enjoy on such a morning. Then our watch are in the sail locker (which I call the Black Hole of Calcutta) owing to its smallness and darkness. We try to find staysails but make no headway, it is pitch black. We steal some more Kerosene this morning for our fo'c'sle and I take some snaps in our free watch this a.m. We commence to change into the tropical staysails.

A lovely morning. Len tells me he kept the course all morning and says it is due to my help yesterday. I hope so. We still have a fine wind and make about 10 knots. Down in the hold chipping rust all afternoon. I help the Sailmaker sewing sails in the morning free watch until my needle breaks, then I sleep one hour. We change three tropical staysails in the afternoon. The Chief Mate is a day man now. Borje cuts his hand badly tonight and as he has dishwasher this week he asks me to do it for him but I refuse, he must get another deckhand. A lot of the boys have sick stomachs (Len included) owing to the food. I again sleep in the sail locker.

Position 28.18°N 20.58°W

Changing sail

Day 30 Saturday November 26th

Our watch change the three big sails, the foresail, mainsail and mizzen sail in the morning watch. The starboard lot did nothing and we worked like slaves in tropical heat and with a rotten breakfast in our stomachs all morning. The 1st Mate kept us at it all the five hours. So we were all done by 1pm only, to our amazement, came the three whistles to help the starboard watch, as usual, this time to shift the three big sails into the sail locker.

A steamer bound North passes us at 10am. We have a sing song before coffee in the afternoon.

A lovely day. One of the tropical staysails, only put up today, blows out at the back. They are so thin you can see the sun through them.
Position 23.42°N 21.18°W

Day 31 Sunday November 27th

At long last we really have a nice Sunday. No taking in and setting sails and so, I wash some clothes first thing in the morning. Then I take snaps of the port and starboard watches and later my poor little 3rd Mate.

Len is laid up in his bunk with back sprain due to lifting those very heavy sails yesterday.

It is a lovely day, sunny and warm and most of the boys and I sit out on deck and read and air clothes. One bird the size of a seagull is seen. I hear we are near St. Pauls Island. Blomquist is a peculiar creature very moody, I ask him the position and he just passes me by without a word as if I were dirt.

We have a lot of visitors in our fo'c'sle in the afternoon and we chat about Finnland, Germany etc. they were Kanerva, Sonntag, Allonen, donkeyman and the sailmaker. The poor little 3rd Mate seems very sad and is becoming a nervous wreck. I feel very sorry for him, a decent lad.

Our watch, self 1st on right

The rest of the day men are chosen and start tomorrow, namely Sonntag, Henriksson, Berntsson (in the port watch) and Blomquist and Finneman (from the starboard watch). We now have six men.
Position 18.55°N 21.7°W

Day 32 Monday November 28th

I slept again in the sail locker owing to the heat, music and talk of the day men. The wheel is very hard and heavy this morning. Down the hold chipping rust all morning. I take some more snaps this afternoon and until coffee time I sit out and read in glorious sunshine. Sonntag and Blomquist are busy all day putting fresh stays to each mast, so evidently "Olivebank" is not going to be scrapped.

The little cat is sick in our fo'c'sle this p.m. but we are not angry, we understand. Borje nearly falls into the hold this a.m. when he stepped onto a plank which was not fast.

There are five men today busy sewing sails on deck. Len turns out again at 4am and the Mate then sends him up to overhaul buntlines. When he got down again and was in the hold the 2nd Mate broke them and called him up again.

Len and I discuss sailing ship life after tea and the moody characters of the Finns.
Position 14.3°N 21.18°W

New stays

_____

Day 33 Tuesday November 29th

At 6am we have a very heavy downfall of tropical rain and we collect fresh water, all the boys getting wet through but we require the water urgently because we only had a little left. Then down in the aft hold clearing bilge water again, there is a lot more again.

A dragonfly is flying around in our fo'c'sle this morning and some small swallow like birds flying aft of the stern, probably stormy petrels.

My bunk is wet through. My blankets and my pillows. The fo'c'sle is a wet damp, miserable place not fit for even pigs. Captain Granith helps this morning with the steering. Another downfall of rain at 10am. We brace a little at 7am. Down in the hold chipping rust again in the afternoon. At 4pm we square up the yards and at 5pm we get another heavy rainfall and I again get wet through. I have a real row with Kullberg this afternoon in the hold. In front of the 3rd Mate he started shouting at me to work harder, a thing he never does except when the Mate is around and he wishes him to think he is a good worker. I tell him to go to hell and he says shut up. Another minute and I should have knocked him into the hold.

A butterfly on deck this afternoon and I see a flying fish while at the wheel. These Finns are sly and untrustworthy. Give me a bunch of Britishers. Captain Granith talks to me at the wheel this afternoon about Isabella and I hear for the first time she has T.B. she told Captain Granith. I again sleep in the sail locker.
Position 10.8°N 22.1°W

[Editor's note: Isabella refers to Isabella Kiernander, a poet and a friend of Geoffrey and his brother Jack. In the front of her book of poems entitled 'Songs of the Tall Ships', she mentions Captain Granith and Geoffrey in her dedication.

The news that Isabella had tuberculosis must have distressed Geoffrey greatly as he had lost his beloved mother 'Honey' to the same disease on 17th April 1937. This news may also account for the 'sadness in his soul' that he refers to in day 52 of this log.]

Day 34 Wednesday November 30th
While at look-out from 12pm to 1am a very heavy rain and hail squall hits us and our watch stand by in case of making fast the royals. I get absolutely wet through. We again collect rain water and our tanks are nearly full. Another rain squall at 4am. Down in the hold scraping rust all morning 8am to 1pm. To show the character of these Finns, although Bjorkman and Kullberg loathe the 3rd Mate they ask him if I am junior man and he says, no. They just wanted him to say, yes, so that I could dish wash. We again have a sing song in the free watch. At 11pm it begins to rain in torrents, the biggest downpour I have ever known and we again collect rain water and fill the tanks. Borje and Bjorkman again start this sly work of shrieking when the Mate is near.
Position 7.12°N 22.21°W

Day 35 Thursday December 1st
At 12 midnight "all hands" brace and then we are free. The wind and rain becomes more furious and we are in the middle of a tropical squall. The Captain comes out on deck and orders the starboard watch to take in all three royals, flying jib and jigger gaff. I felt for them making fast up there in hail and rain. The rain lasted two and a half hours and I could not get to sleep until 2am only to rise again at 3.45am. This is the romance of the sailing ships. I often dream of little Honey (mother) only to wake up and know that she is no longer with us in person but I know she is with us in soul. At 6am we again set the three royals

and flying jib and I overhaul gardings in the fore royal. Three royals were taken in last night for approximately a ten minute squall. Just as I reach the deck again after completing my task up in the royal the 3rd Mate orders me up to overhaul all gardings in the fore mast and yet Bjorkman (a deckhand) is given a painting job. I cannot understand the character of the Finns on this ship they are most

unloyal. I have always worked hard and spoken well of the 3rd Mate and Bjorkman has slated at him behind his back (black and blue). Yet to his face, Bjorkman fusses him up. The 3rd Mate knows all this and yet he gives me the rotten jobs. They beat me completely. My heart is broken of trying to be just and so I work no longer at it. There is no organisation and harmony on this ship compared with the "Ponape".

During the rain squall last night three pin holes appear in my bunk roof and it is just a miniature fountain so I have to putty all my bunk ceiling. I sleep a little in the morning free watch.

Fo'c'sle head from fore mast

Down in the hold chipping rust in the afternoon. Bjorkman is again given a painting job in the hold and the 3rd mate plays up with me over the chipping of one plate although I was not the only one who had chipped there. I am thoroughly fed up and dispirited with it all. Borje again asserts himself at coffee telling me that he and Bjorkman only take a little milk. Yes, but they have two cups. We are becalmed at night. I again go to sleep in the sail locker but am hauled out by the 2nd Mate. Little swallow like bird flying about.
Position 4.27°N 23.14°W

Day 36 Friday December 2nd

At 3am our watch set the mainsail and mizzen sail as there is a little more wind and the 3rd Mate chooses just the time it rains, so again I get wet. Five hours down in the "heavenly hell hole" this morning chipping rust. It rains hard all morning and some of the boys collect rain water for the donkey tank the other two tanks forward are full. We are sailing Bi de Vind and roughly in a direction of South South West.

I have three more holes in my bunk roof and the rain drips down onto my face waking me up at 7am. Poor Len is getting it thick from the 2nd Mate, all the dirty jobs but I go out on deck and just stare the devil out. He hates this.

I take my ukelele to look-out a lovely night until 10.15pm when a very heavy squall hits us and the Captain again becomes nervous and orders the three royals to be taken in. This we do only just as we were about to make fast, we are ordered to set them again. What a joke but really beyond a joke. Lindroos who was at the wheel said he actually heard the captain pray. The squall lasted five minutes.
Position 2.57°N 24.20°W

Day 37 Saturday December 3rd

We have a fairly strong wind all morning and steering Bi de Vind going about South West. Bjorkman again starts his shouting and rushing about. Really he is beyond me, he hates the 3rd Mate for his shouting and yet he is about the greatest shouter in our watch. I loathe the evil sour bugger. I overhaul gardings in the main royal before breakfast. I sleep on my bunk in the free watch in the morning. Starboard watch spread wet sails all over the deck in the morning to

dry and in the afternoon we spend two hours tying them up and putting them in the sail locker.

Drying the sails

Heavy and warm work and I have another row with Bjorkman. We are not on speaking terms. I am tired so fall asleep in the free watch. I am feeling depressed. The black cat is just human with the 3rd Mate, he can make it do anything.
Position 0.40°N 26.11°W

Day 38 Sunday December 4th

I was free all night and slept soundly for eight hours. In the morning I shake hands with Bjorkman and we are again friendly. I wash some clothes in the morning and mostly all the boys do.

A large black bird flying over the ship this a.m. What has happened we get Tomato soup for lunch.

We cross the line at 6am and this afternoon we have the "ceremony". Len, Borje, Bjorkman, Englund and Lindroos are the unfortunate ones. They get a lot of paint over their No. 1 and 2's and I hear Henriksson is in for it for clipping too much hair off them.

I sit on deck in glorious sunshine all day and read. A lovely sunset. I asked Captain Granith if I could buy some drink. He said he had none but would have given me some otherwise.

The little black cat again plays with the 3rd Mate. I write a letter to Arthur.
Position 2.57°S 29.4°W

Crossing the line

Len being taken for baptism

Where paint is essential

Day 39 Monday December 5th

I slept on my bunk in the morning . Although Bjorkman and I were pals yesterday, today he is again funny and will not speak. God only knows why. I have neither said nor done anything since yesterday to upset him. Chipping rust all afternoon on top of holds.
Position 5.12°S 30.36°W

Day 40 Tuesday December 6th

Russia lost Finland December 1918 and so Finland celebrates this yearly with a days holiday and so do we . A lovely day and I sit out on deck all morning and sleep until coffee in the afternoon. We have boxing, wrestling and games on deck after coffee and I box Sontag but he is to big for me but he thinks I am quick. In the evening after tea Sontag and Berndtsson chat about girls etc. in our fo'c'sle and Sontag makes Len and I laugh by saying that he slept at a terrible place in Glasgow one night for a shilling. It must have been a tramps place. A lovely moonlit night. The 2nd Mate (who dislikes the English) and the passenger have a row which can be heard up on the poop.
Position 8.24°S 30.54°W

Day 41 Wednesday December 7th

Last night was a true tropical night, not a cloud in the starlit, moonlit sky with the Southern Cross very clear in the Southern sky. The first time I see it this voyage too. Len tells me the 2nd Mate crept quietly up to look-out while he was there to see if he was awake. He has only done this with Len and I can plainly see that he loathes the English. I sleep on my bunk during free watch 8am to 1pm but none to well on account of the noise on deck, at least three different hammerings going on. While at the wheel from 1pm to 2pm I pick out a sailing ship on the port horizon evidently steering Bi de Vind and we have course South by West. I tell the mate and it is confirmed she is a square rigger with no royals, either "Pommern" or "Lawhill". *[Editor's note: I too am undecided, so this is one photo of "Pommern" and one of "Lawhill"]*

(left) "Pommern" and (right) "Lawhill"

The Captain thinks it is the "Lawhill". We then also go Bi de Vind and slowly overhaul her all afternoon. Down in the hold chipping rust in the afternoon. Borje given painting job but not me, oh no, never any decent job for me but Borje is angry because the 3rd Mate asks him if he can paint. Sonntag comes up to our fo'c'sle in the evening and again teases (in fun) Len and I and boxes

with us again and chats about women. Captain Granith is up until midnight, all excited I suppose over the "Lawhill". Later the Captain and the passenger have an argument.
Position 11.14°S 31.13°W

Day 42 Thursday December 8th
"Lawhill" still in sight at 10am but sailing faster than we are, out of sight by 11am. Down in the hold chipping rust again in the morning watch 8am to 1pm but I don't work hard, I just sit there although the 3rd Mate is there too, I have finished working my best for him, he is not worth it. "Lawhill" deserves to beat us. We have no, as I have said before, no organization at all on this ship, just slap happy.

Within an hour we sail Bi de Vind, square up for course and then Bi de Vind again. I am dog tired by 1pm and famished also and I sleep till coffee in the afternoon. The Cook has given us stale sour bread all week and again for tea tonight. Only I play hell and go to the Steward and get fresh which I eat and yet the Cook says that what he had given us was fresh. What a lie. Borje laid up all day and last night with stomach trouble, no wonder, only selfish as the Finns always are, instead of going back to our real tricks at the wheel etc. It alters for the good of them all and the worse for me.

Donkeyman as usual, after tea, plays his only two tunes on the organ. I am sick of the whole routine and shall be pleased to be off.

A lovely night again.
Position 14.11°S 31.19°W

Day 43 Friday December 9th
I sleep on my bunk during the morning free watch. We brace up twice during the afternoon working watch otherwise we were chipping rust in the hold. It rains a little in the afternoon and at 7.15pm the starboard watch brace, taking the sails to the other side as the wind is now South West only to brace again at 8pm as we once more get our South East Trade Wind back. The 2nd Mate shouts at nearly all the boys in his watch over one thing and another. Very little sleep.
Position 17.26°S 31.18°W

Day 44 Saturday December 10th
We change the very worn tropical foresail for our strong one again this morning and afterwards we cut away the braces as we shall not use the sail again. We put it down in the fore locker to be eventually used for any covering. I then carry coal to the galley.

A lovely day and the South East Trade Wind holds good. A few flying fish seen while at the wheel and I see also my first Cape pigeon this voyage. Cookie and the Steward are mad as somebody has stolen some jam out of the galley. Len, Blomquist and I sit on a hatch and chat after coffee, such a nice fellow at times, in fact one of the best as he is sensible.

I catch a bird about as big as a pigeon while at look-out. It was a land bird as it had no webbed feet. Its body was black coloured and it had a greyish white head with a fair sized beak slightly turned down at the end. I let it go again and it again flies around the ship.
Position 20.15°S 31.5°W

Day 45 Sunday December 11th
I wash some clothes in the morning. Rather a dull day at first but later cloudless and very warm. I sit on deck in the afternoon and both read and chat. The 2nd and 3rd Mates see the "Lawhill" from aloft with glasses, this time aft. So, old "Olivebank" can still beat 'em.

Many boys making models also the 1st and 3rd Mates. I see that bird I caught last night still flying around. One day-man of each watch comes back to the watch again tonight. We water the deck at sunset, and about time too. Donkeyman again keeps us awake at night with his now usual three tunes on the accordion.
Position 22.47°S 29.18°W

Day 46 Monday December 12th
Down in the hold chipping rust all morning. Bjorkman again given a seaman's job helping Blomquist with stays. Passenger starts a model. Little cat sits on the wheel boss from 12am to 1am while I am at the wheel. We are sailing all morning Bi de Vind and going roughly South to West but in the afternoon we get worse going West to South! I sit out on deck in the afternoon and watch Sonntag doing the stays.
Position 24.42°S 28.26°W

Day 47 Tuesday December 13th
At 1am the starboard watch take in the main royal. Len and Laakso make it fast. This is the first royal Len has made fast and this was due to the redoing of the main stays. Rain squalls at intervals. Down in the hold chipping rust from 6am to 8am. In number four hold aft. Clearing bilge water once again until coffee time, then we turn the ship about twice in the space of one hour. The starboard watch in the morning again set the main royal. Decidedly colder. A lovely golden sunset.
Position 26.31°S 28.50°W

266

Day 48 Wednesday December 14th

Down in the hold chipping rust again in the morning and I am actually given a painting job. What a wonder. I sleep on my bunk until coffee in the afternoon free watch. After coffee I am called aft by the Captain. He tells me I am now an A.B. with £2-15 shillings per month. He asks Len and myself for our passports and since we were ready for jumping ship we both wished to keep them. I had to hand mine over but Len says he has not got one. The Skipper is mad and says Len must cable for one at once on arrival in Australia and that he will not be allowed ashore until he has done so. Len is fed up. I am too. Len says he thinks he will have to make the trip home in this hell ship and he blames me, of course. Sonntag visits our fo'c'sle after tea and stays two hours. Len looks worried and says he is finished with sailing ships, the voyages are too long. All the crew seem fed up due, no doubt, to the fact that we are becalmed all day and it is very hot.
Position 27.59°S 28.41°W

Day 49 Thursday December 15th

Still becalmed at 7am but at 7.30am a little wind comes up from aft and we square up. I see my first albatross at 7.30am this morning a large one.

Down in the hold chipping rust until 8am. The hold I call plainly "Heavenly Hell". I sleep on my bunk in the morning free watch. From 1pm to 6pm our watch bend the storm main and mizzen sails. I strain myself lifting the big sail. While at the wheel from 4pm to 5pm at 4.30pm I ring one bell (correctly). Up comes the 3rd Mate shouting and wanting to know what is up. I tell him Captain Granith has told me to ring one bell, which he did. The 3rd Mate went away thinking me crazy and laughing to himself. He goes straight up to the 1st Mate, like a baby, and tells him in a sneering laughing way and also in front of the rest of my watch too. I ask Sonntag if they rang one bell on the "Moshulu" and he replied, always. So did we on the "Ponape". The 3rd Mate has been in sail since 1928 and does not know even this. Sonntag tells me to do my own ways and blow them. He also says not to always overhaul gardings. He is the most loyal and trustworthy friend I have, moreover, he is a real man.
Position 28.58°S 28.9°W

Day 50 Friday December 16th

I was free all night but did not sleep more than four hours. I have a pain in my stomach and rheumatism in both sides of my neck. It starts to rain heavily at 4am and continues until 1pm and both watches collect rain water. I have another row with the 3rd Mate on deck in front of Kullberg and Bjorkman and I tell him some home truths. He tells me to shut up. I tell him he is so weak because the watch laugh at him and to get out of it he makes me the laughing stock. To show what the Finns are made of, instead of supporting me Kullberg and Bjorkman laugh at me too. So this is Finnish friendship.

Chipping rust in the hold again. Sailing bi de Vind about South South West, wind increasing. I have truly finished with Len, he hardly speaks to me, always fussing the other lads up when he really does not like them. Weak and no friend for me. He can go his own way, I have finished with him. We catch a rat in the capstan near our fo'c'sle. Two albatross today.
Position 30.58°S 27.24°W

Day 51 Saturday December 17th
The 3rd Mate sends me up all three masts today to overhaul gardings. Sonntag advises me to leave this ship in Australia and join another. Before breakfast we change the spanker sail and the gardings are all rotten and give way, the 3rd Mate doing all things wrong and blaming others for it but the 1st Mate just laughs.

Sent aloft to overhaul gardings

A fair number of albatross about. A fine morning and still a strong wind. We wash the deck down in the afternoon watch until coffee. My back nearly broke with hauling up buckets continuously for one and a half hours. I am feeling very downcast and thoroughly miserable. I just loathe this ship (all) and at times I do truly feel my head will just split and I shall go nearly mad, fast.
Position 35.36°S 27.42°W

Day 52 Sunday December 18th
I slept very well last night being free all night. The Chief Mate talks to me very friendly and kindly at the wheel this a.m. about Isabella and ships. I am again feeling dreadfully miserable and if we don't reach Australia soon I shall go off my head. I wash a few clothes. The boys in my fo'c'sle are very unfriendly with me. Something has happened I cannot think what, they are dreadful and it is just hell living in this place and Len rarely speaks to me. I just dread the coming of each day. They are nightmares to me. It is funny but people never try to enquire, if a man is quiet, if there is some sadness in his soul. They cannot leave him alone. We see a large number of whales in the p.m. Captain Granith gives matches away after coffee. Towards dark the whales come nearer, some are very large. Captain Granith says he has never seen so many.
Position 39.3°S 26.32°W

Day 53 Monday December 19th

Our watch turn the ship at 5am and we still sail Bi de Vind about North North East but the 3rd Mate says to me we shall today get West wind. We put new wire buntlines to the mizzen course sail, about time, the others were all prickles and rusty. I help with the splicing and the 3rd Mate also has a go but is hopeless and all the watch just laugh. Len is impossible. Whatever I say to him, such as, "How are your boils?", he construes around in a skittish way and then looks to see if the rest laugh. No good friend to me.

Two large albatross about and again a few whales. Down in the hold again in the afternoon. We have six albatross about this afternoon and one very large one has white wings with one black spot on each.

The Chief Mate, at 6pm, asks Lindroos, Kullberg and Bjorkman different ropes. None of them gave them very well and he was a little angry and told them they must learn in the free watch.

The wind dies away towards midnight and again our watch heave up the mizzen and mainsails as they were slatting against the stays.
Position 39.57°S 26.3°W

Day 54 Tuesday December 20th

Kanerva catches a large albatross at breakfast. We have it on deck for a time and then we let it go. We gradually go more North and so at 11am our watch again turn ship and the passenger helps, I am at the wheel. I watch the albatrosses while at the wheel. They fly wonderfully keeping near to the masts on the windward side, (they never flap their wings) then round the bowsprit and so on the lee side (further out) and round aft.

Down in the hold chipping rust again in the a.m. starboard watch change torn outer jib.
Position 39.0°S 24.24°W

Day 55 Wednesday December 21st

When I come to the wheel at 4am we are going course East by North and at 4,30 we square up a little. I clear two gaskets in the mizzen rigging. Then down in the hold chipping rust. At 7.30am our watch again brace this time back to Bi de Vind, it is raining and we get wet through. At 8.15am it is pouring down and the wind is much stronger. The starboard watch take in the mizzen staysail, poor devils wet through. It pours down and the sea is rough and misty. At 9am the starboard watch make fast the three royals and the main gaff. We now definitely have our West wind and commence to "run our Eastern Down". In the hold chipping rust in the afternoon.

We have two men at the wheel for one hour in the afternoon and a look-out all afternoon in case of icebergs. Very heavy sea all day and the wheel is heavy to steer.

A lot of birds about including albatross, Cape pigeons and large black birds. At 6pm our watch square up. At 7.15pm the starboard watch set the main royal. Len goes up to overhaul gardings. The starboard watch square up a little more and they then took in all staysails plus the four on the bowsprit. It is a lovely starlit night and quite unlike 45 degrees South.
Position 40.41°S 20.45°W

Day 56 Thursday December 22nd
Between 12am and 4am our watch set the fore royal and mizzen royal and jigger gaff. Borje is sent up to overhaul fore royal by the 3rd Mate and he just takes his time, three quarters of an hour to let loose the sail, just to annoy the 3rd Mate. Which he did. Bjorkman laid up today, that means three men have laid up in our watch so far. I paint the wires on the stays this morning and later help Sonntag and Berndtsson, so today for a change I was a seaman. We have cocoa for lunch. Good old Cookie. I hear the passenger and the 1st Mate had a fight last night on the poop. Poor fellow, I pity his life back aft. A lovely day and so I air some clothes on deck. Wind from aft again.
Position 41°S 14.30°W

Day 57 Friday December 23rd
A lot of birds about again today including Cape pigeons, albatross and stormy petrels. I slept on my bunk in the morning. In the hold chipping rust in the afternoon. It was great down there today, nobody did any work and four of the boys, instead of knocking rust, knocked to the time of tunes and sang as well. The 3rd Mate was down with us, said nothing and looked foolish. Our watch brace twice.
Position 40°S 9°W

Day 58 Saturday December 24th
I carry coal to the galley and then chip rust in the hold. After dinner we are all free and the captain calls me aft to give me a Christmas present from Isabella, a cap and socks. Later all the boys get a present for Christmas from Captain Gustaf Erikson.

A lovely day but cold.

Four albatross about and plenty of Cape pigeons. We have a sing song in the afternoon. We brace in the morning watch. The wind is now from the port side.

We have a great tea, good meat, herrings, sardines, coffee and H.P. Sauce. The boys asked me to ask the passenger for some drink. I tried until 8pm when look-out, then Len tried and got some. He never gave me a drop and did not even wish me a Merry Christmas, in fact I might not have been there. He got drunk and acted like a mad man.
Position 41.5°S 5.13°W

Day 59 Sunday December 25th Christmas Day

Christmas Day and just plain meatballs for breakfast. Christmas Day but I wash some clothes in the morning. What else can one do in such a hole. The Chief Mate talks to me about Isabella and England while at the wheel.

A lovely day and fine speed. In the afternoon our watch are called out twice, once for bracing and the other to set again the spanker, gaff, four bowsprit sails, main and mizzen staysails.

Sonntag looks very angry and refuses to work hard. At 11pm the flying jib rents a hole and the port watch make it fast also the spanker and gaff sails and at 11.30pm the Captain decides to take in the three royals. God only knows why, there was no stronger wind. The port watch work very slowly and take half an hour to break the buntlines so that at midnight our watch have to make them fast. I go up the fore mast with Allonen and we make fast a sail each and wire a second down.
Position 41°S 1°W

Day 60 Monday December 26th

We have rotten meals all day, just plain working day meals and the boys play hell. In our morning watch on deck on four occasions we have two whistles (although a holiday) three times for bracing and the other for setting the main royal and I go up to overhaul the gardings.

Fog in the early morning and very cold but a lovely day later. Sunshine and warm all day.

Len still very off hand and rarely speaks to me. The boys play cards in the afternoon. Sonntag makes the 3rd Mate go round the capstan this a.m. He is a devil and does not care a damn for anybody.

With the dusk comes rain and squalls and we make fast the spanker and gaff and take in the jigger staysail and royal. Wheel is hard.
Position 41.40°S 7.27°E

Day 61 Tuesday December 27th

Between 4am and 5.30am we brace, squaring the yards a little. It is hellish cold and we have hail squalls. A very heavy sea running and again the wheel is very hard. We brace again at 6am. Down in the hold in the afternoon and we have a lot of bracing.

At coffee time I say, we have been 60 days since Greenock, which is true. Len, in front of the other boys , to be awkward shrieks and argues about it. He is hopeless and the most unloyal friend I could hope to have. He was only my friend prior to joining "Olivebank" when he knew I alone could get him a ship. Len and Len alone has caused this unhappiness here.

A big sea runs all day. All morning there are two men at the wheel in the starboard watch but I proudly bring it back to one man.
Position 42.37°S 13.35°E

Day 62 Wednesday December 28th

Down in the hold chipping all a.m. We have two heavy hail squalls. A large number of Cape pigeons. In the morning watch our lot set the fore and mizzen royals then later the main royal. This time I was not sent aloft. The 3rd Mate, fool that he is, informs the boys in the hold that I was in the "Olivebank" and ran away. (First voyage 1932.)

I actually am allowed to paint again in the hold. It is very cold and yet it is summer time down here.

We all look out for the "Phantom Ship" supposed to be off the Cape of Good Hope, that is to say the "Flying Dutchman" but of course it is only in fun as it is a legend.

We brace twice in the morning watch. The 1st Mate, actually very kindly, gives me some English books - perhaps he wants a drink from me in Australia. We still have no staysails, jib boom sails and spanker sails set as wind is from aft.

We take the cat into the hold to look for rats. I sleep on my bunk in the afternoon free watch. The ship is rolling badly. We pass the Cape of Good Hope at 5pm and enter the Indian ocean 8pm.
Position 42°S 19.51°E

Day 63 Thursday December 29th

Kanerva catches another albatross just after breakfast but lets it go again. I sleep on my bunk during the morning free watch. In the afternoon watch we again set all the staysails, jib boom sails, spanker and gaff and squared up and also brace,

272

due to sailing Bi de Vind. At 7.30pm that night the starboard watch squared up dead aft and so once again they take in the staysails. Then just before 7pm our watch set the three course sails and I overhaul gardings in the mizzen mast.

Course sails set

I paint again in the hold. This ships crew I cannot truly fathom they are not nice and friendly and are untrustworthy as friends.
Position 42.35°S 24.37°E

Day 64 Friday December 30th
We have curry and rice for breakfast, very little too, not enough to fill the belly of a small child and so we are all tired and hungry in the working watch from 8am to 1pm and cannot work good. We have no fewer than seven 2 whistles, twice we turned ship, the other times we braced for just the tiniest puff of wind, when really there was no wind all morning. First we heave up all three course sails, yet just prior to dinner we set them again plus staysails and jib boom sails but not the spanker and gaff. We were all just sick of the bracing and very tired. There was no need for it and we had no sooner reached the hold again when 2 more whistles. At 1pm we got more wind but sailing Bi de Vind. It rains all morning. I am just heartily sick of the ship, work and crew. A rotten lot all.

A few albatross and stormy petrels about.

It rains all afternoon and very hard too. The starboard watch were on deck all afternoon from 4pm to 7pm bracing, carrying water and making fast sails, they get wet through, they also turn the ship. They make fast the three royals, jigger, main, mizzen and fore staysails, spanker and gaff and flying jib. They just finish making fast the royals at 7pm, so saving our watch the job. It was blowing hard but the wind lessens as the night draws on. We sail Bi de Vind all night and we fill the tanks with water forward. Len actually does not go up aloft to make fast a royal, he must be a pal of the 2nd Mate.
Position. (Not given)

Day 65 Saturday December 31st

I wake up with a rotten cold and sore throat so I lay up in my bunk until 1pm and although still poorly I turn out to save my watch the extra tricks at the wheel etc. Before 8am my watch set the mainsail and mizzen sail. Between 8am and 1pm the starboard watch set again the three royals and all staysails bar the jigger which we set at 3pm and before this and until 3pm our watch wash and brush the deck down. We also tighten up on all three royal halyards. The Chief Mate very kindly asks me if I am feeling better. He is not so bad.

I have wheel from 3pm to 4pm And we some times go course East ¼ South but chiefly Bi de Vind. After coffee I write some dance tunes down for Bjorkman. A lovely day but cold.

A large number of albatross about. Wind strong all day until 3pm when it gradually lessens and at 6pm there is very little.

Kanerva cuts my hair in the afternoon very well too.

Very little wind up to midnight. At midnight (New Years Eve) the look-out, according to Finnish custom strikes 24 bells. The 2nd Mate plays hell with him. All the crew are very angry about it.
Position 41.50°S 31.24°E

Day 66 Sunday January 1st 1939 New Years Day

Between 12am and 4am our watch twice get 2 whistles, one for setting the foresail and two for setting the mainsail and mizzen sails, also bracing a little. We also set the spanker and braced to port, I "took over" the jigger topsail (gaff). The starboard watch between 4am and 8am also brace twice lastly bracing the yards nearly to the backstays. We go course East ¼ South with a fair wind and fine day but cold.

I wash some clothes and have my first real wash for three weeks. I chat with Cookie and the Steward. Cookie tells me the 2nd Mate played hell with them for being late in getting up this morning and he went into the galley to play up. Cookie told him he had no job to interfere in the galley and next time he would hit him.

I sleep on my bunk till coffee time. Some of the boys play cards.
Position 41.18°S 36.35°E

Day 67 Thursday January 2nd

At 6am we set the spanker. At 7am we brace port way. There is no wind. The crew is all fed up with this bracing etc. and all say they prefer 50 degrees

274

South and taking in sail to this hellish, everlasting bracing. At 7.30am we set all staysails. Down in the hold chipping rust till 8am.

A lovely day, much warmer, no wind. Seven albatross sit on the water aft. I have hellish cold all day sneezing and nose running and stomach cold, the first I have ever had at sea. There is hardly any wind all day and we brace up the three course sails to the yards. We take in the spanker and gaff and jib staysails bar the fore staysail.

A lot of birds about including albatross, Cape pigeon, mollyhawkes and stormy petrels. A lovely sunset.
Position 42.18°S 36.38°E

Day 68 Friday January 3rd

A have a row with Len today. He and others in the fo'c'sle were acting daft, like a load of babies, and throwing mugs of water about. One landed in my bunk spoiling and wetting Honeys photo and other things. This ship is full of kids.

Down in the hold chipping rust in the morning.

A lovely day, warm and not a cloud in sight and this is 40 degrees South but we are becalmed. Bjorkman, Borje and I catch a very large albatross this afternoon. I take snaps. There was a rare gang chipping rust on deck this afternoon at fever rate, The Captain and the passenger, the 1st Mate, 2nd Mate and Len. The Captain actually swept up the deck later. Len tells me the 2nd Mate is always giving him good jobs and the 1st Mate spoke to him for one hour. The Mates are very good to all of us and to Len and I, all of a sudden, there must be a reason. I sit out on deck till coffee reading and the little cat sits with me, he ate a whole large rat this a.m.

A most beautiful sunset and as the sun sinks down on the horizon the moon came up with her silvery pathway in the East the sky being all shades of the rainbow. After tea we feed the albatrosses which are lying on the water all around the ship. I count nineteen and one small stormy petrel, one Cape pigeon and one mollyhawk. We again catch another albatross at 7pm but let it go again.

The boys play about on deck till dusk. While at the wheel from 11pm to 12pm I suddenly hear Big Ben strike half past ten then the familiar voice giving the news bulletin. It was old England on the Captains wireless and this ten thousand miles away.
Position 42.18°S 37.40°E

Self and Len

Day 69 Wednesday January 4th
Still becalmed up to 11am but at 10am the starboard watch brace a little more aft, the first bracing for two days. After breakfast and during our free watch we tease albatross by dangling pork on a rope over the side. They are all quite tame, quaint creatures and one we had on deck actually ate bread out of our hands.

Down in the hold chipping rust before breakfast. I sleep on my bunk in the morning. In the afternoon down in the hold chipping again and shifting ballast from one hold to another a very dangerous job as one slip could be fatal. Then later we shift mooring ropes onto the deck. We also brace once a little to port. At 7.30pm the starboard watch set the foresail as we have a little wind, but very little. Overcast at night . I have a poisoned hand due to a rusty wire.
Position 42.31°S 39°E
276

Day 70 Thursday January 5th

Wind commences to spring up at 7am but during our watch from 12am to 4am we again heave up the foresail which the starboard watch set at 8pm. Then at 3.30am we "about ship" while I am at the wheel from 10am to 11am as there is now a fair amount of wind. Sailing North East and Bi de Vind. We set the spanker, gaff, staysails, bowsprit sails and three course sails. It is much colder.

Albatross still about also stormy petrels and one large black albatross this morning. Down in the hold chipping, painting and greasing wires. I am again pals with the 3rd Mate. Blomquist gives me Attwells book "Horizon" to read and so I read until coffee, then I sleep until 6.30 pm. We sail Bi de Vind all day going about North North East.
Position 42.8°S 39.18°E

Day 71 Friday January 6th

Our watch at 5am about ship. We always seem to get these bracing jobs while the other watch gets nothing. It is a holiday in Finnland so we get one too, always on the 13th day after Christmas. At 6am the Mate blows two whistles just simply to have us all out to see if we were not asleep and then he sends me up to the main yard to overhaul gardings. Bjorkman and I are always a little nervy in the mornings and we discuss this. I say we understand one another now.

It is foggy all day and we have a look-out until 5pm. We have a little wind all day from port and at 3pm we go course East ¼ North. While I am at the wheel from 6pm to 7pm the 3rd and 1st Mates play and sing sea shanties and the Chief Mate tells me that before 6am we shall have strong wind from aft and the royals made fast. The starboard watch square up at 10pm. I read the book "Horizon" in my bunk all afternoon. Cookie comes and plays cards in our fo'c'sle after tea.
Position 42.28°S 40.28°E

Day 72 Saturday January 7th

It is the first round of the English football cup, how I wish I was in England and to be at one match. In our watch from 12am to 4am we set the spanker and gaff and the starboard watch brace more aft at 7.30am and pull in all staysails. We wake up to a fine day and fair wind course being North East ½ East and while I am at the wheel 11am to 12am we sail 8 knots. In the morning watch I clean the navigation house out and carry coal with Borje to the galley.

One albatross now but three mollyhawkes. Passenger, I hear, will not sit at the same table as Cookie. Why on earth be such a snob on a windjammer. We bend a new jigger staysail and our watch brace at 8pm. I show card tricks.
Position 42.28°S 43.20°E

Day 73 Sunday January 8th

At 5.30am our watch brace from aft to a little starboard as we now have fine wind from port. We set the spanker, gaff, all staysails and jib staysails. At 9am the starboard watch brace a fraction further to starboard. A lot of the boys are making models now. I cut myself in several places while shaving. I read in my bunk in the afternoon free watch till coffee then afterwards we have a sing song. At 6.30pm our watch take in the jigger gaff and the flying jib. Lindroos and I make fast the flying jib. At 7pm all hands take in the three royals but the starboard watch make them fast.

The wind slowly increased all afternoon until by 7pm it was blowing hard and a heavy sea running too. Judging by the wind clouds about we shall still have storm winds before the night is out. Some of the boys play cards after tea. Borje and I play hell about the 2nd Mate who persists in walking up and down above our fo'c'sle and it was impossible to sleep. At 10pm the starboard watch take in and make fast the three upper to'gallants.
Position 43.2°S 46.20°E

Day 74 Monday January 9th

Between 12am and 4am the wind increases to gale force and at 2am our watch take in and make fast the three lower to'gallants. Bjorkman and I make fast the mizzen one and it was a difficult job up there with the strong wind. Also our watch take in the jigger staysail and outer jib. Sonntag and I make fast the outer jib. By 4am the wind was gale force and the ship was lying well over to starboard and we do 11 knots. At 4.30 am the starboard watch take in and make fast the mainsail and the mizzen sail and also the spanker, so that leaves us with only the three upper and lower topsails, jigger, main and fore staysails, foresail and main jib. When our watch rise at 8am it is still blowing hard and raining making things miserable. We are all down in the hold from 8am to 1pm hauling up bilge water. We square up at 10am and at 11am it stops raining and the wind has gone down a lot. At 12.15 our watch set the three lower to'gallants and the main and mizzen sails. It is a lovely sunny afternoon and since I got very wet this morning I put my clothes on deck to dry.

A few albatross about.

When taking in sail last night two buntlines on the main lower to'gallant broke due to rotten wires, this also happened to the main upper to'gallant clew line. I am feeling very tired so sleep on my bunk after coffee but it is a job to keep warm nowadays. Allonen is very moody with me now. I cannot weigh these Finns up,. If they have a grievance against you they never say. At 7.30pm we set the main royal. I overhaul gardings in the rigging.
Position 43.4°S 51.35°E

Day 75 Tuesday January 10th

We have our usual two whistles before coffee and this time to set the mizzen and fore royals. While at the wheel from 6am to 7am we change course five times and I am unable to keep course. The Chief Mate shrieks at me but, let him try. I sleep on my bunk during the free watch in the morning. Down in the hold in the afternoon putting up boards and filling ballast baskets and sweeping etc. Sonntag teases the 3rd Mate about his splicing and says it is no good. Len gets some shrieking from the 2nd Mate while at the wheel and just because Captain Granith was there. In a friendly fight with Sonntag I put my leg out again. At 6pm our watch brace more to port and so set the spanker, gaff and jigger.
Position 43.18°S 58.4°E

Day 76 Wednesday January 11th

I slept very badly last night, only about two hours, due to my leg and the continual walking up and down of the 2nd Mate overhead but I soon shut him up by knocking on the roof. In the hold first thing cleaning etc. We brace three times between 8am and 1pm lastly to nearly Bi de Vind but we still have course, East. We also set the spanker, jigger, mizzen, main and fore staysails. The fore royal clew got twisted and we had a job to straighten it. At 12am we commence that hellish job of washing white paint with soda, ready for Australia. I am feeling very tired and my leg is painful.

I had a good laugh in the hold this morning, for the 3rd Mate was just a big kid, using a whole box of matches to look for a rat in the bilges which he never caught. A quaint lad the 3rd Mate but I like him. We are having very poor food now and the boys are beginning to complain. The 1st Mate talks to me while I am at the wheel from 7pm to 8pm. It has become much warmer.
Position 43.24°S 63.5°E

Day 77 Thursday January 12th

The Captain goes up to look-out at midnight and finds nobody there. The Chief Mate plays hell with Kullberg but Kullberg explains that Johansen says it was alright, so the 2nd Mate goes up to Johansen, plays hell with him and makes him stand four hours at look-out. We square up at 6.30am and from 6am to 8am we carry on washing paint on deck.

I sleep on my bunk in the morning free watch. In the afternoon working watch 1pm to 7pm our watch brace over to starboard and then set all staysails, spanker and jib staysail. We go course, East by South. We carry on washing the white paint with soda and during this the whole of my watch start nagging me that I could not work and for the very first time I lose my temper with them all. They were like a swarm of Bees buzzing round me and so the rottenness of the Finns, I loathe them all. In future England and the English for me, these fellows are

cowards if one starts nagging they all do so until my head nearly splits. Then on coming into the fo'c'sle for coffee Len starts but I tell him straight he is in future no friend of mine. He blames me for waking him up the other night, just to be in with the boys. What a pal, after all that I have done for him. The Finns are friends with you when all is o.k. but only then and yet they say the Danes were untrustworthy. I said never, not so.
Position 43.10°S 67.53°E

Day 78 Friday January 13th
In the morning watch we again wash paint and finish it. A very strong wind blows all morning and increases as the day goes on so that the Captain orders two men at the wheel it looks very heavy today. We square up a little. It is a wonder the royals have not come in yet. Because the Captain is on the poop this morning the Chief shouts at me for nothing. What devils. A little sea comes on board midships.

One albatross today.

Again some bread in my bunk but I just square it, kids they all are not men. It rains hard all afternoon and the wind increases. Starboard watch take in the three royals, gaff, flying jib and fore staysail. We all want to know why, at 7pm, our watch take in the inner jib and square a little. One man at the wheel at 8pm. At 11pm we slaves again take in the outer jib and main staysail.
Position 43.50°S 74.34°E

Day 79 Saturday January 14th
At 7am our watch set all three royals. I again clean out the navigation house and am thus able to take down all positions so far.

There is very little wind now and it is from aft. Course East by South.

Sonntag splices new gardings for the fore and main royals which broke yesterday. Our watch wash down the deck in the afternoon. I have two tricks at the wheel taking Kullbergs trick so that he can finish washing the fo'c'sle. I also give him a hand with this after my wheels but I doubt it is ever received with gratitude. Typical example of the Finns. When I give course in Swedish at the end of my wheel, the Captain was there with the 1st Mate and the Chief says curtly that I cannot say it in Swedish, I must say it in English!

We have a good sing song at night all the boys join in but Len, who never joins in but always breaks it up by butting in with a stupid tune.
Position 43°S 78.34°E

280

Day 80 Sunday January 15th

Between 12am and 4am our watch brace three times, lastly over to port and so we set all staysails.

It is turning much colder. I wash some clothes again today.

Len is very funny again speaking very little to me. I have found him out now. If I am in with the boys he is so jealous he goes all quiet and wont speak except in a curt way. The passenger and the Chief Mate are friends again now laughing and shouting together.
Position 43.0°S 82.59°E

Day 81 Monday January 16th

The 1st and 3rd Mates are drunk this morning friends with the passenger I suppose when they want drink. We have our usual two whistles before coffee.

The 3rd Mate, being drunk, starts throwing his knife about in the hold. I can see a dangerous man when drunk. The boys rag him and one (name unknown) throws a lump of cement at him. It hits him and the 3rd goes looking for the man but does not find him.

We brush up dirt in the bilges. I sleep on my bunk during the morning free watch. In the afternoon we are down in the hold laying burlap round the boards etc. While down there we watch the rats, they are very tame and come up close to us boys. I see my first black one today. A few large albatross some mollyhawkes and one smaller albatross. I start to make a model.
Position 42.42°S 87.11°E

Day 82 Tuesday January 17th

At 12 midnight the starboard watch brace to starboard and so set all jib sails staysails and spanker. During our watch 12am to 4am the policeman forgot to rouse the man for the wheel and so the 1st Mate blew two whistles for all watch on deck. In watch 8am to 1pm we are down in the hold again cementing bilges a rotten job. A few albatross about.

Course East by North. Just because I am feeling happy today and just for fun, said to Len, I was not jumping ship, he says he is and becomes most unfriendly and all the boys notice his attitude. He is forever talking about gentlemen and not being one. Considering all I have done for him he is just a big rotter. After tea we have a great gathering of boys in our fo'c'sle and we chat about the English Navy, Suez canal and politics.
Position 42.42°S 92.58°E

Day 83 Wednesday January 18th

We soda wash the poop before breakfast and I have a row with Borje and Bjorkman. Borje ordered me to haul up water. I refused saying I had done it once and he plays hell with me but I plainly tell him I am a slave no more for people, he soon shut up. At 6am we square up and we thus take in the four jib sails and spanker. I try to sleep on my bunk during the morning free watch but it was impossible owing to the din overhead of the starboard watch soda washing. In the afternoon we finish soda washing the deck only doing to midships. We have a sing song at night. At 12pm Finneman thought it was his watch from 12am to 4am and turned up at the wheel.
Position 42.43°S 97.23°E

Day 84 Thursday January 19th

A sailing ship is observed aft on the port side at 8am. The officers back aft think it is the "Lawhill", "Killoran" or "Winterhude". She is slowly picking up on us and at 12 midday the Captain decides to wait for her by sailing Bi de Vind and thus she comes along quickly and at 2pm she is fairly near. It is picked out to be dear old "Winterhude" and looking very pretty too. I hear she has four English apprentices on board. Our crew are very angry that we wait. Down in the hold finishing cementing the bilges there and after we replace boards. I buy three packets of cigarettes from Allonen for two shillings. At 3.30pm "Winterhude" is aft and eventually and by careful manoeuvring and us going course again she comes along side by 5pm and I take plenty of snaps.

"Winterhude" from "Olivebank"

At first we speak by flags and then as we come along side by megaphone. I shout out ,"Are there any English?", and immediately two hands wave from "Winterhude". Donkeyman plays his accordion for them and "Winterhude" boys dance on the fo'c'sle head.

"Winterhude" boys dance on the fo'c'sle

We shout and speak to them but are soon told to shut up by the Chief Mate. This is worse than prison. They tell us they spoke to the same steamer as we did and passed the Cape the same day too. Their staysails are very patchy and all in holes and our Chief Mate asks why they don't patch them. We begin to draw ahead of them at 6pm and by 9pm she is dead aft her green starboard light showing plainly. The starboard watch brace at 6pm.

In a fun fight with Sonntag he knocks me on the nose and my nose bleeds for half an hour. He doesn't really know how strong he is but instead of always hitting me, the smallest man, he should try someone his own size and he just takes my fags whenever he wishes.
Position 42.56°S 100.21°E

Day 85 Friday January 20th
"Winterhude" has now been left aft about two miles. We square up at 6pm and then go down the after hold wrapping burlap around the stanchions. The 3rd Mate tells me he does not like Borje and calls him a farmer. I see four land birds this morning. We are almost becalmed and the albatrosses are sitting on the water again.

Down in the aft hold shifting bilge water again and I tease Allonen about being a German. Down comes the 3rd Mate and plays hell with us both for talking too much but more so with Allonen and the 3rd Mate was white and shaking in anger, so also Allonen. Both were a funny sight with chests stuck out and fists clenched, a kind of Laurel and Hardy film.

We again wait for "Winterhude" but her Captain has more sense and keeps his course. We are absolutely becalmed at 6pm but "Winterhude" about two miles away has wind from aft. It comes in foggy at night.
Position 42.46°S 101.25°E

Day 86 Saturday January 21st

Although no wind, at 2am we have two whistles and set the four jib sails. I make some coffee. At 3am another two whistles to set the foresail, mainsail and mizzen sail just because "Winterhude" has gone ahead of us. Captain Granith decides to visit "Winterhude" this morning and so our watch get the motor boat out and the Captain, Blomquist, 2nd Mate and passenger go over. The two English boys shout over as "Winterhude" comes near to see if I want any books. At 2pm the motor boat returns plus Captain Morn of the "Winterhude", a woman and a man passenger and their two kiddies. Then at 5pm they return plus our 2nd and 3rd Mates but the motor boat breaks down and they have to row. Our passenger lends a hand with the rowing.

Plenty of bracing on a Saturday afternoon on both ships, in fact plenty of work and just to please Captain Granith, donkeyman plays music on his accordion, as "Winterhude" is a stones throw away. Captain Morn recognises me and comes up to speak to me. Both ships sailing Bi de Vind.

I carry coal to the galley in the morning. The 1st and 3rd Mates and the passenger arrive back at 7pm having rowed back and they are all drunk. The Chief Mate and 3rd Mate act disgustingly to the passenger hauling him about telling him to shut up etc. etc. all in front of the crew and in my opinion done on purpose. Then the crew hauled him up in a rope just like an animal. If the Chief had acted any further then I would have stood by the passenger. I will not see an Englishman treated so. Then he keeps our watch working three quarters of an hour and then we square up. "Winterhude" now ahead.
Position 42.50°S 102.15°E.

Day 87 Sunday January 22nd

When we turn in free watch at 12am "Winterhude" is ahead but at 4am she is aft and yet there is little wind. "Olivebank" is good with little wind. At 5am our watch take in the four jib sails, main and mizzen staysails, as the wind is from aft. I wash some clothes before breakfast. At 7am wind comes again and we do about 4 knots. I sleep on my bunk all morning free watch and read in the afternoon watch until at 3pm we brace more to port and thus set the four jib sails, mizzen and main staysails again.

"Winterhude" leaves us she steers East by South and we North East ¾ East, wise "Winterhude" and I should like to bet she arrives first. While I am at the wheel from 6pm to 7pm just because they have nothing to do the Captain, Chief Mate and 3rd Mate tease the cat (like big babies) by flapping their fingers at its tail. Poor cat it gets a time of it.

Our watch brace still more to port at 6.45pm. More bread in my bunk but I say nothing, babies are not worth the trouble, but very annoying really as I had only cleaned my bunk at 5pm. We get more wind as night settles in and rain too.
Position 42.45°S 105.9°E.

Day 88 Monday January 23rd
We wake up to an Easterly wind and so sail Bi de Vind going about North East. A hell of a job in the hold this morning both cementing bilges and also cleaning stale bad wheat and slush away from other bilges. A stink which could never be worse and just when we have no water. I darn some socks and mend a coat. Passenger and Captain play cards, whot rot after the way the passenger was treated. It blows up a little at night but still we sail Bi de Vind.
Position 42.15°S 108.7°E

Day 89 Tuesday January 24th
I hear Cookie has fallen out with our fo'c'sle crowd. I don't blame him they are a lot, really they are, never friends for more than a day, but what I cannot understand is this, they talk about each other behind their backs but are all friendly to their faces.

We brace twice between 4am and 5.30am also at 4.30am squaring up and taking in the spanker then at 5am just going back to the original and setting the spanker, and the tack is against the backstays. Very little wind but we go course North East ¼ East. The Mates cannot think what work to give us and this morning we just cut rope away from old sails.

A large number of albatross about today also a Cape pigeon, a mollyhawke and a stormy petrel. I sleep on my bunk in the morning and then do a long splice on a wire. I had never done a long splice before and because I was a little bit slow the 1st Mate (for all the boys to hear as usual) shouts that I am slow and would never make a sailor. Where upon I tell him "No never on a Finnish ship because I always get the dirty jobs". A little more wind in the afternoon.
Position 41.57°S 109.34°E.

Day 90 Wednesday January 25th

We commence to oil the deck but only to half way. The Chief Mate again plays up with me and I notice that the boys in the forward fo'c'sle kind of sneer at me. I am disliked I know and somebody has made trouble but the Finns are a rotten lot they hide things behind their backs and never speak their feelings. The Mates are unable to find us any jobs and so the crazy fools actually decide to start painting the fo'c'sles a job which will cause us boys a lot of misery. This job is a trade wind job and it is very cold still here. The boys are angry about it . A lovely day, no wind so we heave up the mainsail, mizzen and foresail.
Position 41.26°S 112.10°E

Day 91 Thursday January 26th

We commence in earnest scraping the rust and paint in the fo'c'sles and what a mess up. Nobody knows where to put stuff. All the boys have decided to sleep in the hold. No wind and twice we heave up and set three big sails. While sleeping in the hold a rat walked over my face and woke me up.
Position 41.56°S 112.26°E

Day 92 Friday January 27th

Carried on painting our fo'c'sle and finished giving it the first coat. We have some fun in the hold in our free watch. The wind is all over the place from East to West. The passenger has not been seen since Sunday. Australia so near yet so far.
Position 41.58°S 113.8°E

Day 93 Saturday January 28th

I am in the coal hole before breakfast filling buckets with coal and Bjorkman is on deck hauling them up. I might just be a bit of dirt down there. He first chucks the rope down any old way and the buckets too, so I protest and come up. He tells me to shut up and get down again but I play hell with him and he shuts up.

We square up after coffee (5.30am) and we now get some good wind. I sleep in the warm hold during the free watch in the morning. In the afternoon till coffee we just brush up the deck and of course brace here and there. At 5pm while bracing the mizzen the starboard brace wire snaps and down comes the block onto the poop with great force luckily nobody was near as they may easily have been killed. Good wind all a.m. increasing at night. We collect much needed rain water at odd times in the day during rain squalls. We are without a drop of washing water. Three albatross and one stormy petrel seen today. Course North East ½ East.
Position 42°S 114.36°E

Day 94 Sunday January 29th

The wind increased all night and in the morning at dawn a very angry red sky. At 8am we have two men at the wheel as the wind is gale force. At 9am our watch take in the gaff, spanker and jigger staysail and at 12.20pm the three royals. I make fast with Bjorkman the mizzen royal and once again the buntlines break (to old, like the ship) and also a clew line in the main royal. Later the mainsail sheet breaks. Captain Granith is very nervy all day. Big sea.

One or two albatrosses about, mollyhawkes and stormy petrels. The stormy petrel I saw yesterday and said to Len meant gales was true after all. Two rats woke me up in the hold, one on my face and one on my leg. At 8pm our watch take in the spanker, gaff, jigger staysail and four bowsprit sails plus the main staysail and mizzen staysail. I make fast the jigger staysail and the four bowsprit sails and while making fast the outer jib the ship suddenly rolls and I am very nearly sent overboard. Just in time I cling to the sail and my feet are hanging overboard. A very lucky escape. Two men at the wheel all night. Very strong gale and sea.
Position 41.38°S 119.31°E

Very strong gale and sea

Day 95 Monday January 30th

When I go to the wheel at 5am the Chief Mate orders one man at the wheel. Before breakfast our watch paint our fo'c'sle with white enamel. In the afternoon watch I am the only one sent down into the hold to shift bilge water, the rest of the watch just paint. So this is Finnish fairness. We brace four times between 1pm and 7pm and at 3pm we set the main royal. At 6.30pm we set all staysails as the wind is from the port side. Now very tired.

One albatross. At 7pm starboard watch set fore and mizzen royals.
Position 39.35°S 125.31°E

Day 96 Tuesday January 31st

Between 8am and 1pm our watch heave up both anchors. This meant four solid hours turning round the capstan and I had no wheel. I then painted the anchor links and so at 1pm I was very tired. Our fo'c'sle is finished at 5pm. I talk politcs with Kanerva, donkeyman, Cookie and Allonen.

Good wind all day and doing about 12 knots.
Position 38.19°S 130.46°E

Day 97 Wednesday February 1st

We commence getting both anchors hanging overboard between 6am and 8am and carry on and finish the job in the afternoon watch. Then we are down in the number two hold shifting chains, wires and wooden planks from ballast. The starboard watch cleared number three hold.

We shift back to our fo'c'sle all our bunk clothes and we are all very pleased. I sleep for an hour on deck in the free watch in the morning in hot sunshine. We are sailing Bi de Vind all morning but at 3pm we go course again North by East ½ East. We sight Neptune Island at 6pm and the light from a light house is seen at 7pm.

Many seagulls come to the ship at 7pm and sit. Blomquist cuts my hair again and that of many other boys.

One albatross with us all day. We square up a little at 7pm and at 8pm Kangaroo Island light is picked out in the distance and at 8.30pm the mainland light. Thistle Island and light is passed on the port side at midnight.
Position 36.5°S 135.6°E

Day 98 Thursday February 2nd
We square up at 1am and at 5.30am all hands are called out to make fast sails.
We are in sight of Port Victoria and we pick out four sailing ships. These are later
confirmed as "Pamir", "Passat", "Pommain" and "Viking" and later "Lawhill"
comes. We anchor at 7am.

AUSTRALIA AT LAST.

*[Editor's note - Geoffrey jumped ship in Australia for the second time on the
"Olivebank" and came home on a steamer not long before the outbreak of
World War Two where he served his country in the Merchant Navy in the
Atlantic convoys, Russian convoys and to and fro South Africa, before being
invalided out of service in 1944. Geoff's love of the sea and sailing ships,
despite the hardships never decreased.*

*The "Olivebank" returned to England in 1939 with Len still on board. He
remained Geoff's friend until he died.Fortunately Len left the ship before
she sailed for Mariehamn.*

*The "Olivebank" was sunk by a German mine off Gotland in September
1939 taking with her Captain Granith and all hands save four, Blomquist,
Bjorkman, Kullberg and Lindroos who died aged 71 in 1990.*

*To them all and to all those who, "went down to the sea in tall ships"
and knew both the comradeship and the frustrations of living in a close
community, where joy and sorrow, pleasure and pain is magnified out of
all proportion to the frustrations and friendly jibes of shipboard life, this
handwritten poem sent to Geoff by Isabella Kiernander sums up all the love
of sail and the great call of the sea far better than I ever could.]*

Lost Shipmates

To Captain Carl Granith and my shipmates of "Olivebank".

Think of me sometimes shipmates
Down where the dark sea's bed
Cradles your last long sleeping,
You, whom the world calls dead.

Where the soft grace of moonbeams
Touches with muted light,
While here I watch their pathway
Gold, in the dark sea night.

Could I but span the distance
And with my shipmates lie
Where my heart is lost forever
Under the sea and sky.

Hear you the muffled ship bells
Call in that lonely deep?
Telling the tale of watches
Kept as you stir in sleep.

Or do you sail my shipmates,
Into some fairer dawn
Out on a sea uncharted
Rounding a kinder Horn?

Out where the long lit silence
Dreams on the dreaming sea
Still does our barque sail onwards
As you tack and wait for me?

Making no other landfall,
Far from the seas we knew
Waiting to make the last great Port
Till I sail again with you.

Isabella Kiernander